Political Philosophy

ROYAL INSTITUTE OF PHILOSOPHY SUPPLEMENT: 58

EDITED BY

Anthony O'Hear

CAMBRIDGE
UNIVERSITY PRESS

CAMBRIDGE UNIVERSITY PRESS
Cambridge, New York, Melbourne, Madrid, Cape Town,
Singapore, São Paulo, Delhi, Tokyo, Mexico City

Cambridge University Press
The Edinburgh Building, Cambridge CB2 8RU, UK

Published in the United States of America by Cambridge University Press, New York

www.cambridge.org
Information on this title: www.cambridge.org/9780521695596

First published 2006

A catalogue record for this publication is available from the British Library

ISBN 978-0-521-69559-6 Paperback

Contents

Preface

The papers printed in this volume were based on lectures given in London as the Royal Institute of Philosophy's Annual Lecture Series for 2004-5. Taken overall, they present a number of contrasting perspectives on political philosophy as it currently stands.

While I would like to thank all the contributors to both the volume and the series, I have, with sadness, to record that Oswald Hanfling died during the preparation of the volume. His contribution to this volume, characteristically careful and forceful at the same time, underlines the loss to the philosophical community which his death entails.

I should also like to thank Marcela Herdova for her help in preparing the volume for the press and also for compiling the index.

Anthony O'Hear

Notes on Contributors

Jonathan Wolff, Professor of Philosophy, University College London

Susan Mendus, Professor of Politics, University of York

Anthony O'Hear, Weston Professor of Philosophy, University of Buckingham, Director of the Royal Institute of Philosophy

Oswald Hanfling, Late Professor of Philosophy, Open University

Michael Otsuka, Reader in Philosophy, University College London

G.A. Cohen, Chichele Professor of Social and Political Theory, All Souls College, Oxford

John Kekes, Research Professor, State University of New York, Albany

Edna Ullmann-Margalit, Professor of Philosophy at the Hebrew University of Jerusalem

Hilary Putnam, Cogan University Professor Emeritus at Harvard University

Robert Grant, Professor of English, University of Glasgow

João Carlos Espada, Professor of Politics, Director of the Institute for Political Studies at the Catholic University of Portugal

Susan James, Professor of Philosophy, Birkbeck College, London

Making the World Safe for Utilitarianism

JONATHAN WOLFF

Introduction

Utilitarianism has a curious history. Its most celebrated founders—Jeremy Bentham and John Stuart Mill—were radical progressives, straddling the worlds of academic philosophy, political science, economic theory and practical affairs. They made innumerable recommendations for legal, social, political and economic reform, often (especially in Bentham's case) described in fine detail. Some of these recommendations were followed, sooner or later, and many of their radical ideas have become close to articles of faith of western liberalism. Furthermore many of these recommendations were made expressly to improve the condition of the deprived, or of oppressed groups. Yet the moral theory which inspired this reforming zeal is, at least officially, utilitarianism, and when we teach this theory to our students we feel it our duty to point out the horrors that could be justified by any theory which assesses the moral quality of actions in terms of the maximization of good consequences over bad. No consequence is so bad that it cannot, in principle, be outweighed by a large aggregation of smaller goods. Hence there are circumstances in which utilitarianism can require slavery, the punishment of the innocent, and redistribution of resources from the poor to the rich, or from the disabled and the sick to the able bodied and healthy. Indeed, in the right circumstances, it can justify pretty much anything you can think of. For all their intelligence and imagination neither Bentham nor Mill seemed to recognise or discuss these catastrophic possibilities.

It is, however, no defence of utilitarianism to say that it was held by people who had fine motives and did not see its consequences. The current orthodoxy is that the central flaw in utilitarianism is that, as Rawls puts it, utilitarianism 'does not take seriously the distinction between persons'.[1] This phrase of Rawls' finds a clear echo in Nozick's remarks that 'There are only individual people,

---

[1]   John Rawls, *A Theory of Justice* (Oxford: Oxford University Press, revised edition 1999), 24.

with their own individual lives. Using one of these people for the benefit of others, uses him and benefits the others. Nothing more. What happens is that something is done to him for the sake of others. Talk of an overall social good covers this up. (Intentionally?)'[2]

Thus Nozick and Rawls both suggest that utilitarianism proceeds as if morality is some sort of generalised prudence. On such a view just as an individual may accept losses for the sake of greater benefits, so might 'society'. Yet, they counter, in reality all that happens is that one person gains and the other loses. This is no moral compensation. The gains do not justify the losses, even when they are bigger.

Consequently utilitarianism has been out of favour in philosophy for some time. It is remarkable that those with moral and political views as far apart as Rawls and Nozick have united to condemn it on apparently the same grounds (although this is less of a surprise when we realise that they both claim Kantian roots for their theories).[3] In its place we find various views which assign rights to individuals which will block at least some, perhaps even all, applications of maximizing consequentialism. This is true even for some views which are still sympathetic enough to consequentialism to retain the name.[4]

Yet while philosophers have turned away from maximizing consequentialism, public policy decision making has embraced it. Many areas of public policy are dominated by cost-benefit analysis, which at least in its purest from is a particularly crude form of consequentialism: consequentialism of money. Many decisions, large and small, are informed by cost-benefit analysis. The topics range from the building of a new airport to the permissibility of performing a particular animal experiment. This is an important example of where what may well be regarded as an outdated and crude philosophical theory has taken hold—almost as a default or standard theory. This should worry philosophers. And, indeed,

[2] Robert Nozick, *Anarchy, State, and Utopia* (Oxford: Blackwell, 1974), 33.

[3] Of course Nozick also believes that Rawls has not appreciated the full force of this objection, for it undermines Rawls' own theory too, so Nozick argues.

[4] See, for example, the rule-consequentialism of Brad Hooker, *Ideal Code, Real World* (Oxford: Oxford University Press, 2000).

some have duly reported themselves worried.[5] Yet how we should respond to this situation is by no means clear.

This paper explores the parallels between maximizing consequentialism in philosophy and cost-benefit analysis in public policy decision making. I believe that each area can cast light on the other. My conclusion—to anticipate—is that these maximizing doctrines are very powerful but also very dangerous. Like a powerful but destructive technology, the task is understanding when to use it and when not to. The danger alone is not a sufficient reason to reject the technology if conditions of safe use can be understood and reliably implemented, especially if we are unable to find an alternative which better meets our needs. Hence I want to produce a highly qualified defence of both utilitarianism and cost-benefit analysis. The qualifications I discuss in this paper are these. First, I defend the theories as *decision procedures* rather than as *moral theories* in their own right. Second, they are adequate decision procedures only under certain highly constrained conditions.[6] Indeed, these conditions may rarely, if ever, be met. However if the main argument of this paper is accepted then we have every reason for considering how we can move to a situation where the conditions are in fact satisfied.

Cost-Benefit Analysis And Its Difficulties

What we can call 'pure' cost-benefit analysis takes the following steps:
(i)   A qualitative statement of all costs and all benefits of a particular course of action (and its main alternatives, including the alternative of doing nothing) is set out.

---

[5]   Elizabeth Anderson, *Value in Ethics and Economics* (Cambridge, MA: Harvard University Press, 1993), and Henry S. Richardson, 'The Stupidity of the Cost Benefit Standard', in *Cost-Benefit Analysis: Legal, Economic, and Philosophical Perspectives*, M.D. Adler and E.A. Posner (eds.) (Chicago: University of Chicago Press, 2001), 135–167.

[6]   There is a third qualification. I believe that in some cases, in order to make adequate decisions, we need to add in factors which would not normally form part of an economic decision making mechanism. This is to say that cost-benefit analysis will often need to be supplemented by other considerations, especially where issues of risk to safety are concerned. This takes us beyond the terrain of this paper. I discuss it in Jonathan Wolff 'Risk, Fear, Blame, Shame and the Regulation of Public Safety', *Economics and Philosophy* forthcoming.

(ii) These costs and benefits are then rendered in quantitative terms.

(iii) These quantities are then converted into a single currency (usually money) and summed.

(iv) A decision is made on the basis of which alternative provides the greatest net benefit in terms of the designated currency.[7]

Any of these steps can be problematic. First coming to a statement of the full consequences of any course of action is difficult. Even when the possibilities are discerned—and this is difficult in itself—many consequences are uncertain and rendering them in probabilistic terms can be arbitrary and misleading. This is particularly so when outcomes will depend on the possible actions of other human beings, including the decisions they make take, including some in response to the decisions they expect us to take. If we really were to take all possible consequences into account we would very soon be overwhelmed. Therefore simplification must be made, and this always has its dangers. Furthermore, there is a potentially indefinite number of alternatives to any course of action. How do we know which to consider? Onora O'Neill has argued that we will tend not even to consider alternatives we consider to be wrong.[8] Hence even at the first step consequentialism appears parasitic on other moral norms. (However this may be less persuasive in public policy, where the constraints may be simply to stay within the law, than in personal morality where many other considerations may seem relevant.)

Even more contested is the step of converting other values into their monetary equivalent. This is often unsettling. For example when carrying out a risk cost-benefit analysis to see whether it is right to spend money to introduce new safety measures there seems no alternative to putting a financial value on reducing the risk of death. For ease of calculation this is rendered in terms of the saving a 'statistical life'. Currently in the UK government policy requires decision makers to operate with a value of life—or rather a value of preventing a fatality—of a little over a million pounds.[9] To some

[7] For this way of breaking CBA into separate steps see J. Wolff and D. Haubrich, 'Economism and Its Limits', in M Rein, M. Moran and R, Goodin (eds.) *Oxford Handbook to Public Policy* (Oxford:Oxford University Press, forthcoming 2006).

[8] Onora O'Neill, *Faces of Hunger An Essay on Poverty, Development and Justice* (London: Allen and Unwin, 1986), 71–96.

[9] Health and Safety Executive, *Reducing Risk, Protecting People*, 2001, http://www.hse.gov.uk/risk/theory/r2p2.htm

this sounds a barbaric way of approaching the issues. A common response is that no price should be put on life. Whether or not one is sympathetic to this claim, and its appropriateness in this extremely difficult context, the fact remains that where values are genuinely unquantifiable or incommensurable cost–benefit analysis will be in grave difficulties. We will return to this below.

Yet even where there is no principled objection to the idea of measurement or conversion, the particular valuations can be highly contested. To give an example a number of studies have tried to estimate the 'cost of a problem gambler' in the context of considering whether the benefits of a liberal gambling regime outweigh the costs. A survey reveals that estimates over the last fifteen years or so, all backed up with detailed costings, and aggressive defence of methodology, vary from an annual cost of £373 to an annual cost of £35,300.[10] It is hard to resist the conclusion that these costings are typically used to support policies advocated on other grounds, rather than being based on some sort of neutral method of valuation.

However even if problems of quantification and commensuration can be solved, CBA may still run into difficulties. Bearing in mind the standard objections to utilitarianism, it is not difficult to see the parallel problems for CBA. A policy could have overall benefits yet be extremely costly to some individuals. Why, it will be asked, should benefits for one party justify costs which fall on others? Consider again the gambling case. Whatever we think about trying to quantify the costs, in qualitative terms they are well understood. Problem gambling can lead to despair, extreme child neglect, family break-up and suicide. Is it really right that we should determine gambling policy purely on the basis of whether the aggregated benefits are greater or smaller than the aggregated costs of the ruined lives of those who suffer? CBA, then, as a form of maximizing consequentialism, shares the defects of other forms.

Now it should at once be admitted that the pure form of CBA is rarely seen. Some theorists and practitioners are often highly

---

[10] Sir Alan Budd, et al. *Gambling Review Body Report*, DCMS 2001, http://www.culture.gov.uk/global/publications/archive_2001/gamb_rev_report.htm Interestingly this highest figure was mentioned on the front page of the Daily Mail on 16 October 2004 as part of their campaign against the liberalisation of U.K. gambling laws. It was not mentioned that this figure was the highest of a range of estimates, or that it was produced by a group of researchers who were trying to convince their audience that an expensive form of proposed therapy for problem gamblers provided good value for money.

sensitive to the problems just outlined, and attempt to take appropriate steps. Consequently it is not uncommon to hear the argument that while political decisions should be informed by CBA it should not be the sole input into decision making.[11] In effect this is to decline to take the final step of the pure model. Others, worrying about the third step—the translation of costs and benefits into monetary terms—have argued that because valuations are always contestable different groups should be encouraged to offer their own CBA of the same scenarios.[12]

To avoid some distributional problems, the government has now proposed adding a further step in which financial benefits can be weighted for different groups.[13] So a benefit to the poor is considered to be of greater value than the same benefit to the rich, on the assumption that it will make more difference to their lives. This turns CBA into something closer to classical utilitarianism. Furthermore additional weights can be added to give even greater consideration to those who fare badly, which will move CBA to something closer to Parfit's prioritarianism.[14] In other cases groups considered particularly vulnerable are given special concern. Their vulnerability could be something to do with their relation to the decision—for example people living in a particular location—or more general, the poor or the mentally ill. Hence, in effect, special steps are proposed to attempt to avoid the problem that society's risks and costs are all dumped on a particular group who do not share in the benefits.

In deference to worries about commensurability sometimes the analysis leaps from the second stage to the last, in which costs and benefits are enumerated and quantified but not placed on a common scale. This is the approach taken with respect to animal experimentation.[15] This then leaves decision making to intuitive judgement rather than to the outcome of a quantified formal

[11] Cass Sunstein, *Risk and Reason* (Cambridge: Cambridge University Press, 2002), David Schmidtz, 'A Place for Cost-Benefit Analysis', *Nous* **35**, No. s1 (October 2001), 148–171.

[12] K.S. Shrader-Frachette, *Risk and Rationality* (Berkeley: University of California Press, 1991).

[13] HM Treasury *Green Book, Appraisal and Evaluation in Central Government*, 2003, Annex 5 http://greenbook.treasury.gov.uk/

[14] Derek Parfit, 'Equality and Priority', *Ratio* **10, No. 3** (December 1997), 'Equality and Priority', 202–221.

[15] Michael Banner et. al, *Animal Procedures Committee Recommendations On Cost-Benefit Assessment Under The Animals (Scientific Procedures) Act 1986*, 2003, http://www.apc.gov.uk/

method. This type of 'soft' cost-benefit analysis may seem more reasonable, but it loses the advantages that led to the rise of CBA. For it is vulnerable to the criticisms that defenders of pure CBA pose; indeed the same objections which led Bentham to utilitarianism. Bentham, rather scandalously, argues that there are only two alternatives to utilitarianism. The first is the principle of asceticism which is the mirror-image of utilitarianism—maximize suffering—and which Bentham plausibly points out has never been seriously maintained.[16] The second is the principle of sympathy and antipathy, which Bentham also calls the principle of caprice. This, Bentham suggests, approves or disapproves of an action 'merely because a man finds himself disposed to approve or disapprove of them.' The problem, Bentham continues, is that 'What one expects to find in a principle is something that points out some external consideration, as a means of warranting and guiding the internal sentiments of approbation and disapprobation: this expectation is but ill fulfilled by a proposition, which does neither more or less than hold up each of these sentiments as a ground and standard for itself.'[17]

It is hard to disagree with the point that without the rigours of some formal approach to public decision making a great deal must be left to individual judgement—or likings or dislikings—of politicians and even unelected officials. Whether or not this is a problem is arguable. Some will say that in reality we never have an alternative to intuitive judgement, and so CBA, at best, is a cloak for individual judgement, hidden away in the details, and at worst a cloak for abuse of power. On the other hand without some form of formal methodology decisions will seem to lack a firm basis, a series of decisions may be inconsistent, and we may decline beneficial schemes in favour of relatively inefficient ones. Leaving so much to individual judgement opens the way if not always to corruption then to prejudice or lazy thinking. CBA and utilitarianism promise discipline. They provide a means of making decisions rooted in an analysis which can be scrutinised, questioned in public, attacked and defended. Bias and abuse of power can be detected by those scrutinising the calculations. In other words it provides public accountability (something everyone wants for others, even if, less often, for themselves).

[16] Jeremy Bentham, *An Introduction to the Principles of Morals and Legislation*, J.H Burns and H.L.A. Hart (eds.) (London: Athlone, 1970,) 17–21.
[17] Op. cit. note 16, 25.

Jonathan Wolff

What Are the Alternatives?

Economists are well-aware of the accusations against CBA. Their defence often is that they would be more than happy to give it up, if only someone would actually tell them what else to do instead of just complaining. Some critics of CBA have risen to this challenge by proposing 'deliberative democracy' or 'public reason' as a constructive alternative. Yet it is less easy to see what to do with this suggestion. Deliberative democracy is an attempt to substitute an *auditable process* for the *auditable application of a formula*. This has undoubted appeal, yet it is hard to see how this could be applied in the case of each and every decision currently taken by public officials. Discussion will rarely lead to a consensus, and it is hard to see how all legitimate interests will be represented in proportion to their weight. Now there is of course a sophisticated emerging literature on the idea of deliberative democracy, and so this should not be dismissed.[18] Yet although deliberative democracy may be highly suitable for very important issues, such as those concerning national sovereignty, or specialised local decisions affecting a defined population, such as new traffic schemes, it is harder to imagine how it can be used case by case to address the welter of mid-level resource allocation and development decisions faced by central and local government departments. Or at least it is hard to see how it could deliver consistent results. Perhaps this does not matter. However if one hopes to achieve some sort of cumulative effect through decision making it seems unlikely that it can be achieved without some more formal methodology.

What, then, is left? Bentham, it is true, identifies the idea of a formal, accountable, methodology with utilitarianism, and does not consider whether alternative formal methods—quantified or unquantified—are possible. Nevertheless, those who oppose utilitarianism or cost-benefit analysis have a tough time. They need either to propose an alternative accountable methodology, or to be prepared to give up accountability, trusting the intuitions and judgements of officials and politicians, and putting up with the risk of undetectable corruption, prejudice, nepotism and what we might call 'policy drift'. This is a version of a familiar dilemma. For example John Rawls opens *A Theory of Justice* by comparing utilitarianism and intuitionism.[19] Utilitarianism is to be praised for

---

[18]   See, for example, A. Gutmann and D. Thomson, *Why Deliberative Democracy?* (Princeton NJ: Princeton University Press, 2004).

[19]   Op. cit. note 1, 19-36.

offering a firm, principled, accountable methodology. Unfortunately it delivers some horrendous conclusions. Intuitionism need never deliver any results we don't like, but in the absence of an accountable methodology provides no argumentative purchase against those who disagree with the conclusion. In the case of CBA, the pure theory represents the analogue of utilitarianism, while the various modifications introduced to make its deliverances more appealing begin to turn it into something closer to intuitionism. For one might have little to say in defence of the exact weights and fiddles used to make the sums come out right when they are disputed. Indeed those who, in a spirit of concession, say that decision making should be informed, but not determined, by CBA are often in difficulties in explaining what else one should take into account, if not costs and benefits.

Rawls can be understood as being motivated by the aim of having the best of both worlds: the rigour of utilitarianism, and the intuitive appeal of intuitionism. And this, indeed, may well be decision maker's holy grail; an accountable decision procedure which produces only ethically acceptable results. This is a motivation for both the form and the content of Rawls' lexically ordered principles of justice.

Rawls' general approach is undeniably attractive and on the face of it, there seems little reason why it should not be translatable into a tool for public policy decision making. As already noted pure CBA is applied utilitarianism, and utilitarianism is out of favour in philosophy. The obvious next step is to state a more acceptable ethical or political theory and apply it to public policy.

Let us put aside the problem that not everyone accepts that Rawls' theory of justice is correct. The question which concerns us is whether it really does provide a feasible alternative to cost-benefit analysis for public decision making. So the question of how Rawls' theory might be applied to public policy is at least worth taking seriously. Indeed one of the appealing aspects, for many, of Rawls' theory is that it is designed, at least according to some interpretations, with the idea of feasibility firmly in mind.[20]

Rawls' theory is, of course, that first we should provide everyone with a fully adequate set of equal basic liberties; second that we should arrange for equality of opportunity; and third we should act so as to maximize the wealth and income of the worst off. Now Rawls is clear that the 'we' who act in such case is not you and me.

[20] C. Kukathas and P. Pettit, *John Rawls' 'Theory of Justice' and Its Critics* (Oxford: Polity Press, 1991).

Jonathan Wolff

Neither is it government officials or policy makers. Rather these are principles for the 'basic structure' of society; principles so fundamental that they inform the content of the constitution. There is no intention that any policy maker should make any direct appeal to the principles of justice. Consequently there is an apparent gap between these principles of justice and any concrete methodology for policy makers.

How can this gap be bridged, and Rawls' principles made to yield a policy makers' handbook? The first thing to note is that a great deal of public policy is addressed to what would fall under the first two of Rawls' principles of justice: the liberty principle and the fair opportunity principle. For example the creation of a secure legal system can be seen as contributing to the implementation of the liberty principle, while education, and at least some aspects of the health system are arguably institutions designed to fulfil the aim of equality of opportunity. In these areas, although there may be questions at the level of the development of detailed policy, the overall guiding aim of the institution should be clear, and so policy makers should be able to follow the principles of their institutions.

The problem I want to bring out centres on the final principle, the Difference Principle, which tells us, to put it crudely, to maximize the wealth and income of the worst off. How can we arrange public policy so decisions will turn out to be of the greatest benefit to the least advantaged in terms of their wealth and income? Now it may seem simple. We should tax the rich and give to the poor. Redistribution will achieve Rawlsian justice. However most public policy decision making, although often redistributive in its effects, will not be redistributive in its intentions. These include, for example, many decisions about management and development, both in economic terms and in terms of the material environment. Brian Barry points out that inflation, in effect, redistributes from those with cash savings to those with cash debts. So a decision to maintain any particular rate of inflation will have redistributive consequences, as may a decision about public transport, a leisure centre or a library.[21] How are decisions such as these to be appraised? Here, then, I am especially concerned with what we might think of as growth and management decisions, rather than those with an explicit redistributive intent and rationale.

[21] Brian Barry, 'Does Democracy Cause Inflation? The Political Ideas of Some Economists', in L. Lindberg and C. Maier *The Politics Of Inflation And Economic Stagnation* (Washington DC: The Brookings Institute, 1985), 280–318.

As mentioned above Rawls does not argue that public policy decision makers should, in each decision, aim to make the worst off as well off as possible. And reflection on examples shows that to do so can be a crippling strategy. In deciding where to put the next airport, should the decision really be taken purely on the grounds of which location (if any at all) would make the worst off best off (assuming that issues of liberties and opportunities were already dealt with or do not apply)? Even if maximizing the advantage of the worst off is one's long term goal—as it should be for a Rawlsian—it is far from clear that it is best achieved through applying a direct strategy of this sort to every case.[22]

There are, in fact, at least two types of problem. The first is relatively straightforward where a short term loss to the worst off will lead to a longer term gain. For example the expense of having to purchase double glazing may be worth it if the new airport will eventually produce new employment opportunities with a higher wage.[23] This should be reasonably easy to deal with. The second, and much more tricky problem, is where a general policy of allowing the possibility of uncompensated losses for the worst off might be of greater medium term net benefit even to the worst off than a policy which allows them only to gain. What they lose on the swings might be doubled on the roundabouts. For a general policy which allows risk may well generate larger gains for everyone. This requires thinking of decisions as forming part of a series, even when they are taken in an uncoordinated way by different decision makers. What is needed is a general policy to cover such cases, which allows short term loss in the expectation that such a general policy will nevertheless be to the advantage of the worst off. We might call this 'Rule-Rawlsianism' where we sometimes allow the worst off to lose. Yet is may not be at all obvious how we can formulate the algorithm for policy makers which will collectively generate the greatest advantage for the worst off.

Now it might be thought that I have exaggerated the difficulties. Any policy maker should do whatever is best to stimulate the economy; this will then expand the tax base and allow for greater redistribution to the worst off. Problem solved. However this ignores the uncertainty of the outcome of decision making. Consider, for example, the decision whether or not to bid for the

---

[22] Still less by deliberative democracy, of course.

[23] And indeed where a large surplus is envisaged compensation to those who lose in the short-term may often be possible (although for some qualifications to this see note 32 below).

Olympics, restricting attention just to financial consequences. The bid will cost money, and it might not succeed. Worse, we may win the bid but find that the economic consequences are negative. Only under the most favourable outcome will the economy be stimulated and generate economic benefits. Under all others it is likely that the poor will be made a little worse off. Considering this, if our concern is to ensure the position of the worst off, we had better not take this gamble. Yet, it seems, this conservative approach could be damaging over time, if generalised. So we are left with this puzzle: what is the right general approach to adopt?

The significance of this point is that while Rawls' theory seems to provide the best hope for a formal, quantifiable, alternative to utilitarianism, and hence by extension to cost-benefit analysis, it falls down at the vital point. If Rawls' theory—a theory specifically designed with issues of implementation in mind—fails to yield a determinate decision procedure for policy makers, what hope is there for other theories? Hence it is easy to have sympathy for the claim that cost–benefit analysis, in some form or other, seems to provide the only determinate methodology we have, in the sense of providing a formal, accountable decision procedure for public policy.

How important is a determinate methodology, bearing in mind that in the case of maximizing consequentialism its cost can be unacceptable results? What good is a method if it doesn't yield what we want? Here we might be reminded of the old joke about a drunk looking for his lost house key in a well-lit street, even though he dropped it in the adjacent dark street, arguing that 'at least I can see properly here'. Certainly he is right that on the whole it is better to be looking for something in the light than in the dark. But if what he is looking for is somewhere else he will have a frustrating night ahead of him. However two points are worth making. Even though it is true that looking for the key in a well-lit street doesn't help you find it when it is not there, this does not mean that the approach is 'refuted' and should not be used when you have reason to believe that the key is there. Second, and to continue to pursue this rather strained analogy, consider breaking the original search into two parts. In the first the contents of the neighbouring dark streets are trawled and dragged somehow into the well-lit street. In the second the light street is searched. Now this doesn't seem so stupid. This is to attempt to convert cases where the method will not work into cases where it will; an ambitious strategy but not one to be disregarded entirely.

Making the World Safe for Utilitarianism

To put this in context, earlier we briefly explored responses to the fact that forms of maximizing consequentialism can yield counter-intuitive results. We can now see that they broadly fall into two types. The first is to modify the theory so it yields better results, through weights and incorporation of other factors. The second is to try to appeal to a different moral theory altogether. Both responses have grave difficulties. In the first case the more we modify the theory to make it more acceptable the more we lose both the benefits of the maximizing approach and the discipline of a formal method. In the second we lose the method, and unless we find another we are sunk. But now I'm suggesting a third possibility: first try to distinguish the types of circumstances under which the method works from those where it fails. Then we use the method where it works. What about cases where it does not work? One possibility, I have suggested, is that we might attempt to convert cases where it does not work into types of cases where the method works—drag them into the well-lit street. Of course conversion is unlikely always to be possible, and so various secondary strategies will be needed. But nevertheless the sensible strategy must be first, to take another look at the variety of cases, and try to achieve a systematic account of when maximizing consequentialism works and when it does not.

When Does Maximizing Consequentialism Work?

To advance the discussion I want to return to Rawls; this time to his discussion of the choice of principles behind the veil of ignorance. It will be recalled that Rawls argues that the question of what is the correct theory of justice comes to turn on the question of rational choice: the choice of those behind the veil of ignorance, who are ignorant of their own characteristics. The principles people would rationally choose in such circumstances are, Rawls argues, the correct principles of justice, at least for societies in the western liberal democratic tradition. The issue of the correct choice of principles, in turn, reduces to the question of the rational principles of choice to apply in the circumstances of the original position.

For present purposes we need only compare Rawls' favoured option—the maximin criterion, which leads him to propose his theory of justice outlined above—with the principle of maximizing expectations, or maximizing average utility (MAU) which would lead to average utilitarianism.

13

Jonathan Wolff

Rawls notes that some will be surprised by his preference for maximin over MAU.[24] For, as Rawls explains, MAU is taken almost as a definition of rational behaviour in many contexts, especially within economic theory. He argues, nevertheless, that the special circumstances of the original position make MAU an irrational approach. For present purposes the most important special features are, first, this is a one-off situation, and second, the choice is highly significant in that if it goes wrong it will go very wrong. There are, Rawls says, 'grave risks'.[25] Consequently, it seems implied by Rawls's discussion, if these features were **not** present then MAU would be much more attractive. That is to say, if the situation was regular and repeating, and losses were not catastrophic, then the economists may well be right: MAU is rational under those circumstances. To illustrate suppose that each week you are faced with a lottery in which you can either have the certainty of £100 or a fifty percent chance of £300 (and a fifty percent chance of nothing). If you really were faced with this choice each week, and you were sure that the odds were genuine, then you would clearly end up better off by playing a regular strategy of MAU—gambling—rather than playing safe with maximin.

We should note that choosing MAU does not entail that you believe that the correct theory of prudence is to maximize the average. On the contrary, you might be convinced that prudence requires one to maximize the worst reasonable possibility (i.e., maximize the worst outcome but ignoring possibilities with freak odds). Interestingly, though, in this case both a reasonably cautious and an adventurous theory converge on the same decision procedure. This is an important, and potentially powerful, result. We can detach the *theory* of maximizing consequentialism from the *decision procedure*, for the same decision procedure may, under certain conditions, be compatible with a variety of theories.

There are, of course, cases where a cautious attitude would dictate a different choice. If, at the time of making a decision, you had no other money, and no way of surviving without money, then

---

[24] Op. cit. note 1, 134.

[25] Op. cit. note 1, 147–8. Indeed after this paper was substantially drafted I noticed that in these pages Rawls attributes a version of the view defended here to Edgeworth, and then points out and challenges the underlying assumptions. Some of the arguments of this paper can, therefore, be read as responses to Rawls' criticisms of Edgeworth.

gambling would be very bold.[26] But the main point is that over a long series, with true odds and no grave risks, the policy of maximizing average expectations—be it money or utility—will almost certainly lead to a policy of maximizing actual money and utility.[27] Under such conditions the policy of making the worst thing that can (reasonably) happen as good as possible tells you to follow a maximizing strategy. Consequently, to put it starkly, there are times when a Rawlsian should adopt the methods of a utilitarian.

Can we be more precise about these circumstances? Four conditions seem to stand out:

1. There need to be regular opportunities of a similar nature. (Call this the assumption of 'many chances'.)
2. No single loss (or likely repeated series of losses) creates a type of level of harm for any individual from which recovery is very difficult or impossible. (The assumption of 'recoverable loss'.)
3. There is no reason to doubt that the probabilities run true. (The assumption of 'true odds'.)
4. All relevant gains and losses can be quantified and compared to each other. (The assumption of 'weak commensurability'.)

Each of these conditions requires elaboration. First, 'many chances'. Clearly it will be rare that anyone will be presented with exactly the same type of decision time and again. Rather what I have in mind, in relation to public policy, is some sort of 'routine decision for government and its agencies' so that the decision whether or not to bid for the Olympics, whether to build a high-speed rail link, whether to build a shopping centre, and what

---

[26] However although a different choice is called for, it is less obvious that this case shows that the policy of maximizing average utility has been abandoned. Those with no money at all have steeply diminishing marginal utilities for money, and so 50% chance of £300 will, under these circumstances, have less utility than £100.

[27] Can it be that the policies of maximizing expected money and maximizing expected utility come apart? In the short term this is possible, and it is even possible to think up examples in which one maximizes actual utility by following the policy of maximizing not expected utility but expected money (where marginal utilities decline one will refuse risks that would be profitable in utility terms in a longer series). However in a longer series the calculations are more awkward as the utility of money depends not only on how much you receive in total but whether you receive it when you need it or can otherwise make good use of it.

interest rate policy to pursue all fall within the scope of the class to be taken collectively. One-off decisions, in the intended sense, may be much rarer, and may include such things as a decision to go to war, although even this, arguably, could be included. The excluded class also includes those decisions taken explicitly to achieve aims of social justice.

The second assumption of 'recoverable loss' needs further thought, as no path through life is risk free, and maiming or death is not recoverable for the individual involved. Everyday we are exposed to myriad tiny risks; risks tiny enough that we can discount them for most practical purposes. Yet many public decisions will lead to deaths. If we win the Olympic bid and engage in major construction, it is close to certain that at least one construction worker will die. Nevertheless we are unlikely to think this a sufficient reason for not making the bid.[28] Clearly we need to formulate the assumption in such a way that very small risks are permitted, yet it remains a puzzle how to deal with this in detail.[29]

The assumption of true odds also needs explanation. In the case of tossing a coin, where there are true odds one can expect to be a winner roughly as often as being a loser, at least in the longer run. True odds would be violated if it turned out that men, or white people, or the educated, or the rich, won more often than women, or black people, or the uneducated, or the poor. Another way of putting the assumption is that it holds only if in the longer run one's actual payout will come close to matching the statistically expected payout.

Now it may be that this assumption may be quite unrealistic. Indeed I have argued elsewhere disadvantages tend to cluster together, and those who do badly in some respects will come to find that they do badly in others in others.[30] Where we have a society where some groups tend to win and others tend to lose, then the application of cost-benefit analysis can continue to reinforce this. Such clustering of disadvantages needs to be addressed directly as part of a social justice agenda. Hence the arguments of this paper in defence of cost-benefit analysis are most pertinent when we have

---

[28]   Does this reveal some sort of class bias? Martin O'Neill asks whether we would accept the loss so easily if we could predict the death of a teacher or doctor?

[29]   For further discussion see Wolff, op. cit. note 6.

[30]   Jonathan Wolff and Avner de-Shalit, *Disadvantage* (Oxford: Oxford University Press, forthcoming 2006). For similar arguments, see Brian Barry, *Why Social Justice Matters* (Oxford: Polity Press, 2005).

reason to believe that clustering effects will not skew the odds, or for a hypothetical future where we have overcome such effects. We will return to this.

Finally, I have referred to the fourth condition as 'weak commensurability', allowing for sufficient comparability between different goods so that cost–benefit analysis can be applied. Philosophically this is often regarded as highly dubious,[31] yet it is important to understand what exactly is at stake.

For the purposes of making decisions, values of different sorts have to be compared in order to decide where our priorities lie in cases of conflict over use of resources. As we noted, for example, in safety decision making, a monetary value of around one million pounds is put on saving a life. Yet we should not assume that means that as a society we put a monetary value on each life, and that value is one million pounds, as if one million pounds somehow equates to a life and compensates for a death. It seems important, then, that we regard this as an equation used for making safety decisions rather than an all-purpose identification. Indeed this form of what I call 'weak commensurability' is consistent with what we could call 'weak incommensurability', which is the idea that the loss of one good—health say—cannot properly be made up for by any amount of some other good, such as money. Many people may be prepared to assent to this form of incommensurability. Nevertheless, the acceptance of such a doctrine does not stop us from arguing that some health interventions provide good value for money while others do not. Yet that judgement, of course, seems to presuppose weak commensurability. Hence it is possible to accept both weak commensurabilty (comparisons for some purposes) and weak incommensurability (non-comparisons for other purposes).[32] We could define the strong versions of each as the denial of the weak version of the other.

---

[31] See, for example, A. Sen and B. Williams, Introduction to *Utilitarianism and Beyond* (Cambridge: Cambridge University Press, 1982). And, indeed, I have argued for incommensurability myself, see Jonathan Wolff, Addressing Disadvantage and the Human Good, *Journal of Applied Philosophy 2002*, **19**, No. 3, (2002), 207–218.

[32] If this is right then it explains why the apparently appealing idea of 'cost-benefit analysis with real compensation'; (i.e., those who would lose are compensated with money so that no one actually loses) is more problematic than it may seem. Of course compensation with money can be better than no compensation (although not in every case, see Bruno Frey,

Jonathan Wolff

Consequentialism Reassessed

It appears that the notorious counter-examples to maximizing consequentialism occur under circumstances when at least one of the first three assumptions—many chances, recoverable loss, and true odds—are violated. The classic 'scapegoating' objection to utilitarianism—hanging the innocent to calm the mob—probably violates all three in its classic version: it is one-off situation, the loss of being hanged is irrecoverable, and a person is picked not at random but because he is a member of a suspected group. Let us call circumstances in which these three assumptions, plus the further assumption of weak commensurability, hold 'fortunate circumstances', and where at least one is violated 'unfortunate circumstances'. Of course unfortunate circumstances come in degrees. When several of the assumptions are violated—as in the case of scapegoating—the circumstances are deeply unfortunate.

In fortunate circumstances—where the assumptions hold—gambling and the preparedness to lose from time to time pays. To put this another way, the strategy of taking the rough with the smooth should ensure more 'smooth' over the medium and long term, even for the worst off, than following any other strategy, such as the direct maximin policy of always trying to make the rough as little rough as possible.

With this in mind it is worth revisiting the 'separateness of persons' objection to utilitarianism. Nozick and Rawls, we saw, argued that utilitarianism falsely assumes that one person's gain can morally override another's loss. However we now see that in fortunate circumstances no such assumption is required. One person's loss will be, if not compensated, than in some sense outweighted by that same person's gain sometime earlier or later. When this is true, utilitarianism—as a decision strategy—really is prudence. There are gains which outweigh the losses within each life. However, in unfortunate circumstances—when the assumptions do not hold—the criticism is apt. Some may suffer uncompensated losses, of a very significant nature. How should we respond to these difficulties?

At least within philosophy, the most common response is to treat the lack of generality of utilitarianism as a reason for rejecting it.

Not Just for the Money (Cheltenham: Edward Elgar, 1997)) but unless strong commensurability holds it will not 'return' people to their baseline situation.

For if it can lead to unacceptable consequences it cannot be true. However, rejecting a theory is not, in itself to provide an alternative. And although there are plenty of more appealing approaches to personal morality, we do not seem to have many candidate alternatives for public policy decision making, as we have already seen.

A second alternative is to adjust the theory so that the difficult cases cannot, or are least less likely, to occur. As we saw the, the idea of weighting benefits to the poor may avoid some unfairness, and this approach has been explored in Treasury advice.[33] Unfortunately, though, there are two problems. First, and most obviously, unless some weights are absolute, horrors can still occur. Second, and more subtly, while weighting in one-off cases is to be recommended, to adopt weighting in what I have termed fortunate circumstances will do more harm than good, over time, even for the worst off. For it will impede risk-taking that would reasonably be expected to benefit everyone over time, including the poor (remember that in fortunate circumstances probabilities run true). Now if we are never in fortunate circumstances then this is less of a concern. But if we are to adopt weighting as a universal rule we begin to drain away some of the benefits of maximizing consequentialism.

These two problems push in opposite directions. To deal with the problem of catastrophic consequences we may wish to assign very strong individual rights. However once we trim the scope of consequentialism in this way we will lose even more of its benefits. Indeed giving people rights not to lose even in what I have termed fortunate circumstances is highly problematic. We are used to hearing about the tragedy of the commons—that land owned in common will be over-grazed, that oceans owned in common will be over-fished etc—and that private property rights of some sort are the necessary remedy. What we need to hear more about is the opposite—the tragedy of privatisation. Indeed there may be several tragedies of privatisation, but here I mention only one, concerning risk. Suppose, as is increasingly common, people are not prepared to accept the risk of (non-disastrous) loss or harm. In the earlier image, suppose people are simply not prepared to take the rough with the smooth, and insist on rights against even modest damage, rather than 'pooling' exposure. Well, the smooth will not be so smooth for anyone. It will no longer be the case that 'what you lose on the swings, you gain on the roundabout'. Making sure you never

---

[33] See note 13.

lose out means that you will lose out, compared to what might have been. Policy making will become more risk-averse, and in what I have called fortunate circumstances we can all expect to lose over time.

Consequently assigning rights seems not to get us where we need to be. How about the strategy hinted at above, of conversion—dragging everything into the well-lit street? The idea, then, would be not to adjust the decision procedure but to adjust the world so that it fits the procedure. How can this be done? The main problem we face may well be the fact that disadvantages cluster which makes the assumption of true odds unlikely to be true. Now it seems to me that we have independent reasons, based on distributive justice, to wish to challenge and break up such clustering and thereby help bring about true odds. Although it may be utopian to think we can ever complete such a task, the closer we get to it, the more appropriate it will be to use cost-benefit analysis, for the benefit of everyone.

Hence if we cannot bring about favourable circumstances—and in fact even if we could—it is worth considering the possibility of approaching decision-making through two waves of policy. The first wave uses cost-benefit analysis; the second mops up afterwards, or even better acts concurrently to ensure that no harm is done to those already relatively badly off. Some time ago I proposed a version of this, calling it a 'weak equity axiom'; that is 'If a change generates a surplus then those already towards the bottom of the distribution should not suffer as a result of the change.'[34] I would now want to interpret this as allowing loss in the short term, but not the medium. Having thought of this as a modification to utilitarianism, I was rather astonished to discover that Bentham had made a similar point. When advocating the introduction of the printing press in Tripoli and Greece, he warned 'care should be taken that the employment given to it should not be

[34] Jonathan Wolff, 'Rational, Fair and Reasonable in P.J. Kelly (ed.) *Impartiality, Neutrality and Justice* (Edinburgh: Edinburgh University Press, 1998), 35–43. This is, of course, very similar to the idea of cost-benefit analysis with real compensation, mentioned in footnote 32.

such as to throw out of employment any of the existing scribes, except in so far as other employment not less advantageous is found for them'.[35]

From a classical utilitarian point of view, why worry about the scribes? Bentham, no doubt, had some idea of indirect maximizing strategies in mind: noting the value of security, and also appreciating that mitigating the loss of the scribes—which they will feel very heavily—will cost relatively little. But this type of secondary policy can be supported on Rawlsian as well as utilitarian grounds, and is appropriate in large, one-off, cases and circumstances where probabilities do not run true. Indeed it may be no accident that Rawls sees as possibly the most plausible alternative to his theory a hybrid view in which a liberty principle is supplemented by utilitarianism subject to a social minimum.[36] Perhaps several theoretical approaches, including Rawls's own concern for the worst off, all converge on the same decision procedure for public policy.

The idea of two waves of policy may bring to mind Musgrave's classic distinction between the allocative branch and the distributive branch of economic governance. Clearly there is a great deal in common between my approach and Musgrave's.[37] However, there are also differences worth emphasising too. My account does not appeal to the value of efficiency in its own right at any point. Hence, unlike Musgrave I make no observations about personal incentives, labour supply, marginal tax rates, and so on. Rather I point out that in order to make the worst off as well off as possible society needs to take risks which may in fact, over the short term, make the worst off worse off. Hence my concern even at the first stage is distributive. For that reason it is important that we have already taken some steps to bring us closer to fortunate circumstances, especially in relation to clusters of disadvantage. Efficiency, then, turns out to be a very welcome by-product. However given that we are unlikely to meet all the conditions of favourable circumstances, and, even if we were improbable runs of

[35] Jeremy Bentham, *Securities Against Misrule and Other Constitutional Writings for Tripoli and Greece*, (ed.) Philip Schofield (Oxford: Clarendon Press, 1990), 38. I thank Philip Schofield for drawing my attention to this text.

[36] Op. cit note 1, xiv.

[37] I am very grateful Shepley Orr for bringing this to my attention. Richard Musgrave, *The Theory of Public Finance* (New York: McGraw Hill, 1959).

odds may leave some people badly off, a second wave of policy, as for Musgrave, will be needed to mop up ill effects of the first. So there are differences and parallels between Musgrave's ideas and those presented in this paper.

Conclusion

By way of conclusion it is worth reflecting on Will Kymlicka's interesting diagnosis of the problem with utilitarianism.[38] According to Kymlicka the fundamental impulse of utilitarianism is Bentham's dictum that everyone is to count for one and no one for more than one. Bentham, argues Kymlicka, was too quick to interpret this egalitarian premise in additive terms, summing advantages. The problem, we have seen, is this leads to unacceptable outcomes in certain types of case. Kymlicka's response is that Bentham should have been an egalitarian in the tradition started by Rawls and completed by Dworkin. My reply is that the counter-examples are good reasons for limiting utilitarianism's scope as a decision procedure, but need not force its complete rejection. There are two reasons why this is welcome. First, no one else has told us how to approach public policy decision making (except decisions of an explicitly redistributive kind, typically involving transfers of money). Second, we can all be better off Bentham's way. Under fortunate circumstances Utilitarianism—and with it cost-benefit analysis—can make us all better off.[39]

[38] Will Kymlicka, *Contemporary Political Philosophy,* 2nd edition (Oxford: Oxford University Press, 2001).

[39] I would like to thank audiences at the R.I.P. lecture in London, and Cambridge for their comments and criticisms. I would especially like to thank Veronique Munoz Darde, Martin O'Neill, Shepley Orr, and Michael Otsuka, for extremely helpful written comments.

Innocent Before God: Politics, Morality and the Case of Billy Budd[1]

SUSAN MENDUS

I begin with the story told by Herman Melville in his short novel, *Billy Budd*.[2] The year is 1797. Britain is engaged in a long and bitter war against France, and the British war effort has been threatened by two naval mutinies: the Nore Mutiny and the mutiny at Spithead. The scene is His Majesty's Ship, the *Indomitable*, and the central character is Billy Budd, sailor. Billy Budd is a young man of exceptional beauty, both physical and moral, whose only flaw is a stammer. He is loved by all his fellow sailors except the master-at-arms, John Claggart. The incarnation of evil, Claggart recognises in Billy the incarnation of goodness, and is consumed by a jealousy which leads him to accuse Billy (falsely) of inciting the crew to mutiny. Alone with Claggart and the ship's Captain, Edward Vere, Billy hears the lying charge against him. He is enraged, but his stammer prevents him from responding in words. He strikes Claggart, and the blow is fatal. Billy Budd, sailor, has killed the master-at-arms of one of His Majesty's ships on active service, and the penalty for this is death.

It now falls to Captain Vere to judge Billy Budd's case. He knows Billy to be innocent of incitement to mutiny, but he also knows that Billy has committed a capital offence. How is he to proceed? Melville writes:

> In the jugglery of circumstances preceding and attending the event on board the *Indomitable*, and in the light of that martial code whereby it was formally to be judged, innocence and guilt ... effectively changed places. In the legal view, the apparent victim of the tragedy was he (Claggart) who had sought to

[1] Earlier versions of this paper were delivered at the Universities of Durham, Lancaster, Oxford, Southampton and York. I am grateful to all the participants for their incisive and helpful comments.

[2] All references are to Dan McCall (ed.) *Melville's Short Novels* (New York: Norton, 2002).

23

victimise a man blameless (Budd); and the indisputable deed of the latter, navally regarded, constituted the most heinous of military crimes.[3]

Billy Budd is indeed 'innocent before God', but before man he is guilty. At the Last Assizes he will assuredly be acquitted, but it is God alone who can acquit—man must condemn and, reluctantly, Captain Vere condemns. He sentences Billy Budd to be hung at the yard-arm in the early morning watch. Billy's dying words are 'God bless Captain Vere'.

In Melville's novel a good-enough man, Captain Vere, condemns to death a moral innocent, Billy Budd, and is prompted, perhaps forced, to do so by the lying words of a villain, John Claggart. This is the story of *Billy Budd*. It is the story of innocence condemned, of evil condoned, and of the 'jugglery of circumstance' that surrounds and prompts both.

In the 80 years since its first publication, Melville's novel has been subjected to intense, even obsessive, critical attention by moral philosophers, political theorists, lawyers and literary critics:[4] some read it as a version of the story of Christ, and as a warning that the world of politics cannot accommodate moral purity. In politics, the good must die. So Billy dies, as Christ died before him, a sacrificial lamb on the altar of political necessity. Others read it as a commentary on homosexual love, and construe Claggart as the spurned lover seeking vengeance in return for rejection. Yet others read it as a reminder of the limitations of human law: 'the law, moving between crime and virtue, cannot recognize what is beyond it' wrote Hannah Arendt, 'and while it has no punishment to mete out to elemental evil, it cannot but punish elemental goodness'.[5] Man's law (our law) demands the death of the morally pure (of Billy Budd), while remaining impotent in the face of unalloyed evil (John Claggart).

All these interpretations focus on the fate of the morally good in a world that is partly, if not largely, evil. My focus, however, is a different one. It is not on the elemental goodness personified by Billy Budd, nor on the elemental evil of John Claggart, but on the dilemma that confronts Captain Vere. For *Billy Budd* is in essence a novel about politics and about the responsibilities of political office.

[3] Op. cit., 148.
[4] See the critical essays in Dan McCall (ed.) *Melville's Short Novels* for some examples of the range of critical responses to the novel.
[5] Hannah Arendt, *On Revolution* as quoted in McCall (ed.) *Melville's Short Novels*, op. cit., 397.

Captain Vere is a naval officer in time of war. He 'wears the King's buttons' and owes a political duty to the King. When faced with a choice between hanging an innocent man and obeying the King's edict, he chooses the King. Is his choice a morally defensible one?

Melville ponders this question and concludes, not with an answer, but with a reflection. He writes, 'Forty years after a battle it is easy for a non-combatant to reason about how it ought to have been fought. It is another thing personally and under fire to direct the fighting while involved in the obscuring smoke of it ... little wean the snug card-players in the cabin of the responsibilities of the sleepless man on the bridge.'[6] But what are the responsibilities of the sleepless man on the bridge? How are we, the snug card-players, to understand Captain Vere's dilemma and how, if at all, are we to judge his decision?

Captain Vere stands in a long line of political actors faced with hard, even tragic, choices between official duty and moral conscience: Pontius Pilate condemned Christ to death on the cross and then 'took water and washed his hands before the multitude, saying I am innocent of the blood of this just person; see ye to it'.[7] Like Captain Vere, he ordered the death of an innocent man, and he did so for reasons of political necessity. History has not, on the whole, forgiven him. Similarly, German judges who had been appointed under the Weimar Republic found themselves required to administer increasingly anti-Semitic laws under the Nazis. Like Captain Vere, they punished the innocent, and did so for reasons of political necessity. History has not, on the whole, forgiven them, either. The moral appears to be that in politics the innocent will not always be protected. Sometimes they will die precisely because they are innocent, and the question, simply put, is: on what grounds, and by what right, do we judge those who condemn them to death? What, to repeat, are the responsibilities of the sleepless man on the bridge?

In this paper I will focus on that question and I will canvass two possible answers to it. The first is that it is his responsibility to do whatever his official duty dictates: faced with a choice between official duty and personal morality, he (and we) should choose official duty. The second is that his responsibility is to arrive at his own moral judgement, independent of the requirements of official duty. The duties of office are subservient to the dictates of private conscience. Neither of these answers seems to me to be adequate:

---

6   *Billy Budd*, 156.
7   St Matthew 27:24.

the former makes Vere a good officer, but a poor man, while the latter makes him a good man, but a poor officer. The challenge for Vere, however, is to be both a good man and a good officer. I will conclude, therefore, with a third answer to Melville's question, one which (I believe) enables us to see how it might be possible to be both.

I begin by foreshadowing that third answer, and I take my cue from Peter Winch who writes:

> I could not have acted as did Vere ... I should have found it morally impossible to condemn a man 'innocent before God' ... I should find the considerations connected with Billy Budd's peculiar innocence too powerful to be overridden by the appeal to military duty.[8]

This suggests that Winch believes Vere to have done wrong when he sentenced Billy Budd to death. But this is not so, for Winch goes on to say that although he himself would have found it 'morally impossible' to condemn Billy Budd to death, it does not follow, and it is not true, that he believes Captain Vere to have acted wrongly. He writes:

> The story seems to me to show that Vere did what was, for him, the right thing to do. But what makes me say this is not anything I see in the situation different from what I have imagined myself to be faced with ... if A says 'x is the right thing for me to do' and B, in a situation not relevantly different, says 'x is the wrong thing for me to do', it can be that both are correct.[9]

For Winch, then, there is no simple answer to the question 'what are the responsibilities of the sleepless man on the bridge?': Vere's responsibilities as Captain of HMS *Indomitable* are to comply with the requirements of the English Mutiny Act and condemn Billy Budd to death. But Winch's responsibilities, if he were Captain of HMS *Indomitable,* would be to reject the requirements of the English Mutiny Act and spare the life of a man known to be innocent. The responsibilities of the sleepless man on the bridge vary, it seems, according to who the sleepless man is, and it is important to note here that Winch is not claiming simply that he could not have brought himself to condemn Billy Budd to death. He is claiming that it would have been *morally wrong* for him to do

---

[8]   Peter Winch, 'The Universalizability of Moral Judgements' in Winch, *Ethics and Action,* (London:Routledge, 1972), 163.

[9]   Op. cit., 164.

so, while also claiming that it was *morally right* for Vere to do so. This is, to say the least, a puzzling conclusion, and yet I think it is the correct one. However, in order to explain why I think it is correct, I need first to discuss the two more 'standard' responses to the question: the first, to recall, holds that Vere ought to give priority to the duties of office, while the second holds that he ought to give priority to his own moral beliefs.

The Responsibilities of Captain Vere

The view that political agents ought to give priority to the duties of their office is not one that currently commands much support. It conjures up an image of the political actor as mere functionary, hiding behind the demands of his official role with the largely disingenuous claim 'I was only obeying orders'. In his book, *Political Ethics and Public Office,* Dennis Thompson gives short shrift to this claim. He writes: 'because personal responsibility attaches to persons, not to offices or collectivities, it follows officials wherever they go ... even if officials do the best they can in circumstances not of their making, they do not escape blame if they simply and indefinitely accept those circumstances'.[10]

This response, however, is not one that has been deemed appropriate through the ages. The Victorian writer, James Fitzjames Stephen, was clear that the duties of office take absolute priority over private conscience, and he offers reasons for that view which are interesting and instructive. Discussing the case of Pontius Pilate, (the case on which some say *Billy Budd* is based) Fitzjames Stephen writes:

> The point to which I wish to direct attention is that Pilate's duty was to maintain peace and order in Judea and to uphold the Roman power.... . To a man in Pilate's position the morals and the social order which he represents are for all practical purposes final and absolute standards.

And he continues:

> If this should appear harsh, I would appeal to Indian experience. Suppose that some great religious reformer—say, for instance, someone claiming to be the Guru of the Sikhs, or the Imam in

[10] Dennis Thompson, *Political Ethics and Public Office* (Harvard: Harvard University Press, 1987), 64.

whose advent many Mahommedans believe—were to make his appearance in the Punjab. Suppose that there was good reason to believe that whatever might be the preacher's personal intentions, his preaching was calculated to disturb the public peace and produce mutiny and rebellion: and suppose further that a British officer, instead of doing whatever might be necessary, or executing whatever orders he might receive, for the maintenance of British authority, were to consider whether or not he ought to become a disciple of the Guru or Imam. What course would be taken towards him? He would be instantly dismissed with ignominy from the service which he would disgrace, and if he acted up to his convictions, and preferred his religion to his Queen and country, he would be hanged as a rebel and a traitor.[11]

And Fitzjames Stephen clearly implies that this response would be the correct one.

It is tempting to dismiss these remarks as simply an expression of Victorian jingoism—exactly the views one would expect from a nineteenth century defender of Queen and Empire. And in part, that's what they are. They do, however, have an interest beyond the parochial. Fitzjames Stephen's conclusion that politics is of supreme importance is based on a general, moral claim that 'to a man in Pilate's position the morals and the social order which he represents are for all practical purposes final and absolute standards'. To hold an official position (a political position), whether as Roman Governor of Judea, or as Captain of HMS *Indomitable*, is not simply to have official (in these cases, political) duties, it is also to represent, in one's own person, the moral standards of the society to which one belongs. On this understanding, Pontius Pilate, as Governor of Judea, is the personification of Roman morality and Roman views about justice. Similarly, Captain Vere is the personification of the moral values that prompted and informed the war against France.

This may seem hideously overstated: surely, it cannot be the case that in taking on an official responsibility one becomes nothing other than the mouthpiece of the establishment? We may be inclined to think that it cannot, but I believe that we are in part deceived and that Fitzjames Stephen articulates an important truth, which is that when we accept official roles, we thereby become, to some degree, the representative of the body that appoints us. As

[11]   James Fitzjames Stephen, *Liberty, Equality, Fraternity* (Cambridge: Cambridge University Press, 1967), 114–115.

Roman Governor of Judea, Pontius Pilate speaks for Rome in Judea; as Captain of HMS *Indomitable,* Captain Vere speaks for the King. To move from the sublime to the ridiculous, as the Head of Department, I speak for my department and, crucially, I do that (or should do that) independent of whether the views of the department are my personal views. For sure, I need not think that I am the mere puppet of those in whose name I act, but equally, having taken on an official role, I cannot simply distance myself from the views of those whom I represent. And 'cannot' here means 'morally cannot'.

To see how this is so, consider the moral status of resignation. It is sometimes (often) said that, where a person's official or political role requires him to do things he believes to be morally wrong, then it is always open to him to resign and thus, the implication is, to escape responsibility for what subsequently happens. This strikes me as both false and naïve. There can of course be cases in which resignation exculpates, but more often responsibility survives resignation, even though the responsibility is of a rather different kind.

In his discussion of the problem of dirty hands, Martin Hollis considers those German judges referred to earlier, who were appointed under the Weimar Republic and subsequently found themselves called upon to administer anti-Semitic laws. He notes that:

> Some resigned but others, reckoning that they would merely be replaced by ardent Nazis, stayed on, grimly trying to do some slight good. Whether or not they made the right choice, they were certainly right about the responsibility. Those who resigned escaped the office, but not the responsibility ... Once a dilemma has been posed for a person in office, integrity does not demand that he keep his hands clean by stepping aside. It is too late for clean hands, whatever he does.[12]

There are, it seems to me, two ways in which this is true—two ways in which responsibility survives resignation. First, when we accept official positions we know that they carry responsibilities with them and, unless we are very naïve, we know that those responsibilities may require us to do what we believe to be morally wrong. To agree to take on an official role just is to accept that one will be bound by

---

[12]   Martin Hollis, 'Dirty Hands', in *Reason in Action: Essays in the philosophy of social science* (Cambridge: Cambridge University Press, 1996), 143.

its duties even when they are morally disagreeable. Of course, there are limits to this, and when those limits are exceeded, people may feel that the only honourable course is resignation. However, and this is the second point, even when the limits are exceeded, responsibility does not fail to apply, for one continues to bear some responsibility for what happens as a result of one's own refusal to carry on. It is important to note that this is not a defence of utilitarianism. I am not suggesting that, in general, when I refuse to do something I believe to be wrong, I am thereby responsible for the terrible things that other people do in response. What I am suggesting, however, is that official duties make a difference and that, when I resign rather than do what my official duty dictates, I cannot 'wash my hands' of the consequences that follow from that resignation, for resignation is, by its nature, a rejection of the moral duties I took upon myself when I accepted office. It may be that it is justified. It may be that it is the honourable thing to do. Nonetheless, the man who resigns, and thus abdicates responsibility, is not, and cannot be, in the same moral position as the man who never accepted that responsibility in the first place.

To summarize, then, the view that the sleepless man on the bridge has a responsibility to do what the duties of his office dictate, and that he has that responsibility even when the duties conflict with his own conscience, is not without merit. Nonetheless, it is not, to my mind, fully satisfactory, for the initial objection— that this threatens to make the officer a mere functionary or puppet—persists.

This brings me to the second of the two possibilities mentioned at the outset: that the responsibilities of the sleepless man on the bridge are responsibilities to do what his own conscience dictates. In this case, that means that his responsibility is to refuse to sentence Billy Budd to death.

The Responsibilities of Edward Vere

In 'Truth and Truth as Predicated of Moral Judgements' David Wiggins criticizes Vere's decision to obey the dictates of office and to sentence Billy Budd to death. He writes:

> Even if Vere would have put his commission at risk in not proceeding so summarily against Billy Budd (because there was some just appreciable risk of indiscipline or disorder ensuing, for which he would have been held responsible), well—in the name

of natural justice, never mind Vere's mental dispositions or the orderly unfolding of his life-plan (doomed in any case, to judge from the story)—perhaps that risk ought to have been taken. And the thought that it ought to have been taken was open to Vere.[13]

By contrast with Fitzjames Stephen, Wiggins insists that it is appropriate, indeed morally obligatory, to take a 'provisional' attitude towards the duties of one's official role. They are, of course, moral duties, but we must always reserve the right to renounce them if they conflict with our understanding of natural justice. Pilate should not see himself simply as Roman governor of Judea, nor should Vere see himself simply as captain of HMS *Indomitable*. Each should remain himself and should be ready to bring the moral demands of office before a higher court—the court of his own moral judgement.

Again, this understanding of the relationship between self and official role is intelligible and has merit: as noted earlier, when we appoint people to public office we want them to be more than mere conduits for the demands made by that office. There is something alarming about a person who is never prepared to put into question the obligations that fall upon him in his official capacity and, more than that, there is reason for not entrusting such a person with public office in the first place.

However, Wiggins' appeal to conscience is not without difficulty, and we should hesitate before embracing it. Wiggins suggests that Captain Vere should have taken a 'provisional' attitude towards his official duties, and by this he means that he should have been ready to reject its demands when they conflicted with natural justice as revealed by the dictates of his own conscience. But there are at least two problems with this approach: the first is that individual conscience is notoriously unreliable, and indeed duties of office are themselves a way of trying to limit the scope for its exercise. This may be because political agents have to act, as did Vere, in the 'obscuring smoke' of battle: we all know that our own judgement is unreliable when we are 'under fire' whether the fire is physical or metaphorical and, for that reason, the moment when we are tempted to ignore the duties of office is likely to be the moment when we need them most.

Beyond that, however, we have reason not to appoint a man who declares in advance that, when the duties of office conflict with

[13] David Wiggins, 'Truth and Truth as Predicated of Moral Judgements', in *Needs, Values, Truth: Essays in the Philosophy of Value* (Oxford: Blackwell, 1987), 180.

conscience, he will follow conscience. This is not simply because such a statement suggests that he does not take his office and its duties morally seriously, it is also because we have no assurance that conscience tells him (or us) the right thing.

There is a classic statement of this problem in Mark Twain's *Huckleberry Finn*. Set in nineteenth-century Missouri, the novel tells how a young white boy (Huck Finn) helps Jim, the black slave, to escape from his owner, Miss Watson. As the raft sails down the Mississippi, bringing Jim closer and closer to freedom, Huck realises what he has done. He has stolen someone else's property. Here are his thoughts:

> Jim said it made him all over trembly and feverish to be so close to freedom. Well, I can tell you it made me all over trembly and feverish, too, to hear him, because I begun to get it through my head that he was most free—and who was to blame for it? Why, *me*. I couldn't get that out of my conscience no how nor no way ... it hadn't ever come home to me before what this thing was that I was doing. But now it did; and it stayed with me and scorched me more and more.[14]

Conscience speaks clearly to Huck and tells him that he has done wrong. Things get worse when Jim announces his intention to buy his wife and children out of slavery; and then adds that, if the children cannot be bought, he will steal them. Huck is horrified:

> Thinks I, this is what comes of my not thinking. Here was this nigger which I had as good as helped to run away, coming right out flat-footed and saying he would steal his children—children that belonged to a man I didn't even know; a man that hadn't ever done me no harm.
>
> I was sorry to hear Jim say that, it was such a lowering of him. My conscience got to me and stirred me up hotter than ever, until at last I says to it; 'let up on me—it ain't too late, yet—I'll paddle ashore at first light and tell'. I felt easy, and happy and light as a feather, right off. All my troubles was gone.[15]

---

14   Mark Twain, *Huckleberry Finn* (London: Dent, 1950), chapter xvi.
15   Ibid.

We are, I take it, glad that Huck dismisses the claims of conscience, for conscience can be a bad guide as well as a good one, and we do well to remember that before we rush to applaud the person who 'follows conscience'.[16]

For these reasons, then, we should treat with caution the suggestion that the responsibility of the sleepless man on the bridge is simply a responsibility to follow where his conscience leads, and to renounce duty when it conflicts with conscience.

My question, to recall, is 'what are the responsibilities of the sleepless man on the bridge?', and I have expressed doubts both about the claim that his responsibility is to do whatever official duty dictates, and about the claim that his responsibility is to do whatever conscience dictates. Moreover, I indicated at the outset that, in my view, his responsibilities vary depending on who he is: what it is right for Vere to do, as Captain of HMS *Indomitable*, may be wrong for Winch were he captain of HMS *Indomitable*. However, the preceding discussion rules out the possibility that, by this, I mean simply that each should follow his own conscience. Conscience, I have suggested, is an unreliable guide. What, then, do I mean?

The Responsibilities of Edward Vere, Captain

The explanation requires a rather abrupt change of gear. So far, I have been discussing a distinctively political problem—the problem of political action. But in discussing the political problem, I have used the resources of moral philosophy. That is to say, I have treated the case of Captain Vere as a case of individual moral dilemma. And so it is. However, it seems to me that, in order to answer the question posed by moral philosophy, we need to appeal to the resources of political philosophy, and in particular to modern liberal political philosophy. In this final section, therefore, I shall try to explain how political philosophy may resolve the problems posed by moral philosophy.

In *Political Liberalism* John Rawls notes, and insists upon, the 'permanence of pluralism' about the good. He takes as his starting point the fact that the modern world is characterised by people with very different, and conflicting, understandings of the highest good and of the right way to lead their lives, and he goes on to insist that

---

[16] For an illuminating discussion of this case see Jonathan Bennett, 'The Conscience of Huckleberry Finn', *Philosophy*, **49**, (1974), 123–34.

this pluralism is characteristic of modern democratic societies and that it is unlikely to disappear or diminish. Thus:

> A modern democratic society is characterized not simply by a pluralism of comprehensive religious, philosophical and moral doctrines but by a pluralism of incompatible yet reasonable comprehensive doctrines. No one of these doctrines is affirmed by citizens generally. Nor should one expect that in the foreseeable future one of them, or some other reasonable doctrine, will ever be affirmed by all, or nearly all, citizens.[17]

Of course, in insisting on the permanence of pluralism, Rawls is referring primarily to the fact that different *groups* of people have competing ideas about what is good: Muslims differ from Christians; the Amish differ from secular liberals; hedonists differ from stoics. What is also true, however, is that individuals differ, and may legitimately come to different conclusions about what it is good to do in any given situation. Recall John Stuart Mill's famous claim:

> If a person possesses any tolerable amount of common sense and experience, his own mode of laying out his existence is best, not because it is the best in itself, but because it is his own mode. Human beings are not like sheep, and even sheep are not indistinguishably alike. A man cannot get a coat or a pair of boots to fit him unless they are either made to his measure or he has a whole warehouseful to choose from; and is it easier to fit him with a life than with a coat?[18]

What is right for one man may well be wrong for another; what is right for Vere may well be wrong for Winch. Or so Mill implies, and Rawls concurs when he notes that one reason why we cannot expect convergence on moral judgement is because 'different conceptions of the world can reasonably be elaborated from different standpoints and diversity arises in part from our different perspectives. It is unrealistic—or worse, it arouses mutual suspicion and hostility—to suppose that all our differences are rooted solely in ignorance and perversity, or else in the rivalries for power, status, or economic gain.'[19]

---

[17]   John Rawls, *Political Liberalism*, (New York: Columbia University Press, 1993), xvi.
[18]   John Stuart Mill, *On Liberty*, (London: Penguin, 1974), 132–3.
[19]   John Rawls, op. cit., 58.

Again, what is right for Vere, given his standpoint and perspective, may be wrong for Winch, given his standpoint and perspective. This is not a thought that has commended itself to moral philosophers, who tend to insist that if something is right for one person, then it must be right for anyone else similarly situated. It is, however, a basic premise of modern liberalism, with its commitment to the permanence of pluralism, that something may indeed be right for one person, given his perspective, dispositions, character, cultural background etc., but not right for someone whose perspective, dispositions, character, and cultural background are different.[20]

Two points should be noted here: the first is that liberalism's commitment to pluralism about the good is more than and different from a mere appeal to conscience; the second (though this is more contentious) is that moral philosophy is often conducted in a manner that does not reflect the realities of modern political life. To explain these two points, let me return to Fitzjames Stephen's judgement on Pontius Pilate. Fitzjames Stephen wrote:

Suppose that some great religious reformer—say, for instance, someone claiming to be the Guru of the Sikhs, or the Imam in whose advent many Mahommedans believe—were to make his appearance in the Punjab. Suppose that there was good reason to believe that whatever might be the preacher's personal intentions, his preaching was calculated to disturb the public peace and produce mutiny and rebellion: and suppose further that a British officer, instead of doing whatever might be necessary, or executing whatever orders he might receive, for the maintenance of British authority, were to consider whether or not he ought to become a disciple of the Guru or Imam. What course would be taken towards him? He would be instantly dismissed with ignominy from the service which he would disgrace, and if he acted up to his convictions, and preferred his religion to his Queen and country, he would be hanged as a rebel and a traitor.[21]

---

[20] In making this claim I am, of course, assuming that a distinction between the right and the good can be drawn, and that the fact of pluralism is confined to pluralism about the good. This claim is contestable—see, for example, Jeremy Waldron, 'Rawls's *Political Liberalism*', in Waldron, *Law and Disagreement,* (Oxford: Oxford University Press, 1999), 149–63.

[21] James Fitzjames Stephen, *Liberty, Equality, Fraternity* (Cambridge: Cambridge University Press, 1967), 114–115.

When I first introduced the quotation, I said that we might be tempted to dismiss Fitzjames Stephen's claim as no more (nor less) than we would expect of a Victorian defender of empire. And I remarked that, in a sense, that's what it is. All I want to do now is urge that although it is that, it is not *merely* that.

When people are appointed to public office, they are appointed within a context that defines—to a greater or lesser extent—not only what the duties of office are, but also, and crucially, how they themselves should relate to those duties. Moral philosophers, including the ones I have discussed here (Winch and Wiggins), tend to proceed as though the duties of office are given and it is then a matter for each individual to consider them and decide what his relationship to them will be: whether and when he will obey them, whether and when he will follow his own conscience. But this is not always the way things are. When I take on an official role, I accept specific duties—so much has been noted already. However, I also accept, or offer, an understanding of my relationship to those duties, and that understanding will differ from one historical moment to another, from one cultural context to another, and from one individual to another. For a man in Pilate's position, the duties of office were indeed absolute. In becoming Roman Governor of Judea, he undertook to speak with the voice of Rome. For us, things are different: we have different duties and, crucially, different understandings of our relationship to those duties. These are the differences of standpoint or perspective which underpin the permanence of pluralism. However, and to repeat, they are not differences that amount simply to differences of conscience. They are differences that inform our understanding of the moral status of the exercise of conscience.

To put the point differently, when we appoint people to public office we do so against a background understanding of both their own personality (their perspective or standpoint or conception of the good) and the stringency of the requirements of the post. Sometimes, we appoint those who are more likely to exercise their own judgement; sometimes we don't. Sometimes we ourselves are appointed because we are independent spirits; sometimes we are passed over for that same reason. Having once been appointed because we have a particular standpoint or perspective, it is not open to us to deliberate, as if *de novo,* on our relationship to the duties of office. That was, in part, something we committed to at the outset.

The dilemma of Captain Vere arises most acutely when he is appointed because he is, or is deemed to be, a man of judgement, and not a mere 'rule follower', for now he has specific duties arising from his role as captain of the *Indomitable* (the duty to comply with the requirements of the Mutiny Act), but he also, and legitimately, has an understanding of himself as someone who has been made captain *precisely because* he will not always obey those duties. For such a man, the question is not 'what is it right for the Captain of HMS *Indomitable* to do?', nor is it 'what is it right for me to do?'. His question is, 'what is it right for me as Captain of HMS *Indomitable* to do?', where that question emphasises both that he has official duties and that he has been appointed because we know that he will perceive those duties from his distinctive perspective or standpoint. And if he were not inclined to do that, we would not have appointed him in the first place.

What, then, are the responsibilities of the sleepless man on the bridge? It depends. I make no apology for failing to provide a neat, and definitive conclusion, for part of my argument has been that those who do so fail to understand the complexity of the case. They fail to see that the duties of office must be interpreted, and that the interpretation must flow in part from the character of the officer appointed.

More generally, and more worryingly, those who insist on a definitive answer deny the legitimacy of declaring that what is right for one person may be wrong for another, but that belief, though almost heretical in modern moral philosophy, is the very stuff of modern political philosophy. Indeed, it is the background assumption against which modern political philosophy begins its work. This tension between moral philosophy, which demands convergence, and political philosophy, which assumes permanent divergence, is disconcerting. It raises important but (for me) unanswerable questions about the relationship between the two areas of our discipline, and it prompts unease about whether they can 'speak' to one another.

That, however, is for another day. For now, I return to the snug card players in the cabin, and to Herman Melville, who reports the official naval judgement on the case of Billy Budd. It ran as follows:

On the tenth of the last month a deplorable occurrence took place on board HMS *Indomitable*. John Claggart, the ship's master-at arms, discovering that some sort of plot was incipient among an inferior section of the ship's company, and that the ringleader was one William Budd, he, Claggart, in the act of arraigning the man before the captain was vindictively stabbed to the heart by the suddenly drawn sheath knife of Budd ... the criminal paid the penalty of his crime. The promptitude of the punishment has proved salutary. Nothing amiss is now apprehended aboard HMS *Indomitable*.[22]

We, and Captain Vere, know different. Captain Vere did what was right for him, given his peculiar standpoint and perspective. He was, we may suppose, appointed partly because he had that standpoint and perspective, and he interpreted his duties from that standpoint and perspective. However, and following Rawls, we must also acknowledge that his was not the only perspective, nor even the only reasonable perspective. Different people might reasonably judge differently and, as a result of their different judgement, they might have different duties. The responsibilities of the sleepless man on the bridge depend, in no small part, on who that sleepless man is.

[22] *Billy Budd*, op. cit, 168.

Democracy and Openness

ANTHONY O'HEAR

During the recent Iraq war there was a great deal of discussion of the desirability of bringing democracy to Iraq, and indeed to other countries which were suffering under ruthless and oppressive dictatorships. There was also the thought that if Iraq had a flourishing democratic system, its benefits would become evident within the Middle East, and other peoples in the area would be encouraged to press for more democracy in their own countries. And critics who expressed doubts about any of this were accused of treating the people of the Middle East in a patronising way, implying that they were not able to do what we in the West have managed for some time.

I certainly do not want to appear patronising, nor indeed do I want to reject the idea that democracy may be the best form of government for everyone, everywhere. And I think that it evinces a form of pessimistic determinism to say, as many do on both left and right, that there may be countries too poor or backward to become democracies. But I do want to raise a number of questions in order to make slightly more precise just what might be meant by democracy, or by the sort of democracy it might be advisable to spread around the world.

Consider the following cases

1. In an Islamic country, there is a bitterly fought and often violent election. The election is won by the radical or fundamentalist party, who have made it clear that they will institute Sharia law and various other practices regarded by others inside and outside the country as repressive. The army steps in and annuls the election, setting up a military dictatorship with its own different type of repression. One effect of this is that the country become a major exporter of asylum seekers, some of whom join Islamic terrorist groups outside the country around the world.
2. An African country is divided on tribal lines. People in that country vote almost entirely on tribal lines. One tribe is significantly larger than the others. There are democratic

elections, but they are always won by one party, so democratic tribalism leads to a one party state.

3. A central European country is suffering from a continuing economic and social crisis following a disastrous war. Elections happen frequently, but tend to produce weak governments, which simply exacerbates the crisis. A new party arises, led by a strong leader, who identifies groups to blame for the continuing crisis. He promises to rid the country of instability and to curb the influence of the offending groups. The voters give him this power, and he then uses his majority in the democratically elected parliament to he set himself up as dictator.

4. Another Western country has for a number of years (with just one break) been run by a party of the social-democratic left, which has won a series of elections. This party is in fact financed by the trade unions and led by a combination of doctrinaire socialists and rabble rousing populists. The state runs pretty well everything including what their official doctrine refers to as 'the commanding heights of the economy' (i.e. decrepit, inefficient and over-manned steel, coal, aircraft, rail and motor industries, to say nothing of telecommunications and other public utilities), and controls (or attempts to control) the whole economy. Nevertheless, despite or perhaps because of all this, there are damaging strikes every year in both public and private sectors, which usually end in 'meaningful' settlements after 'contructive' negotiations (i.e. pay rises for the strikers of between 10 and 20% or more). Inflation is rampant, 20% or so per year; taxes are as high as 98% on the highest incomes; there is capital flight; in some cities the dead are unburied and rubbish is uncollected for weeks; the government has to go the IMF to get baled out and is forced to institute draconian economic measures. It loses the next election, after its leader and the country's Prime Minister has returned from a mid-winter holiday in the Caribbean uttering the immortal phrase 'Crisis? What crisis?'

A few preliminary comments on our cases

The first case is based on the current situation in Algeria, following the success of the Islamic Salvation Front (FIS) in the first round of elections in 1991, and the army's cancelling of the second round in 1992, in which the FIS was heading for a clear majority. One lesson which might be drawn from it is that the effects of violent political events in one country may not be confined to that country. In this sense, then, and in line with one of the themes of this meeting, we all have an interest in what happens in Algeria; we all have to consider whether democracy is or is not desirable in such a country, and whether we would support the intervention of the army in an election in circumstances like those which obtained in Algeria. (It is worth noting that free and fair elections in Egypt, Pakistan and elsewhere in the Islamic world, including possibly Saudi Arabia, would probably see victories by fundamentalists; but it is also worth noting that the allegedly 'secular' government currently ruling in Algeria is actually a brutal and ruthless dictatorship, and that in its attitude to women is currently trying hard to appear as hard-line as its fundamentalist critics.)

The second case might be Zimbabwe (or many other African states). But let us suppose it is Zimbabwe over the past twenty or so years. Actually in 2002 even some of the President's own supporters were beginning to turn against him, and he was in some danger of losing the election that year. Whether he would actually have lost it or not in a genuinely free election, we will never know, because the population was assisted in its democratic deliberations and in its vote-casting by groups of the President's supporters, armed thugs known as 'war veterans', whom the police, far from controlling, actually helped. But this was only the final stage on Zimbabwe's route from democracy to a one-party state with no respect for human rights and in effect a president for life or for as long as he feels like staying on. We need to ask whether this passage was inevitable in the circumstances, and also perhaps about the meaning of fair elections.

The third case is a somewhat simplified sketch of Germany in 1933. The National Socialists under Hitler together with the parties which supported the Nazis did win an election that year, the last election in Germany until after the war. A democratically elected leader did then annul democratic procedures (by means of the Enabling Act, which gave the Chancellor power to make laws without consulting Parliament), leading to what philosophers have dubbed 'the paradox of democracy': that is, a democratic system democratically voting away its own right to operate democratically. In this context we might also note what has happened more recently in Europe; when the European Union attempted in effect to negate the democratically decided inclusion of Jörg Haider's Freedom Party into the Austrian government, and also when, in the French Presidential election of 2002, the whole apparatus of government and the media abandoned all pretence at impartiality and directed itself, unfairly many thought, to defeating Le Pen. So should democratic institutions act undemocratically in attempting to defeat those they see as enemies of democracy and likely if they got power to undermine democracy?

The final example is sketch of my own country in 1979 and the atmosphere leading up to 1979; unlike the other stories, it does have a reasonably satisfactory ending. The new leader was Mrs Thatcher who, among other things, took on the trade unions and curbed their undemocratic power. She got inflation down, privatised much of the economy, including the public utilities, and she reduced taxes generally (while actually generating more revenue for the government). But perhaps we could also consider the less happy case of Chile under Allende where a democratically elected government appeared to its critics to be expropriating private property on a large scale and was plunging the country into severe social instability. But when does a democratic re-distribution of wealth become expropriation, and when does giving workers their legitimate trade union rights become syndicalist abuse of a labour monopoly (in which collectivised labour can hold a country to ransom, by means of closed shops combined with aggressive and often violent strikes in key industries)?

Aristotle and Plato

So from our examples, we have a budget of questions, too many and too complex to answer here or even discuss in any detail. But clearly they all show ways in which democracy is not just being used to further undemocratic ends—which it clearly is in the cases considered—but more precisely, democratic structures are being used to decrease openness and freedom in the society as a whole. Underlying all the questions and cases is the meaning of a distinction made first by Aristotle in his **Politics** (1279a16). In Aristotle's own words 'it is clear that those constitutions which aim at the common good are right, as being in accord with absolute justice; while those which aim only at the good of the rulers are wrong. They are all deviations from the right constitutions. They are like the rule of the master over the slave, whereas the state is an association of free men.'

While it is easy for us in the twenty first century to see in dictatorships and oligarchies the type of deviation from the good constitution of which Aristotle speaks, it is less natural to see democracies in those terms; less natural, perhaps, but as our examples suggest, not necessarily incorrect. For Aristotle there are two ways in which rule by the majority can turn out, the first which he calls polity and the second he calls democracy. Polity is political control exercised by the mass of the populace in the common interest, whereas democracy is when the mass uses its power to further the sectional interests of the many, or as Aristotle says, of the men without means. Democracy is when the poor and numerous hold office, and use their office for the benefit of the poor and numerous, often by punitive taxation of the better off (what might be called redistribution, but which may actually be little better than the legalised theft and the expression of the primitive resentment of the less well off against those who may well have worked hard to achieve their positional and economic superiority).

Democracy, as opposed to polity, may then lead to that characteristic vice of the many, a spirit of small-mindedness and its working up by demagogues. Here, of course, Aristotle walks in the footsteps of his teacher, Plato. In Plato's **Republic** we find an almost wholly negative characterisation of democracy. Democracy arises in the first place when the majority in an oligarchic society begin to realise that the minority of wealthy people who are ruling are in fact no better than the majority, and because of their corruption by wealth, weak too. So in a movement which anticipates the awakening of the slave class in Hegel, the poor use their numerical might to take over from their masters. A form of egalitarian diversity and liberty ensues, which is close to anarchy in that there is no real authority and no hierarchy of value. There is no real constancy, either individual or collective; the same people appear one day as sybarites, the next day as ascetics; one day they praise military virtue, the next business values, the next study, and so on; and the same goes for the fashions in society as a whole. Those rule who manage to convince the majority that they are the 'people's friends'.

Among the people themselves, in the name of liberty, lower passions begin to dominate, and there is also a cult of youth: 'the parent falls into the habit of behaving like the child, and the child like the parent; the father is afraid of his sons, and they show no fear or respect for their parents in order to assert their freedom ... the schoolmaster timidly flatters his pupils, and the pupils make light of their masters as well as of their attendants. Generally speaking, the young copy their elders, argue with them, and will not do as they are told; while the old, anxious not to be thought disagreeable tyrants, imitate the young and condescend to enter into their jokes and amusements.' (**Republic**, 563a-b) Eventually, in the ensuing lawlessness, democratic despots become dominant, paving the way for straightforward tyranny.

We do not need to accept everything Plato says to see that, phenomenologically speaking, he acutely captures some of democracy's inherent dangers and possible outcomes, a point to which we will return. But he is too negative, in part I conjecture because he holds a false view of political truth. It will be recalled that for Plato the ideal republic was one which would be ruled by philosopher kings, intellectuals who had devoted their lives to the study of dialectic, cut off from the rest of humanity and from ordinary human concerns. They would acquire a form of wisdom superior to the rest of humanity, and, armed with this wisdom, they would be able to rule and administer society with perfect justice. From this perspective any attempt to involve the majority of ordinary people without philosophical training in matters of government would necessarily corrupt the pure truth of the philosophers, and it would also mean that society would be dominated by factions and self-interest (much like what Plato saw in the Athenian Assembly, where those he believed signally unfitted to govern held sway, and, whose court of 501 jurors had, of course, condemned Socrates to death).

But Plato's model of ethical knowledge is fatally flawed. Morality and justice are not *a priori* concepts, discoverable by dialectic or pure reason alone. Without denying their objectivity, it is important to appreciate that what we know about these things emerges from human experience and from what we discover about human flourishing through the experience of life. They are, to that degree, empirical matters, constrained to a considerable degree by what we learn about the experiential interplay between human possibility and human limitations.

But even if this were not so, Plato's model of politics is also fatally flawed. For his rulers to be able to rule successfully, they would have to have knowledge of the whole of society, in order to see what policies were needed and how those policies turned out. It is just this knowledge which they are denying themselves by failing to involve the whole population in their decision making. For, however well intentioned and learned legislators might be, all actions and policies have unforeseeable and unintended consequences. To take a simple example, it might be felt that in a situation of housing shortage, private landlords are taking unfair advantage of their tenants by pushing rents up too high and threatening those who do not or cannot pay with homelessness. So the government acts to control rents and tenure to protect the security of tenants, which would in all probability be both just and popular democratically. But unfortunately the landlords respond by ceasing to let their property to secured tenants, whose situation is actually worsened as the supply of property to rent dries up.

No doubt it would be said that all this is now well known. Any future rent acts would be drafted to close off this eventuality, and that is no doubt true. But what is now well known was not well known when, in response to public pressure, British governments did first introduce rent acts in the 1960s, with the effects I have just described. And no doubt future rent acts will have other, as yet unpredictable, consequences. The general point being made here is that the successful ruling of any society will require a constant flow of information to the rulers from the ruled, both in order to decide policy, but even more important to learn the effects of policies. It is just this flow of information which Plato's rulers are denied by their situation, and it will also be denied to any self-enclosed group of rulers who are insulated from the general public by groups of flatterers, place men and intermediaries who tell them only what they want to hear (which will be the inevitable effect of any dictatorship). Effective rule requires openness in the body politic, an openness which democracy is well suited to supply.

This was well understood by Aristotle in his defence of polity. In general, according to him, when there are many people, each is likely to have some share of virtue and practical wisdom, which is why he wants matters of value generally to be decided by the consensus of the many and the wise; the wise, to be sure, but also the many because of their experience, individual and collective. And although individually each of the many may be inferior in understanding to the experts, collectively they are likely to be as good or better.

Negatively, too, if we exclude the mass of people from politics we are likely to be incubating a 'huge hostile element in the state' (1281b31). True enough, but the positive argument is stronger and more interesting. It is precisely the point we have been making, that those who best understand the effects of policies are those directly affected by them: 'there are tasks of which the actual doer will be neither the best nor the only judge ... An obvious example is house building: the builder can certainly form an opinion on a house, but the user, the household manager will be an even better judge ... and it is the diner not the cook that pronounces upon the merits of a dinner.' (1282a17–23) In our days of arrogant architects raised to peerages and celebrity chefs, Aristotle's common sense is salutary. And anathema as it might be to politicians and bureaucrats, in evaluating practical matters and particularly in public politics, the user or consumer should be in pole position and not the producer or planner.

Then again, while Aristotle is unillusioned about the possibilities of democratic corruption and the buying of votes, he also points out that the more power is diffused, the less the possibility of corruption; many are less easily corrupted that one or a few (and, as we have learned, corruption can take many forms and also can occur even among the most incorruptible once they have got power). But, more than that point, obvious enough to us if not to Plato, Aristotle also points out that if the people in the middle of society take a hand in politics, the results are likely to be better than if either the arrogance of the rich or the envy of the very poor are in the ascendant. 'Where the middle element' as he puts it, 'is large, there least of all arise factions and divisions among the citizens' (1296a8), and this desirable condition is more likely to obtain in large democratic states than in any other type of constitution, given the natural tendency of oligarchies, aristocracies and monarchies to concentrate wealth and honours on the few—and hence to prepare the way for factional strife.

But this middle element, if mature, numerous and powerful, will also be able to counter-balance the tendency in democracy to egalitarianism of a radical sort, which is inherent in the democratic assumption that at a certain level every man—and opinion—is equal or deserving of equal attention. What we are calling openness does indeed demand an assumption of this sort, because, for reasons already touched on, we do want every voice to have some sort of say and we do not want people to be dismissed and treated as non-persons; the difficulty is to maintain this fundamental premise without lapsing into the potentially rancorous egalitarianism which would treat all opinions as equally worthwhile or valid, and dismiss any differences of wealth and position, however obtained, as in themselves objectionable. And it is at this point that a strong and stable middle group in a society may be able to steer policy and practice in directions which are both democratic and measured in value and judgement. Of course, as Aristotle hints in his negative remarks about the bad form of democracy, a successful middle group and a successful polity will be far easier to establish in a society in which everybody has a degree of economic stake in that society and economic security to boot. The historic connexion between liberal democracy and the ownership of property is not coincidental.

In sum, then, Aristotle, while no uncritical admirer of democracy, actually gives us some very substantial reasons for thinking that the beneficent form of democracy—polity as he puts it, a democracy dominated by a secure and stable middle group—is likely to produce better decisions, better feedback, less corruption and more political wisdom overall than rule by one man or a few or by some faction simply pursuing its own interests unchecked or by rulers unprepared to listen to all those they rule. This point in Aristotle is so strong that given the high likelihood of corruption and stupidity in both monarchy and oligarchy, one wonders why he did not come straight out and declare polity the best form of government *simpliciter*. But it would, of course, have to be a polity in which general consensus through the middle group restrained the brute exercise of power by a bare majority acting purely in its own narrow and immediate interests.

De Tocqueville

Not even the most superficial consideration of democracy can avoid a brief reference to de Tocqueville's unparalleled analysis of democratic mores and the democratic temperament (in **Democracy in America** referred to here in the Fontana Press edition, translated by George Lawrence, 1994). De Tocqueville was, of course, talking about early nineteenth century America, a society he admired for its peacefulness, its community spirit and for its way of settling differences. Nevertheless he did have considerable reservations about some aspects of democratic America, mostly based on its tendency to a form of egalitarian culture. In this he was following in Plato's footsteps, for Plato had also criticised the egalitarian tendencies of democracy, as we have seen, but in one significant respect de Tocqueville departs from the Platonic analysis, and arguably he is more accurate at least as far as modern democracies go. For where Plato sees democracy as characterised by a scandalous diversity of taste, morality and attitude—a sort of Nietzschean pandemonium of free spirits—de Tocqueville emphasises democracy's tendency to conformism beneath any superficial diversity.

Where a society is stratified and men are unalike, the few who are really enlightened and learned may be accepted as such, and so become able to wield great power; whereas 'the nearer men are to a common level of uniformity, the less they are inclined to believe baldly in any man or class. But they are readier to trust the mass, and public opinion becomes more and more the mistress of the world'. (435)

In a democracy, although people hate being thought worse than their neighbour and dislike obeying superiors, because of the general egalitarian spirit each person actually has a low opinion of himself and 'thinks that he is born for nothing but the enjoyment of vulgar pleasures' (632). Democracy dislikes the idea of high ideals beyond those of material self-interest—which is why democracies tend to be unwilling to go to war—but the obverse of this good quality is that all too easily in a democracy a spirit of cultural and moral mediocrity reigns. So along with the dogma of intellectual equality goes a practice of universal weakness. In democracies individuals are weak and conformist, and expect the whole to do for them what they should be doing for themselves did they really respect themselves or their freedom.

And this paves the way for what de Tocqueville memorably referred to as democratic despotism, a society ruled over by a schoolmaster rather than a tyrant, but despotic nonetheless in its combination of centralisation and popular sovereignty. Over this society and its people

> stands an immense, protective power which is alone responsible for securing their enjoyment and watching over their fate ... It would resemble parental authority if, fatherlike, it tried to prepare its charges for a man's life, but on the contrary it only tries to keep them in perpetual childhood. It likes to see its citizens enjoy themselves, provided that they think of nothing but enjoyment. It gladly works for their happiness but wants to be the sole agent and judge of it ... Thus it daily makes the exercise of free choice less useful and rarer, restricts the activity of free will within a narrower compass, and little by little robs each citizen of the proper use of his own faculties ... It covers the whole of social life with a network of petty, complicated rules that are both minute and uniform, through which even men of the greatest originality and most vigorous temperament cannot force their heads above the crowd. It does not break men's will, but softens, bends and guides it; it seldom enjoins, but often inhibits action; it does not destroy anything, but prevents much being born; it is not at all tyrannical, but it hinders, restrains, enervates, stifles, and stultifies so much that in the end each

nation is no more than a flock of timid and hardworking animals with the government as its shepherd. (691)

De Tocqueville is, of course, sketching an ideal type here, the way he thinks that a certain type of egalitarian democracy is likely to go. Much of what he says has come to pass in Western Europe, with its social chapters, its universal provision of state welfare, its incessant regulation of more and more tracts of our lives and its obsessive paternalism masquerading as health and safety. Despotism may be a strong description of our form of life, surely too strong if one thinks of Saddam Hussein's Iraq, say, and it is certainly not a tyranny. But that there is a servile spirit in our commonly held assumption that the state will look after, regulate, determine and protect our lives and behaviour in ever increasing detail is less easy to deny. We might also recall that in **On Liberty** (Ch 5), John Stuart Mill warned that a universal state education would be little more than a device for moulding all men alike, inherently mediocre, essentially conformist, and fundamentally illiberal. Yet in many of our societies and for many of our citizens, universal state education (or at least a heavy preponderance of free state provision in a mixed system) has come to seem a cornerstone of civilised existence (along with analogous state health and welfare schemes). Deaf to the warnings of nineteenth century commentators like de Tocqueville and Mill, we are then surprised when the results of state education are dire throughout Europe and the USA.

Critical as he is of some tendencies of democracy, it seems to be that in one respect de Tocqueville is not critical enough. He clearly thinks that, as part of its general softening effect, democracy will actually make people more humane and gentle, with their passions 'naturally restrained, imagination limited and pleasures simple'. (690) He may be right in his expectation that public policy in a democracy is likely to pay lip service at least to values of humanity and even gentleness, but unlike Plato he clearly did not foresee the extent to which egalitarian assumptions in the populace at large, unchecked by standards of the right way to behave might well issue in individual and group behaviour infused with anger, aggression and resentment; and he paid little attention to the role the mass media, that quintessentially democratic phenomenon, might play in undermining standards of behaviour and conduct. And neither Plato nor de Tocqueville spent much time considering the effect egalitarian assumptions about value might have in a society in which there is not just one, but many so-called cultures jostling for position in a confined social space – maybe because neither would have thought such a society possible, let alone actual.

Democracy, Freedom and Openness

Our initial examples suggested that democracy is not in itself sufficient for good government. Majority rule can be used to tyrannise, to quash good government, to restrict freedom and to close down openness in a society. Both Aristotle and Plato show us why this will happen when a majority uses democracy to further its own interests at the expense of the whole.

But, unlike Plato, Aristotle gives us some strong reasons to think that, generally speaking, democracy might be the best form of government, provided that there is openness within the democracy and provided that there is within that society there is a middle consensus or a consensus of the middle about what is or is not tolerable, and provided that such a consensus generally prevails.

One could argue that in our first three examples of disordered democracy (a Sharia ruled Algeria, Zimbabwe, Weimar Germany), there was or would be neither openness nor the sort of middle consensus Aristotle is seeking, and that in our fourth example there was danger of the essential consensus failing, but that Mrs Thatcher, by her apparently tough and, among substantial sections of the population, deeply unpopular measures, restored it. That may seem a surprising thing to say of a leader who publicly professed to despise consensus and who, according to opinion polls and to what one hears on television, is personally still the most hated British prime minister of recent decades; but it is worth recalling that Tony Blair, for some time the most popular of recent prime ministers and with a huge parliamentary majority to boot, has felt no impulsion whatsoever to reverse her policies on trade unions, inflation or privatisation. In other words these supposedly controversial measures, despite initial appearance, actually reflected the consensus in British society, but one which had been hidden and distorted by political activity over some two or more decades.

In fact de Tocqueville gives us a useful clue to analysing the apparent paradox of some unpopular reforms actually being more consensual than what they replaced. The democratic state, as depicted by de Tocqueville, has a tendency to take over more and more of the lives of the citizens. But the more the state grows, the more power and money it has at its disposal. This over-weighty state then becomes a prize to be fought over by any and all vested interest groups, by all in fact who seek power, wealth and influence in the society. So far from incarnating or mediating consensus within a society, the state and its institutions become prizes to be fought over and won. Reforms, such as Mrs Thatcher's which weaken the power of the state or the inequitable legal status of bodies such as trade unions, then remove a damaging degree of conflict from the political arena, and leave it to the citizens to fight their differences out among themselves; in these circumstances the state becomes more like a referee in the fight, rather than yet another player in the game, whose decisions will be (more or less) accepted in a consensual spirit, provided only they can be seen to embody a degree of impartiality.

This analysis, encouraging as it may seem, however does rest on one assumption: that at a deep level, at a level deeper than day to day politics, there is within a society consensus on basic values, attitudes and behaviour. To what extent does de Tocqueville's conformity of public opinion represent such a consensus? There are two reasons to be cautious here. First, for the reasons already looked at, a bloated de Tocquevillean state is likely by its very existence and nature to promote divisions within society, and so to undermine consensus, at least on the surface. But more profoundly, the public opinion which holds sway in such a state is likely to be both fickle and, ultimately at least, subversive of long-term standards of value. This is because of its egalitarian roots: any view is as good as any other, and the only way of deciding between views is majority opinion. Majority opinion is not determined by long-lasting standards and criteria, but is notoriously subject to media manipulation and distortion, as Plato recognised. And in a society which is dominated by majority public opinion, traditional values and standards are likely to come under assault, particularly if they seem to be standing in the way of instant gratification or egalitarian attitudes.

From this point of view and in an egalitarian democracy, public opinion is likely to destroy the roots of a true 'middle' consensus in a society, one which is based on long-held and settled values, which are taken within the society to have the sanction of some hierarchy of value beyond mere majority opinion as manufactured in the mass media. As Aristotle notes, 'the most extreme democracy, in which all share, is something which not every state can tolerate; and it is not likely to last unless it is well held together by its laws and customs' (**Politics**, 1319b) and, he would no doubt add, by the weight of a middle group reasonable in it attitudes and respectful of those laws and customs. I have been reluctant to speak of this middle group as a middle class, not only because there is no guarantee that with a certain sort of education (or mis-education) the middle classes, as defined in socio-economic terms, will not become highly subversive of law and custom; but, even more, because there can be occasions when it is precisely the working classes which have the most solid and unspoken regard for settled law and custom, as conservative politicians from Disraeli to Mrs Thatcher have recognised. But it is just this often unspoken respect for laws and customs, together with a sense of value beyond what we chose for ourselves on the basis of our own decisions which binds a society together which is going to be missing in a society run by public opinion.

This thought takes us on to a further consideration of openness. I have argued that some formally democratic societies fail through lack of openness (as do many undemocratic societies as well, of course). This might be particularly the case when a majority insist on imposing their religion or moral code on minorities and reject any criticism or feedback on the effect of their codes and policies. For all its democracy, such a society might well be as repressive and unfree as other countries which are formally dictatorships.

The question, though, is how we are to secure openness in a society. Some who have heard what I have been saying about openness and democracy will be aware that Aristotle is not its only source. In the background of my remarks about the unintended consequences of policies and about the need for openness to correct their defects is Karl Popper's **The Open Society and Its Enemies** (London, 1945, & subsequent editions). Popper was also very aware of the possibility of democracies lacking openness, but he was also sceptical of the efficacy of formal ways of securing openness. For openness is a question fundamentally of attitude within a society and among its rulers. For Popper constitutions guaranteeing fundamental freedoms, just as democracy itself, can have a role to play in a tolerant and humane society, but they are certainly not enough to guarantee it, as numerous examples from the apparently liberal Soviet constitution of 1918 to the current wrangling over the European constitution are enough to show. In Popper's own terminology, if you want openness in an institution you need a spirit of openness in those manning it – and, I would add, if you think that spirit is likely to be found among Europe's current commissioners and fonctionaires, who have for decades floated in a culture of secrecy, evasion and unaccountability, whatever the formal constraints on them, then you are likely to be disappointed.

Multiculturalism and Democratic Consensus

It is, of course, a further question as to whether a spirit of openness on its own is enough to foster a tolerant and humane society, and one which is becoming increasingly relevant because of a further development in democracy. The development to which I refer is institutional multi-culturalism, that is the notion that one can have different groups, with very different values and world views, all accorded equal standing as groups within a single society. Multi-culturalism is usually contrasted with mono-culturalism, according to which, while individuals qua individuals have equal rights under the law, it is assumed that the public institutions and values of the society will reflect those of some dominant and homogeneous group. In a mono-cultural society, immigrants from different groups may well be admitted and even welcomed, but in the public sphere they will be expected to conform to the nation's public attitudes and values.

In practice, of course, few, if any, societies are (or have ever been) wholly mono-cultural, but it is only recently that multi-culturalism has begun to be advocated as a positive value in itself. One recent effect of democratic egalitarianism within the liberal democracies of the West has been to weaken assumptions of superiority about any values, including often the public values of one's own society, and this weakening of faith in current values may also include scepticism about liberal individualism itself (often said to be just the value of the dominant culture(s) in the West). At the same time, whether as effect or cause, there has been a growth of identity politics, the belief that individuals are constituted as individuals by the groups with which, by ethnicity or religion they do identify. Mass immigration and a realisation of the extent to which specific groups within apparently mono-cultural societies have been done down in the past have combined to produce a growing clamour in many Western societies for recognition of group rights and exceptions from national norms in fields such as employment, health, welfare and above all education. The multi-cultural position is that group rights and differences should be recognised in law and practice more generally, and, in the jargon, 'diversity celebrated', not just in peripheral and private things like restaurants and clothes shops, but in the public institutions the very heart of our democracies.

How would a multi-cultural society with differences recognised in all its institutions and welcoming even radical differences among its citizens in such things as religion actually hold together?

Anthony O'Hear

According to Professor Lord Parekh, an influential proponent of such a view, commitment to the political community itself would be enough to hold a society together, where that politics is itself conceived in terms of a commitment to hold dialogue on differences between groups and positions, rather than resorting to violence or to marginalising dissenters or (if one does belong to a dissenting group) retreating into a self-imposed ghetto. This commitment does not presuppose any shared cultural, ethnic, religious or any other characteristic, nor does it 'involve sharing common substantive goals ... nor a common view of (the country's) history which they may read differently, nor a particular economic or social system about which they may entertain different views'; and it can go along with criticising 'the prevailing form of government, institutions, policies, values, ethos and dominant self-understanding in the strongest possible terms', but none of this should be regarded as disloyal 'so long as their basic commitment to dialogue is not in doubt'. (Bhikhu Parekh, **Rethinking Multiculturalism**, Houndmills, 2000, 341–2)

That a commitment to a certain form of openness alone might be sufficient to bind a community together is both radical and reductive. In response, it might be observed first that dialogue alone will not necessarily prevent either sharp divisions or feelings of being marginalized. In all sorts of areas decisions have to be made in a society, and particularly where fundamental moral differences are at issue (e.g. on abortion, women's rights, arranged marriages, euthanasia, and so on), at least some may feel unable to accept them, even after as much dialogue as anyone could want. Perhaps this might seem initially to imply a minimal state, where very few decisions have to be made, and this would certainly be in line with what I suggested earlier in discussing de Tocqueville, but before one becomes too sanguine about that remember that a minimal state would itself be morally unacceptable to those who believe in a socialistic concept of social justice.

But even leaving aside the problem of disputes irresolvable by dialogue, we need to consider whether any human group could function effectively as a society without something more held in common than a shared commitment to the political process. All the societies of which we have knowledge have, to a greater or lesser degree, had shared sentiments, shared allegiances, shared traditions and shared values. Whether a society would be possible which dispensed with all of this—as Parekh and the multiculturalists advocate—might fairly be said by its advocates to be something which we could not know in advance of an experiment along these lines. But that does not, I think, get to the root of the problem.

What the multiculturalists need to consider are the conditions required for the successful operation of the type of politics they advocate. The type of dialogue—and of tolerance and openness— which they see as underpinning the ideal political set-up is not something which comes from nowhere. As our earlier examples of flawed democracies indicate, much more is needed for a successful democracy than a formal commitment to majority rule. And as Aristotle and Plato and de Tocqueville show, democracy itself has certain inherent tendencies which militate against what might be called societies of free and responsible citizens, living in harmony and fruitful dialogue. In order to counter-balance these tendencies, Aristotle's insistence on a secure and stable middle group in society —no doubt appealing to some settled values and sentiments within that society—seems plausible enough.

But the existence and influence within a society of such a group within a liberal democracy itself depends on the sharing of certain values in that society. These values will typically be those of liberal democracy itself, values which will permit a society to be open, flexible, reasonable and tolerant on the one hand, but without compromising its fundamental stability and commitment to certain conceptions of human autonomy and flourishing on the other. These liberal democratic values historically are Western values, deriving from a long history, with its origins in Greece and Rome, in Christianity and in a history of religious wars and persecutions from which emerged ultimately a culture of rights and tolerance. These values are not necessarily so esteemed in other places and traditions, where our stress on autonomy, tolerance and human rights **can** seem like yet another manifestation of Western imperialism. (On this point see Samuel P. Hungtington, **The Clash of Civilisations and the Remaking of World Order**, London, 198, 194.) In other words, the form of politics which the multi-culturalists see as potentially bridging the gap between Western and other world-views itself depends on acceptance of a substantive set of values, which in history have emerged most notably within the Western world, and which for that very reason may well be denied by other potential participants in the multi-cultural democracy.

I am not saying that these values cannot be accepted by others and in other traditions. As I happen to think that these values have a more than local validity, and that they are actually justifiable in terms of certain basic requirements for human flourishing in

Anthony O'Hear

general, I think it patronising to say any such thing, as I said at the start. But we should not expect them, and the political institutions they have given rise to in the West, albeit intermittently and imperfectly, to take root elsewhere or even to flourish in our own societies without certain conditions being fulfilled. And chief among these conditions are a general agreement on what I have been calling liberal democratic values, such as tolerance and respect for individual freedom, together with a middle group in society both large enough and confident enough to ensure that these values persist. But it is not possible for such a middle group to flourish unless its members feel an allegiance to and a stake in their country in a more substantive way than the bare commitment to engage in a Parekhian political discussion. Being a multi-cultural 'community of communities' as Parekh advocates, or simply imposing majority rule will not be enough to get the virtues we really want when we advocate democracy as a form of government. We need a population broadly secure economically and also able to identify positively with the history and core values of their community; and, for a successful democracy not prone to the defects of our four initial examples, among those core values will have to be those of tolerance, of openness in the sense discussed earlier, and, within the limits imposed by the need to share what Aristotle calls the common view necessary to bind any community together, of liberal individualism itself.

Rights and Human Rights

OSWALD HANFLING

Doubts about rights

The concept of rights, as has often been noted, became prominent at a particular time in our history. It is associated especially with seventeenth and eighteenth century political ideas about the rights of individuals versus those of governments, and with such notable events as the American Declaration of Independence. It was at this time, too, that debates about rights of property and liberty became prominent. What was the role of this concept in earlier times? Has it always existed? Does it have a permanent place in our moral thinking? According to H.L.A. Hart,

> the concept of a right, legal or moral, is not to be found in the work of the Greek philosophers, and certainly there is no noun or noun phrase in Plato or Aristotle which is the equivalent of our expression 'a right', as distinct from 'right action' or 'the right thing to do'.[1]

A bolder denial has been made by Alasdair MacIntyre, according to whom

> there is no expression in any ancient or medieval language correctly translated by our expression 'a right' until near the close of the Middle Ages: the concept lacks any means of expression in Hebrew, Greek, Latin or Arabic, classic or medieval, before about 1400.[2]

These claims have not gone unchallenged, however. Thus it has been argued that rights play a prominent and essential role in Aristotle's *Politics*.[3] It is in any case hard to see how the concept of a right could be lacking from human relations. The creation and recognition of rights is no more avoidable than the making of promises, for rights are created in the very act of making a promise. The obligation of a promise 'is the very same moral relation,

[1] *Essays on Bentham* (OUP 1982), 163.
[2] *After Virtue*, (Notre Dame 1981), 67.
[3] Fred D. Miller, Jr., *Nature, Justice and Rights in Aristotle's Politics* (Oxford 1995), ch. 4.

viewed from the point of view of the promiser, as the *right* which the promisee has with respect to the promiser.'[4] If A promises X to B, then he gives B a right to receive X, and to complain if he does not receive X; and perhaps, as the case may be, demand compensation. This does not depend on the existence of particular words or phrases ('a right', 'I promise') in our language, or their equivalents in other languages. What matters is the recognition of A's complaint or resentment against B as reasonable, on the basis of what had been said in a suitable kind of situation.[5] Thus it can properly be said that Achilles was exercising a right—in this a right to keep what belonged to him according to accepted rules of warfare ... and objecting to the those who tried to prevent him from exercising his right.

Scepticism about rights has sometimes been concerned with the role of rights rather than with their existence. Thus it has been argued that the term 'rights' is not, like 'right', 'wrong' and 'ought', a fundamental feature of moral discourse. According to R.M. Hare, the word 'rights' needs to be 'translated' into those other words before it 'can be a dependable prop for moral arguments'; and 'till that happy day comes, we shall get the issues in better focus if we discuss them directly in terms of what we ought or ought not to do, or what it would be right or wrong to do'. (He proceeded to suggest how this might be done, so that talk about rights could be seen to amount to nothing more than talk about right and wrong.)[6]

Now it is true that there are logical entailments from 'rights' to the words favoured by Hare. Thus if someone has a right to to be given X, then he *ought* to be given X and it would be *wrong* not to do so; etc. But it does not follow that the meaning of 'rights' can be reduced to the meanings of those other words. For to speak of 'rights' is to refer to a special kind of moral situation, in which a special kind of moral dialectic is appropriate, including such utterances as 'I have a right to ...', 'You have no right to ...' and 'What gives you the right to ...?'.

The importance of rights has sometimes been discounted by advocates of utilitarianism who see here a rivalry between two

[4] A.I. Melden, *Rights and Persons* (Blackwell 1977),40 (italics added).

[5] The importance, to the concept of rights, of grounds for resentment, was noted by S.I. Benn. See his 'Human rights—for whom and for what?' in E. Kamenka (ed.), *Human Rights* (Arnold 1978); also his *Theory of Freedom* (CUP 1988), ch. 13.

[6] 'Abortion and the Golden Rule' in James Rachels (ed.), *Moral Problems* (Harper & Row 1979),153, 154.

fundamental principles of ethics; but there is no need to regard either rights or utilitarian considerations as fundamental. 'The greatest good of the greatest number' is a principle that has an undeniable place in moral reasoning, but a right may be decisive against that principle, and in such cases 'rights are trumps'[7]. In other, however, they are not. Take the redistribution of wealth. In taking my money and spending it on other people, the government overrules my right of property; but this may be defensible on the utilitarian ground that those people are in great need of help. It might be said that, this being so, the government has *a right* to take my money. But here the term 'a right' would be used in a 'diluted' sense: it would mean no more than that *it is right* for the government to do what it is doing.

It might still be said that in taking such measures a legitimate government would be exercising *its right* to make such choices. But this is not a relevant kind of right. The government's right is a right to make choices, but this does not determine *what* they ought to choose; so that if, for example, they choose to redistribute wealth, they would be expected to have suitable moral reasons for making that choice (and thereby overriding a right of property). (Such reasons might be put forward when presenting their intentions (or justifying their actions) to the public—especially to people whose property rights are affected.) Another example is the right of liberty, which may be appropriately overridden, in many cases, on utilitarian grounds.[8]

The roots of rights

How does the concept of rights come about? Human beings are vulnerable. They can be harmed and hurt, both physically and mentally; their plans can be frustrated and their reasonable hopes and expectations disappointed. To these vicissitudes there are reasonable reactions, both active and emotional. One may take action to improve a situation or prevent it from arising; and one

[7] Ronald Dworkin, *Taking Rights Seriously* (Duckworth 1978).

[8] According to Dworkin, 'the prospect of utilitarian gains cannot justify preventing a man from doing what he wants to do' (op. cit., 193)—in this case, exercising his right of free speech. But it is not clear why he thinks this. (In another passage he concedes that the prevention could be justified in order to 'obtain a clear and public benefit', but not on 'minimal grounds' (193–4).)

may feel emotions such as disappointment, regret and grief in reponse to what has happened. Now these reactions are subject to logical conditions and assessment: the actions and feelings should be appropriate to what has happened. A feeling of regret, for instance, requires a suitable object: there must be something *regrettable* to which the feeling is directed. Failing this, an expression of regret would not be intelligible. And if this condition is satisfied, there remains a question of assessment. Someone who has experienced a trivial loss may be criticized for grieving over it to an excessive extent; while another person might be criticized for 'a lack of feeling' if he dismisses a serious loss too lightly. And similarly with action: a person who goes to excessive lengths to counteract his loss or to protect himself against future losses or harms may be criticised for that reason. In a wide range of cases, however, these criticisms would not be appropriate: in such cases a person's reactions, whether of feeling or of action, are clearly reasonable in the light of what has happened or might happen to him.

The points I have made are applicable to various kinds of harm and disappointment: sickness and bereavement, the vagaries of the weather, and so on. But when we consider harms that are due to human agency, new kinds of reactions, both emotional and active, enter the field, and with these come new ramifications in the assessment of reasonableness. If some person has harmed or hurt me or frustrated my desires, then I may reasonably feel regret or disappointment; but I may also feel *resentful* against that person for what he has done and, where appropriate, take action to defend myself against him.[9]

Resentment, like the other emotions I have mentioned, may be unreasonable or disproportionate, but in many cases it is neither of these; and the same is true of self-defence. There are important differences, however, between resentment and the other emotions; and this again is a matter of logic. It makes no sense to speak of resentment against the weather for letting me down or against the microbes who make me ill. Resentment belongs to a language-game which includes the exchange of justifying reasons between those who suffer harm and those who inflict it. If I express resentment against you, you may ask for my reason. What do I have against you? And when you know my reason, a number of defences may be

[9] In my use of 'resentment' in the following discussion I have been influenced by P.F. Strawson's well-known 'Freedom and Resentment' (*Freedom and Resentment and Other Essays*, Methuen 1974).

open to you. You might argue that your behaviour was justified for such and such reasons; or you might produce an excuse for what you did (you had no choice; you were not aware that your action would harm me). And these defences might, in their turn, be subject to critical discussion. Or again, you might try to defuse my resentment by offering an apology or compensation. I, on the other hand, would be justified in complaining to you, and about you, if such responses were inadequate or not available. And in so complaining I would be expressing *a right* not to be treated as you treated me. A person has a right not to be treated in ways that give rise to reasonable resentment; and he has a *justified grievance* against those responsible, unless they can produce a suitable defence or apology.

Here lies the difference between blaming another person and 'blaming' the weather. If I know that you, knowingly, are the cause of my pain, frustration or disappointment, then I may reasonably resent what you have done, and I would have, prima facie, a justified grievance against you; and you, if you are rational, would have to recognize that this is so. How you would in fact defend your behaviour, or whether you would bother to defend it at all—this depends on what kind of person you are and other circumstances. But however this may be, you could not deny that I have a justified grievance against you if you know that I am a being with desires and feelings who believes that you have harmed me when you could have refrained from doing so, etc.

I have traced the existence of rights to the natural reactions of beings who (a) can suffer harm, frustration and disappointment, and (b) belong to a community of which the members can feel resentment against, and demand justification from, one another. These feelings and demands may be justified; and if they are, then a right has been infringed. Now it might be suspected, especially by those who uphold the is/ought principle, that there must be a circularity here. If my grievance against you is justified, must this not be *because* you have infringed a right of mine? But if this is so, then the existence of rights would not have been explained by my account. The account would come (putting it simply) to this: X has a right not be harmed because he would have a justified grievance against anyone who harmed him; and his grievance would be justified because such harming would be an infringement of his right.

This is not, however, a correct rendering of the account I have given. According to that account, my grievance against you would be justified *because you harmed me* (and did so without justification).

It is true that in acting as you did you would have infringed my right against being harmed, but this right is nothing other than the right to feel aggrieved and behave accordingly. My grievance would be reasonable and justified in the same way as that in which one's feelings about natural harms can be reasonable and justified. It is not as if the use of 'rights' imported a normativity that would not be there without it: the relevant normativity is already present in the use of 'reasonable' and 'justified', and these concepts are essential to an understanding of agency and resentment.

Rights and language

I have claimed that rights belong to a language-game which includes the exchange of reasons. Does this mean that the possession of language is a necessary condition of having rights? If so, are animals excluded? The fact is that the term 'rights' has been applied to animals, and the expression 'animal rights' has become established. But when the term is used in this way, it does not have its distinct meaning, and what is said in this context can just as well be said in terms of 'right' and 'wrong', etc.—as when we say that it is wrong to inflict gratuitous pain on animals and that we ought to treat them in appropriate ways. It is only when we attribute rights to speakers of a language that the term has its distinct meaning. Rights, it has been pointed out, can be 'claimed, demanded, asserted, insisted on, secured, waived, or surrendered';[10] they can also be disputed and bestowed; but these things cannot be done by non-linguistic animals.

Rights are ascribable to beings who can feel resentment; and the ascription of resentment is dependent on certain logical conditions. These include the awareness of harm done by a person who could have chosen to act differently, and who is himself aware of other people as responsible agents who can engage in exchanges of justifying reasons. But there is no purchase for these notions in the case of animals. There is no reasoning, moral or otherwise, among animals or between animals and human beings. Real animals, unlike those imagined in *Animal Farm*, cannot participate in the language-game of rights; and to say of animals that they have a right to such and such treatment is no more than to say that we ought to treat them in that way. The introduction of 'rights' into this context may seem to strengthen our reasons for treating them

[10] Alan R. White, *Rights* (OUP 1984), 90.

decently, but they do not need to be supported in that way. As Hume observed, 'we should be bound by the laws of humanity to give gentle usage to inferior beings', though we are not 'under any restraint of justice with regard to them, nor could they possess any right or property'.[11]

The members of a human society are bound together by a network of rights and duties, but this cannot be said about animals. If one blackbird enters the territory of another, is that an infringement of the latter's rights? Does a cat have a right to kill birds, or do birds have rights against cats? Can the owners of animals have rights against them?

According to a recent writer, 'it seems unsatisfactory to allow the morally significant question of who can possess rights to be determined by conventions of language'.[12] It is, however, a mistake to oppose 'morally significant questions' with 'conventions of language' in this way. The possession of language is a *necessary condition* for various moral ascriptions, and this is not a matter of convention. The rights and duties of promising, for example, can be ascribed only to beings who can perform and understand the speech-acts of promising; and moral responsibility, in the sense of being held to account, can be ascribed only to beings who can *give* an account of what they are doing and why they are doing it. What is at issue here is not a 'convention of language', but the *possession* of language, and language of a suitable kind. Thus the denial of animal rights is not based on a mere convention.

In the following discussion I try to show how various kinds of rights can be accounted for as inevitable features of human life and language. The rights concerned will be treated under two main divisions: benefit rights, and rights of non-interference.[13]

[11] *Enquiry concerning the Principles of Morals*, ed. Selby Bigge, 190. The passage is quoted by Melden, op. cit. 17.

[12] Peter Jones, *Rights* (Macmillan 1994), 68.

[13] My classification of rights is not meant to be comprehensive and neither is it in competition with the comprehensive and much-debated classification of rights by W.N. Hohfeld in his *Fundamental Legal Conceptions* (London, 1919). Hohfeld's system was inspired largely by juristic considerations, and I have not found it useful for my purpose. My main purpose is to show (a) how kinds of rights, and the concept of rights in general, originate, and (b) to compare rights with other kinds of moral reasons.

Oswald Hanfling

Benefit rights

By 'benefit rights' I mean rights to receive goods or advantages of some kind; and the relevant grievance in this case is due to the disappointment of reasonable expectations. This can come about in a number of ways.

Speech-act rights

A right to receive a benefit can be created by an act of promising. By promising Mary to provide benefit B, John leads her to expect to receive B from him; and she will have, prima facie, a justified grievance against John if he does not provide B. But what is meant here by 'expect'? The sense of 'expect' in this case is both predictive and normative. What John conveys to Mary is not merely that she is *likely* to receive B from him, but that she will be entitled to complain if she does not. She can expect *that* John will provide B and also expect it *of* him to do so; and to justify his behaviour if he does not.

A similar case is that of giving permission. By saying 'You may use my bicycle whenever you like', I give you the right to use my bicycle whenever you like. In that case you may reasonably expect to be able to use it at any time, but you will also be entitled to complain if I prevent you from doing so.

In some cases the two kinds of expectation (predictive and normative) come apart. A teacher tells his class: 'I expect you all to behave well this afternoon.' (Perhaps they have heard that an inspector will be coming.) Does the teacher think that they will really behave well? Not necessarily: he may have little confidence that they will. If the class fails to behave as desired, he may say he is disappointed. Yet he and the children would know that this is not really true. When the teacher said that he expected them to behave well, he was using 'expect' in the sense of a moral demand. He was warning the children that he would have a right to rebuke them if they did not behave 'as expected'.

In most cases, however, both senses of 'expect' are relevant. If you promise to do X for me, then (in the absence of special reasons to the contrary) I may properly expect you, in the predictive as well as the moral sense, to do X for me. If this were not so—if people did not generally keep their promises—then the practice of giving promises could not exist. The two senses of 'expect' also occur in the case of 'customary' rights. Thus if I have long been accustomed to enjoying certain advantages or benefits from someone, I might reasonably expect that they would in fact continue; but I might also, in suitable cases, come to expect them as matters of right and complain accordingly if they were discontinued.

Another 'speech-act' source of rights is the enactment of laws, though in this case printing is likely to take the place of speech. Statements of the form 'It is hereby enacted ...', when published by a legal authority, can lead citizens to expect certain benefits and the citizens concerned can reasonably complain if the benefits are not provided. An important difference, however, between this case and that of promising, is that whereas latter is an inevitable feature of human life, this is not so with the enactment of laws. What both cases have in common, on the other hand, is that the relevant expectations and consequent rights are *deliberately created* by those who make the promise or introduce the law.

In contrast to the above, there are rights that are not created. These include customary rights and relationship rights, as well as rights of non-interference.

Customary rights

In any human society there are bound to be regularities of interaction between the members. These lead to expectations of 'what is done' and 'what is not done', so that someone who fails to behave as may reasonably expected may be guilty of causing a disappointment and hence the object of a reasonable grievance.[14] Suppose that in a particular society neighbours are expected to make a certain donation whenever someone gets married. The practice may have begun with a spontaneous action from someone or some group, without being regarded as a duty. Gradually, however, it is copied by others and finally hardens into a duty, with a corresponding right on the part of the married people. In such cases a non-recipient might reasonably resent the behaviour of a defaulting neighbour, claiming that he was entitled to the donation; and this might be confirmed by other members of the community. In such contexts we may use such expressions as 'what is done', 'what we do' and 'it isn't done', and these again can have both a

---

[14] The importance of 'Established Practices' is discussed by T.M. Scanlon in 'Promises and Practices', *Philosophy and Public Affairs*, *19*, 1990, 199-226.

normative and an empirical meaning. It would be a matter of empirical fact that people usually behave in the relevant ways, but they would also be under an obligation to do so.

Another example of 'customary' rights is that of rights of way. A typical case is that of people who have become accustomed over many years to using a route over land belonging to others, without complaint from the latter; and in due course they are deemed to have a right of way which could properly be set against the owner's right if he now tried to prevent them. (In societies with a suitable legal system such rights of way may be confirmed by law in accordance with prescribed periods of usage and other conditions.) Here again it is the coming into existence of reasonable expectations, and the harm done by frustrating them, that accounts for the right concerned. On the other hand, if such a right has long been unexercised, then the expectation of being able to do so may have faded and a right that was based on it may have withered away. A custom that is 'more honoured in the breach than in the observance' ceases to be a custom, and the same fate can overtake customary rights.

A related case is that of absentee landlords. Suppose the owner of a property has long been absent from it and others have occupied it for a long time. In that case we may recognize that the latter have at least some right to the property, which may need to be balanced against that of the original owner. This also happens in the case of territorial disputes between whole populations, where a conflict of rights has often led to fighting.

Relationship rights

Whereas the practices that are behind customary rights vary greatly with different societies, relationship rights are based to a large extent on universal features of human nature. Such are the relations that exist between parents and children. There is natural tendency for parents to give preferential treatment to their children, and vice versa, and this makes it reasonable to expect such treatment, and to complain if it is not given. There are, in other words, *rights* to preferential treatment between parents and children; and there are similar relationships among siblings or friends. These rights and expectations also vary according to custom to some extent, but the variation is limited by the natural concern and affection that people feel for those close to them. Given this fact of human nature, we have a right to expect preferential treatment (including affection itself) from people close to us, and to complain if this is not given.

A similar point may be made about neighbours and colleagues, and members of one's community, for it is natural both to have greater concern for such people than for others, and to expect greater concern from them than from others. These expectations, again, give rise to reciprocal rights, so that if they are disappointed, one can properly complain that one's right to special consideration has been disregarded by the people concerned.

Rights of non-interference

A benefit right, such as those described above, involves a relation with three terms: a claimant to whom the benefit is due, the party who is obliged to provide it, and the justification for the claim. The latter is required in answer to the questions 'What gives you the right to receive ...?' and 'What gives you the right to expect ...?'—in reply to which the claimant might refer to a promise he had been given, a special relationship, an established custom, etc. And if these replies are adequate, then the disappointed claimant may have a justified grievance against the party who fails to provide the benefit.

This is not so with rights of non-interference. In this case the harm is done, and the justified grievance incurred, by acting and not by failing to act (or failing to provide what is due). And here justification is demanded, not from right-holders, but from those accused of infringing their rights. A typical complaint here is 'You have no right to do that to me'. Such rights may be described, accordingly, as 'no-right' rights.[15]

It has been argued[16] that the distinction between negative rights and benefit (or 'positive') rights is untenable, because rights of the first kind may entail rights of the second. Thus my right to be free from interference may entail a positive right to be protected by the police against interference. It does not follow from this, however, that the distinction between negative and positive rights is untenable. A way of drawing it in the present example is by reference to logical priority: it is *because* I have a right to be free

---

[15] Cf. K.R. Minogue, 'Natural Rights', in E. Kamenka (ed.), *Human Rights* (Arnold 1978), 19. The expression 'no-right' also occurs in Hohfeld's classification, loc. cit., but not with the same meaning.

[16] Henry Shue, *Basic Rights* (Princeton 1980).

from harm or interference from others that I have a right to protection by the police, and not conversely. (The first entails the second, and not conversely.)[17]

There is also a disparity between non-interference and benefit rights with respect to duties. If I have a right to benefit B, then someone, or some agency, has a duty to provide B to me. It is sometimes thought that there is a similar correlation of negative rights with negative duties. Thus it is said that we all have a duty not to interfere with the liberty of others, not to violate their property, not to torture them or kill them, etc.[18] On this view, the fact that I have a right to my belongings entails that all other persons have a *duty* not to take them from me, and likewise in the case of other rights of non-interference. It follows that each of us has all the corresponding duties towards all the others. But this is a distortion of the concept of duty. A duty is a reason to act. Having promised you to do X, I have a duty—a reason—to do X; so that if I am asked why I am doing X, I can reply by reference to that duty. But there is no counterpart to this in the case of rights of non-interference. Suppose I am walking down a busy street and do not punch anyone on the nose. Would this be a case of fulfilling a duty? Or should we say that I abstain from punching anyone on the nose because I have a duty to abstain? But in this case there is neither acting nor abstaining. Asked for what reason I do not punch anyone on the nose, I might reply 'Why should I? What do you mean?' It is true that that question might be in order if I had a reason *for* punching someone. But even if this were so, the straightforward answer would not be that I have a duty not to do it, but that I have *no right* to do it.[19]

This is not to deny that a duty can consist in refraining or abstaining from some action, as opposed to acting. I have, for

---

[17] For a different way of defending the distinction, see Onora O'Neill, *Towards Justice and Virtue* (CUP 1996), 131.

[18] Here I disagree with O'Neill's remarks about rights and obligations. According to her, 'any right must be matched by some corresponding obligation ... Unless obligation-bearers can be identified by right-holders, claims to have rights amount only to rhetoric ... This condition can be met for *universal rights* when they are matched by corresponding universal obligations that are allocated to all others ... Liberty rights provide a paradigm of universal rights.' (*op.cit*, 129).

[19] 'What corresponds to 'I have a right to do X' is not 'You have duty to let me do X' but 'You have no right to stop me from doing X', where the emphasis in the sentence may fall on on the 'you' or on the 'right' according to the point that is being made ...' (Minogue, op. cit., 19).

example, a duty to my neighbours to abstain from making too much noise; and in this case their negative right to be left in peace entails a negative duty on my part. But this is a relation between specific people and not people in general—as is the case with rights of non-interference that are of universal scope.

Non-interference rights, I said, are characterised by such challenges as 'You have no right to do that' and 'What right have (or had you) you to interfere?', and it might be assumed that these call on the respondent to invoke *a right* to defend his interference. But this is not always so. Suppose I discover that a man entered my garden without my permission and I put it to him: 'What right did you have to enter my garden without my permission?' The answer might be that he was a police officer in pursuit of a criminal. In this case he had a right in virtue of his office to enter my garden, and this would be a suitable justification for the trespass. But what if the man was a passer-by who thought my house was on fire and wondered whether to call the fire-brigade? He too would have a satisfactory reply to the challenge 'What right did you have?'. But would he be invoking a right? It is true that the expression 'a right' would not be out of place here: we might say that he had a right to act as he did. In this case, however, the expression 'a right' would not have its distinct meaning: we would be saying no more than that it *was right* (or not wrong) for him to act as he did.

Correlated with rights of non-interference is *the right of self-defence*. This is perhaps most commonly invoked in the case of physical attack; but it is applicable to all kinds of interference, or threats of interference, with a person or his interests. In such cases there is a suitable ground for resentment, and if this cannot be countered by sufficient reasons for the interference, the victim has a right to defend himself against it. The right of self-defence is a right to defend one's rights.

The right of property

Let us now consider some particular rights of non-interference. We can harm a person or his reasonable expectations by taking away or interfering with his property, and such a person may have a justified grievance against us. But how deeply is the concept of property, and the right it entails, rooted in the human form of life? Is property itself an institution that needs justification? Property, it has been argued, is the source of much evil. It divides people from one another, produces envy and leads to warfare. Should not the earth and fruits thereof be there for all to enjoy? Would not human life be happier if land and goods were shared by all?

The concept of property, of 'mine and thine', is expressed in our language by genitives and possessive pronouns, and moral principles are implied when we apply these words to objects. In describing this spade as 'mine' and that one as 'yours', I imply that I have certain rights with regard to this spade and acknowledging that you have similar rights with regard to that one; so that, in the absence of other moral considerations, it would be wrong for either of the spades to be taken from us without our consent. But what is the basis of these ideas? Is property an inevitable feature of human life, or is it no more than a matter of convention?

Hume, in his discussion of property, spoke of a 'stability of possessions', whose origin he ascribed to a convention. We live, he said, in a world of competition for scarce resources, and our selfish nature leads us to get whatever we can for ourselves. Yet advantages are to be gained for everyone if there is stability of possessions. But how is this to be achieved in spite of our selfish tendency? 'This can be done after no other manner than by a convention entered into by all the members of the society to bestow stability on the possession of ... goods and leave everyone in the peaceable enjoyment of what he may acquire ...'[20]

In a later passage he spoke of this as a 'voluntary convention and artifice of men' (T 533), as if someone, or some group, hit on the idea that stability of possessions would be to the advantage of all, and then got others to agree to bring this about. But how is this supposed to have happened? He illustrated his idea as follows:

I observe that it will be for my interest to leave another in the possession of his goods, *provided* he will act in the same manner with regard to me. He is sensible of a like interest in the regulation of his conduct. When this common sense of interest is mutually expressed, and is known to both, it produces a suitable resolution and behaviour.

This, he said, 'may properly enough be called a convention or agreement betwixt us ...' (T 490). Now it is clear that two people may arrive at an agreement about respecting each other's possessions if this is in their mutual interest. But this can only happen if the idea of possessions (of 'his goods' and 'my goods') is already in being; it cannot serve to bring that idea, and the presupposed stability of possessions, into being—either in that

---

[20] *Treatise* (ed. Selby-Bigge), 'Of the origin of justice and property', 490.

instance or in general.[21] In any case, respect for property is not contingent on such bargains. I do not respect your possessions *provided* that you will respect mine, and your right to keep what what you have is not contingent on your undertaking to do the same for others.[22]

Hume thought that there must have been an originating event of the kind he described, and we might wonder where and when he supposed it to have taken place. But even if there had been such an event, this would still leave the question why people, such as ourselves, who did not take part in it, should be bound by 'a convention that was entered into' by those who did take part.

Another thinker with ideas about the 'origin of civil society', including property, was Rousseau:

> The first man who, having enclosed a piece of ground, bethought himself of saying 'This is mine', and found people simple enough to believe him, was the real founder of civil society. By how many crimes, wars [etc. etc.] might not any one have saved mankind, by pulling up the stakes ... and crying to his fellows: 'Beware of listening to this impostor ...' (J.J. Rousseau, *The Social Contract and Discourses* (transl. G.D.H. Cole), Dent 1973, 76).

Now it is true that people might be mistaken, and perhaps simple-minded, in believing a man who declared a piece of ground to be his; but then again they might not. In either case, however, they must already have the concept of property: they must know the difference between cases in which 'This is mine' is true and cases in which it is not; and this knowledge cannot have been created by the action of a 'first man' such as that described by Rousseau.

Hume also, however, thought of the stability of possessions as coming about in a spontaneous way, as when he tells us that it 'arises gradually, and acquires force by a slow progression' and without any explicit agreement (490); and this may seem a more realistic suggestion than those quoted earlier. But is the stability of

---

[21] Hume also says that the 'convention or agreement betwixt us' would come about '... without the interposition of a promise'. But such an agreement would have to be *understood* as a promise. If each of us merely expressed an interest in not having his possessions disturbed by the other, this would not yet amount to an agreement.

[22] A similar objection is made by Melden (op. cit. 94–5) to Rawls's account of promising.

possessions a matter of convention at all? A convention is a state of affairs that might have been different or absent. Is this true of the stability of possession?[23] Stability is part of the very concept of possession. An object would not be a possession if it could be taken or used by anyone at will. Let us consider, then, how it comes about that there are possessions. An individual or a community is likely to occupy a particular territory and to do so with some degree of permanence. This is because it is more convenient, on the whole, to stay where one is unless there are special reasons moving away. Given such an occupation, we may say that they are *in possession* of that territory. But is this the same as to say that it belongs to them? We might say of a group of squatters that they are in possession of a property, without implying that it belongs to them. In this case, however, there would be someone who already owns the property. But if there is no such owner, what reason could there be for denying that it belongs to those who occupy it? It would be reasonable for them to treat it as belonging to them, and to regard attempts by others to dispossess them of it as unjustified. This is so because the latter would be *harming* them by interfering with their reasonable expectation of continuing to enjoy the property, whereas no such harm would be done to the invaders by keeping them out.

Similarly, an individual is likely to have on or around him various goods, such as tools, food and clothing, which he keeps in convenient places and expects to be able to use as convenient. Assuming, again, that there are no other claimants, those goods may be said to *belong* to him, and he would be justified in resisting attempts by others to take them or use them without his permission. Such belongings occur spontaneously even within a household, where it is usual for particular implements, pieces of furniture and items of clothing to be treated as belonging to particular individuals. There are natural advantages in staying where one is and using what one has, rather than disturbing the reasonable expectations of others with respect to *their* possessions; and this is not a matter of convention. A reason would be needed

---

[23] In a further passage Hume compared the human situation with regard to property to that of 'two men who pull the oars of a boat' (490). They do it, he says, 'by an agreement or convention, though they have never given promises to each other'. Presumably Hume was thinking of a situation in which progress would be impeded or impossible if the men did not pull together. But in that case, the 'agreement or convention' would amount to no more than a natural reaction to those physical conditions, without any need for a convention or artifice.

for *not* respecting the possessions of others—for disturbing the normal conditions. And this, again, is not a matter of convention.

In some cases the sense of possession is strengthened by the effort that was necessary to acquire or modify the goods concerned. Perhaps the possessor actually made them; perhaps, as in the case of land, he put work into them, thus making them more valuable. In such cases we might say, in Locke's phrase, that he 'mixed his labour' with them. We need not, however, agree with Locke that the mixing of labour is what *makes* the goods into possessions of the person concerned. An object can become my property merely because I was the first to find it, and without any labour on my part. Locke asks how it comes about that a person who finds apples in a wood 'appropriates them to himself' and he regards 'the labour of gathering them' as being sufficient to explain why the apples become his property. But it would be absurd to describe as 'labour' the action of picking up an apple and putting it in my pocket. What would make the apple my property rather than yours is simply the fact that I found it and you did not. 'Finders are keepers'. Having found the apple, I could reasonably expect to enjoy it and resent attempts on your part to take it away from me.

So much for the origin of possessions and the stability that this involves. Now this stability may be threatened by intruders or robbers, and may need to be defended against them. In modern societies this can be done by means of artificial institutions such as the law and the police, while in a primitive state of society it may require physical measures, such as erecting barriers, standing guard, or the use or threat of violence. Now if such struggles were a constant feature of life, and if intruders and robbers were just as likely to succeed as defenders, then there might not be any stable relations between people and land and goods, and no place for the idea of possession. It is not the case, however, that such struggles are a constant feature of life: on the whole, and to a sufficient extent, people are able to stay in the places they occupy and keep the goods they have. And thus the existence of possessions can be seen as following from general conditions of human life, from human needs and tendencies and the advantages to be gained by staying where one is and holding on to what one has in preference to disturbing the reasonable expectations of others.

In the defence of possessions there can be an important role for conventional measures: this happens when physical defences come to be replaced by conventional signs of warning. Such signs are conventional, but their usefulness is a consequence of conditions of human life that are not conventional. In these respects the human condition is comparable to, and (in evolutionary terms) continuous with, that of many animals. A territory, a lair, a cache of food—these may be said to belong to an animal because it occupies them or knows where to find them; and, where appropriate, is able to defend them against intruders. But there is also a role here for 'conventional' signs, such as scent markings and the song of birds -'conventional', because other smells or sounds would have served equally well.

It is, then, a condition of normal human life that we can, on the whole, expect to keep what we have, and organize our lives accordingly. Such expectations are reasonable and this gives us the right to defend what we have. If someone tries to take away the goods in my possession, it is reasonable for me to resent his action and repel the intruder; whereas the latter would have no such justification for his action. The latter would be *harming* me by taking away my belongings, but I would not be harming him by keeping him away. Because these goods are mine, I have a right to resist attempts by others to take or use them without my consent; and this cannot reasonably be denied by them. A similar role is played by the frustration of reasonable expectations in the case of broken promises. In this case, however, the expectations have been *created* by the offender, whereas in the case of property they exist before any offender appears.

The right of liberty

By 'the right of liberty' I mean the right to behave as we choose, without compulsion, hindrance or disturbance by others. This includes the right to do nothing as well as to do something, and to live quietly as well as to make a noise.

The existence of property, as we have seen, has been regarded as being in some way artificial, but this could hardly happen in the case of acting and choosing. Acting is more basic to human life than owning. A new-born child cannot be said to have property except in a legal sense; but he begins to act long before that. From a very early age he reaches for things, grasps them and puts them in his mouth; he also expresses displeasure, and perhaps rage, when someone tries to prevent these activities.

In due course the child can be *told* what he must not do, as opposed to being prevented physically. But—and this is a general feature of language—what is told can also be questioned. And the child who has learned the language of prohibition also comes to learn the language of objecting to prohibitions: he learns to ask 'Why can't I?' and 'Why shouldn't I?'. And with these questions he begins to express his right of liberty. The parent is now challenged to justify the prohibition, failing which he or she can appear to be acting unreasonably. In due course the child learns that he too is exposed to this challenge when he tries to interfere with the actions of others—when, for example, he tries to prevent his brothers or sisters from doing what *they* want to do.

The extent to which reasons are given to or demanded from a child must depend, obviously, on the nature of the environment into which he is born and in which he lives thereafter. But if the child has mastered the language-game of practical reasons, he must have learned the use of 'Why shouldn't I ...?'—or some expression to this effect—as addressed by one person to another who is trying to interfere. And he must also have learned what might count as a reasonable answer to this question—one that a reasonable victim of interference might be expected to accept. If A tries to prevent B from doing what he wants, then B has a reasonable ground for resenting A's interference; but he must understand that this would no longer be so if he were informed of a suitable reason for the prevention. On the other hand, A must understand that B would have a justified grievance if A's reasons were unsuitable or non-existent; failing which, A could not have mastered the language-game of practical reasons.

Human beings act as they do for various reasons and sometimes merely because they 'feel like it'. Some actions are spontaneous, others the result of more or less deliberation; some are important, others trivial; some are directed at long-term objectives, others are not; and so on. But however this may be, our emotions are apt to be engaged if there is interference. If I want to do X and am prevented from doing it, then I have reason to feel frustrated; otherwise I could not be said to have wanted to do X. And if I know that you are the agent of my frustration, then it is, prima facie, reasonable for me to resent what you have done; while you, if you are rational, must understand that this is so.

The right of liberty is typically expressed by such expressions as 'Why shouldn't I do what I want?', 'Why must I do X when I want to do Y?' and (as with the right of property) 'What right have you to interfere?' These are typical questions that we put to those who interfere with what we are doing or intend to do; and similarly with past acts of interference. And to these questions various kinds of answers might be given. They might refer to other people's rights; to one's own good; to the good, in some sense, of people in general;

to the justice of retributive punishment; and so on. There is obviously much scope for disagreement here, both about the principles involved and the importance of particular circumstances; but this does not affect the right to demand justification from those who interfere and to complain if such justification is not available.

I have treated the right of liberty as a right of non-interference. But a person may be prevented from doing what he wants, not by interference from others but by lack of means. Let us refer to the liberty he lacks as 'means-liberty', as opposed to 'non-interference liberty'.[24] Do we have a right of means-liberty? Suppose someone has a strong desire to travel in a space-craft but is prevented from doing so by lack of means. It would be absurd to regard this as an infringement of rights; and the same is true of various more moderate desires that people are unable to satisfy due to lack of means. An infringement of rights presupposes someone who is guilty of the infringement. In the case of rights of non-interference this is the person who interferes; in the case of benefit rights, the person who fails to provide the benefit. But who would it be in the case of means-liberty? What is true is that if people are prevented by lack of means from satisfying basic needs, this is a *reason* for helping them; but it does not follow that they have a right to such help.

In the UN Universal Declaration of Human Rights (Article 22) it is stated that 'everyone, as a member of society, has the right to social security ...'. Now it is true that human beings are essentially social, and to that extent everyone is 'a member of society'. But a society need not be such as to entail rights and duties about the provision of social security. Such ideas would, indeed, hardly have occurred in most societies other than those in the modern western world. There may be good reasons for *creating* rights to social security, but they are not rights that we have merely by virtue of being human.

It has been argued that the right to social security might be justified in the case of citizens belonging to 'a politically organised society' with a 'tacit or hypothetical social contract by which the state is morally bound' to provide such security'.

---

[24] The former should not be confused with Berlin's 'positive freedom' (Isaiah Berlin, 'Two Concepts of Liberty' in *Four Essays on Liberty* (Oxford, 1969)).

The citizen is normally a participant in the cooperative economic endeavour of the society, and as one bearing his fair share of its burdens, has a moral claim to a fair share of the benefits of economic cooperation.[25]

Now this description of rights and burdens might be suitable if being a citizen were like membership of some cooperative enterprise such as the communes established by Zionist pioneers. In this case it was clear that people who chose to join did so on the understanding that they were, indeed, joining a cooperative endeavour with appropriate burdens and rights. But the sense in which we are all citizens is not like this. Most people are citizens of a particular country or city merely because that is where they were born or where they live (or because of the passports they hold). And while it is true that citizens are subject to the laws and customs of their country, this does not imply the existence of a 'cooperative endeavour' such as would generate rights to benefits. The mere fact that one is a citizen of some city or country is not sufficient for that; but it is only in this (ordinary) sense of 'citizen' that we are all citizens.

Liberty and autonomy

The right of liberty, as I have understood it, is the right to behave as one chooses, without hindrance or compulsion by others. There is, however, another kind of interference with liberty which is different from these two. Suppose I plan to repair my car next week-end and you force me to do something else instead. This would clearly be a case of compulsion and in that way contrary to my right of liberty. Suppose, on the other hand, that I happen to be away at the week-end and you repair the car during my absence. Perhaps you think this would be doing me a favour and giving me a pleasant surprise. And this might really be so, but then again it might not. For it might be that what I wanted was not merely to have the car repaired, but to have it repaired *by me*. In that case I would have reason to resent your intervention even if it was well meant. Or again, suppose I have started to repair the car and you show me that there is a better way of doing it. In that case I might be grateful for your advice, but then again I might not. For it might be that I want to be left to work out how to do the job in my own way. Here again it might be reasonable for me to resent your

---

[25] Carl Wellman, *An Approach to Rights* (Kluwer, 1997), 115–6.

intrusion—not because I don't believe your method to be better, but because I want to do the job in my own way.[26] The right to do so, which I call 'the right of autonomy', is a variant of the right of liberty.

The kind of autonomy that is undermined here finds expression in such phrases as 'running one's own life' and in such rebuttals as 'I know there may be a better way, but I want to do it in my way'. Here also is one root of the objection against 'prying into one's affairs' even when this does no harm. One may resent such prying because one does not want others to be in a position to criticize one's management of one's own affairs. Sometimes, no doubt, one is glad to resign one's affairs to the charge of others, but such resignations of autonomy must not go too far. When they do, the person concerned commits a kind of suicide: he gives up an essential ingredient of human life. That is why old people are often reluctant to go into institutions where 'everything is done for them'.

This kind of motive also accounts for the requirement of patients' consent to medical treatment. There is a natural reluctance against resigning one's physical welfare to the charge of another person, even when that person is a doctor who may be presumed to be far more competent in judging what is best for a patient.

The desire to do things for oneself also accounts for a kind of perversity that we find in children when they reject the well-meaning advice and help of their parents. Thus a child may 'resent the indulgent ... 'Yes dear, but Mummy knows best', even in the case that Mummy does'.[27] The child's behaviour, irritating though it can be for parents, is rooted in exigencies of natural selection; and again the point is well made in proverbial expressions, as when we say that we want the child to 'learn from his own mistakes' and 'stand on his own feet'—recognizing that this is necessary if the child is to hold his own in later life. Thus well-meaning parents often find themselves torn between a desire to give help and advice and a recognition that this may not be in the child's best interest in the long run. Or they may be deterred from

---

[26] Cf. T.M. Scanlon, *What We Owe to Each Other* (Harvard, 1998), 253: 'I want to choose the furniture for my own living room, pick out the pictures for the walls and write my own lectures despite the fact that these things might be done better by someone else. For better or worse, I want them to result from and hence to reflect my own taste, imagination, and powers of discrimination and analysis.'

[27] S.I. Benn, *A Theory of Freedom* (CUP, 1988), 105

interfering by the child's own natural resentment of interference. On the other hand, the practice of choosing is itself inculcated by parents into their children, especially in societies such as ours. From an early age children are confronted with questions such as 'Which one do you want?' and 'Do you want to do A or B?'; and they become accustomed to the need to answer such questions. And when they do this, their emotions are apt to become engaged in favour of their chosen option, even if they had no preference for it before being confronted with it by the parent.

The details of these interactions must vary according to the characters and circumstances of the people involved; but whatever these may be, a normal, mature human being is expected to have learned to 'stand on his own feet', 'lead his own life', etc.; making his own decisions and carrying them out in his own way; and he may reasonably feel resentment against those who want to 'take over', even if they mean well. He may also object, reasonably, to the presence of 'prying eyes', even if they do not prevent him from doing what he wants.[28] The omnipresence of Big Brother in Orwell's *1984* would have been a cause for resentment for this reason alone.

The right of autonomy is also connected with the right of democratic participation. It is a near universal feature of human life that there are people in positions of leadership who make decisions that others have to follow, and in this way their liberty to decide for themselves is curtailed. Such curtailments can be justified by reference to benefits such as law and order, defence against outside threats and (in modern societies) relief of hardship. Now all of these can be achieved, with a sufficient degree of efficiency and justice, without democratic participation; but it is reasonable for people to be allowed some participation in decisions that affect them. This is one reason, at least, in favour of democracy.

The right to life

The right to life has often been regarded as the most important of rights. But how are we to account for this right and the importance attributed to it? Is a person harmed by having his life terminated? What Cain did to Abel was not to harm him but to kill him. What is

---

[28] Cf. Benn, *A Theory of Freedom* (CUP, 1988), 270ff.

wrong, then, with killing a person if we leave aside the pain that this may, but need not, involve? Has a right of that person been infringed?

The prohibition against killing is sometimes explained by speaking of life as if it were a kind of valuable property. Thus it is said in taking a person's life we take from him something that is supremely good; and this is supposed to explain, not only why there is a right to life, but why this right, and infringements of it, are supremely important. But is it true that life is supremely good? Is it even true that life is good? This claim has been denied at least as often as its opposite. And if Schopenhauer did not succeed in demonstrating that life is, on the whole bad, he showed at least that the contrary claim is questionable; and he was able to quote from an impressive array of writers in support of this conclusion.[29]

Others have pointed out that life is a *precondition* of both good and bad experiences, and of supreme value for that reason. But what follows from that premise is not that life is of supreme value, but only that its value cannot be ranked alongside the value and disvalue of good and bad experiences.[30]

The right to life is also unlikely to figure in the original learning situations that confront an infant in the context of a family. It is not as if the killing of other people were something that infants normally attempt, or as if the killing of people by one another were a normal and frequent event in a normal infant's experience, suitable to serve as a paradigm for an initial understanding of rights.

The right to life can, nevertheless, be understood as a right of non-interference. It is the right to be allowed to go on living if that is what one desires; and the corresponding 'no-right' is the right that others do *not* have to interfere with this. In this case, of course, there cannot be retrospective resentment and complaint (about having had one's life terminated), but these reactions are applicable to *attempts* to terminate it. Given that I want to go on living, I have reason to resent attempts against my life.

On this view, however, the right to life must also include the negative option: it must include the 'right to die' for those who desire the termination rather than the continuance of life. The right to die is the right to take one's own life, or to let dying take its

---

[29] A. Schopenhauer, *The World as Will and Representation* (Dover 1969), 586–8.

[30] For further discussion, see O. Hanfling. *The Quest for Meaning*, chs. 4–5.

course, without interference from others; and in this case, as in others, sufficient reasons must be produced if this right is to be overridden. (One such reason is to allow for the possibility that the preference for dying may be only temporary.)

It might be objected that to account for the right to life as I have done makes it appear unduly derivate. The very attempt to *account* for that right might be regarded as betraying a kind of moral insensitivity—a failure to understand what morality is about. Now it is true that life has a special 'preconditional' status, as stated above; and also that violations of the right to life are irreversible in a way that other violations of rights are not. These facts explain why the right to life has a special importance, but not why it should be thought to be of *supreme* importance. And neither do they explain how we come to recognize such a right and how it is related to other rights.

The right against unreasonable punishment

So far I have followed my main classification of rights into benefit rights and rights of non-interference. The two rights that follow do not fit well into this classification, but they are too important to be left out. The first is connected with what is sometimes called 'equality before the law'; but the right described in my heading provides a better focus for my discussion.

A person is harmed by being punished, and he may have a grievance against those who punish him. Whether the grievance is justified would depend on whether the punishment was deserved. It would be justified if the punishment were unduly severe or if the offence for which the accused was punished had not been committed by him at all.

In determining the severity of punishments, the principles of *consistency* and *proportionality* are important. The first of these is invoked when we say that a given person should be given the same treatment as others if what he did, and other relevant circumstances, are the same in his case as in theirs. What is to count as 'relevant circumstances' is often a matter of debate, but this does not affect the principle. And if there are circumstances that justify a difference of treatment, then those responsible for the difference should be able to say what they are.

The principle of proportionality, on the other hand, is that punishments should be proportionate to the offence that was committed. Thus it would be unreasonable to inflict a severe punishment for a minor misdemeanour, and the person concerned would have a justified grievance against those responsible.

There is an asymmetry, however, between negative and positive offences against these principles. Someone who has been treated more severely, or less favourably, than others in a similar situation has a right to complain; but complaints would not be in order for someone who had been treated *more* favourably than the others. Such treatment would still (in the absence of special reasons) be unreasonable, but the fortunate recipient of it would not be in a position to complain. And the same is true of the person whose punishment is unduly lenient for the gravity of his offence.

A precondition of respecting the above rights is that of establishing the truth about what happened: whether the defendant was guilty at all and, if so, to what extent. And from this follows the need for 'due process' in courts of law and other tribunals.

The source of the present right lies in the nature of man as 'a rational animal'—an animal whose actions are subject to principles of rationality such as those I have mentioned. Someone who acts inconsistently is liable to the charge that he is being unreasonable, and this would lay him open to a justified grievance in the cases I have mentioned; and the same is true of someone who acts for the reason that p without taking sufficient steps to establish that p is true. And these principles cannot be denied by anyone who belongs to the community of rational beings.

The right to be treated with respect

Suppose my neighbour has an all-night party with fireworks and thereby prevents me from sleeping quietly in my home. He may be accused of violating my right to be left in peace. But at the same time he may be accused of failing in his duty to *respect* me, and this lack of respect may hurt me in addition to the loss of sleep. In such cases we might say that the infringement of the right of respect *supervenes* on an infringement of the right to be left in peace.

Again, suppose you forget to keep your promise to provide something for me. In that case you violate my right to receive what you promised, but you also indicate a lack of respect. If—I might reasonably complain—you respected me as you should, then you wouldn't have been so careless about keeping your promise. In this example, again, infringement of the right of respect presupposes an infringement of a first-order right—to receive what was promised. And my justified grievance about your lack of respect could remain even if the breaking of the promise turned out to be unimportant in itself (as when I no longer need what you had promised).

The right of respect is similarly connected with other infringements of rights, such as occur in the violation of property, physical violence, lying and others. In each of these the harm of lack of respect may be additional to the harm done by those offences themselves.

Violations of this right may be either aggravated or mitigated by words from the offender. The first occurs if he expresses unconcern, perhaps even contempt, for his victim's position; the second, if he offers an apology or expresses remorse. Another kind of mitigation is by means of warning, as when my neighbour warns me in advance of his party. In this case the first-order harm will still be done, but the offence of lack of respect may have been mitigated or even defused. 'At least we were warned', one might say in such a case, or: 'It made no difference to the noise, but at least he showed respect'. (In this case the first-order harm may also be less because it would not come as a surprise.)

A more direct infringement of the right of respect is that of being insulted. According to the proverb, 'sticks and stones may break my bones; but words will never hurt me'. It is not true, however, that words cannot hurt me. A person who has been insulted might properly complain of having been hurt, and he might speak of this as an infringement of the right of respect. 'You have no right to talk to me like that' would be a suitable response in such a case.

How is it that mere words can hurt us? Why should we feel hurt and resentful in that case? There is a primitive, natural preference for being addressed kindly rather than harshly, with smiles rather than with frowns, and with expressions of affection rather than of dislike. These preferences first appear in the interaction of parents with their children. It is in the nature of parents to react with expressions of pleasure and affection when their children behave well, and with contrary expressions when they do not; and it is in the nature of children to receive these reactions with pleasure or displeasure. And these reactions continue into later life and into the wider community.

There is also a connection between respect and *self*-respect. The latter depends on the extent to which we can feel *worthy* of respect; and to determine whether, or to what extent, we are worthy respect, we must rely both on self-reflection and on the respect shown to us by others. Thus our self-respect may be undermined by their failure to treat us with respect, and in this way they may be guilty of inflicting gratuitous harm on us.

There are still other ways of respecting or failing to respect another person. Suppose I think poorly of the quality of a colleague's paper. I might not have any hesitation in mentioning this to a third party; but what if the author himself asked for my opinion? In that case I would probably give a less frank reply then when speaking to a third party. But would this be right? The right to be treated with respect includes a right to be told the truth about oneself. In failing to be frank we may offend against a person's autonomy—his right to deal with his situation as it really is. Perhaps we also imply that he is not capable of doing so properly, which would, if he found out that we had not been frank, undermine his self-respect. Yet, on the other hand, telling the truth, or the whole or unvarnished truth, might be inconsiderate, and contrary in *that* way to the other's right to be treated with respect.[31]

Human rights and undeniable rights

Where, in my review of the sources of rights, are we to look for human rights? A variety of rights purporting to be 'human' have been declared by agencies of one kind and another, including some whose meaning is unclear. An example is 'the right to freedom of opinion and expression'.[32] To be free to *express* one's opinions is clearly a right of non-interference, but the idea of interference with opinion itself is far from clear. Another dubious example is the right to 'the pursuit of happiness', as listed in the American Declaration of Independence. Presumably it is open to anyone to *pursue* happiness, even if his condition is such as to make success unlikely. The pursuit of happiness is compatible with a life of actual misery.

---

[31] Sometimes an ambiguous wording can help. I once heard a play in which an aspiring poet asks a repected aunt for her opinion of his latest product. Her cautious answer was: 'You should work harder at your poetry'. Was her point that his work was deficient, or that it was worthy of more work?

[32] Article 19 of the UN 'Universal Declaration of Human Rights' of 1948.

In other cases there are doubts about the status, rather than the meaning, of proposed rights. Such rights as those of paid employment, social security, education and trade unions have been put forward in human rights declarations by the United Nations and other bodies. But, we may ask, why should they be accepted as human rights? There may be good reasons for *creating* such rights—reasons connected with human flourishing, the relief of hardship, etc.; and such reasons, as well as less respectable ones, might be used to persuade governments to sign declarations in which the rights are proposed. But if they do so, would it follow that they are *human* rights?

Human rights, it is often said, are rights that every human being has merely in virtue of being human. In the case of such rights there should be no place for the question 'What gives you the right to ...?', for in posing such a question one would *presuppose* that the addressee is human, and hence endowed with the right concerned. Human rights are thus undeniable and universal. But then it would follow that they do are not dependent on the signing of a declaration. The declaration may be an act of recognition of rights that exist independently of it, but it could not serve to create those rights.

Persons with suitable authority can create rights by signing a declaration, and such acts are akin to those created by promises. The signing may be done for various reasons, including a desire to appear in a good light to more powerful nations; but whatever the reason may be, the signing creates a right, just as promising to do X creates an obligation to do X. But such rights are morally binding only on those who sign, and not on those who do not. The former may accuse the latter (or the governments they represent) of 'violations of human rights' if their behaviour is contrary to the rights contained in declarations that others have signed, but this is not a description that they need to accept.

Suppose, however, that such a declaration has been signed by every single government (or its representative). Would that make a difference? The UN declaration of 1948 is entitled 'Universal Declaration of Human Rights'. What this means is, presumably, that it was signed by all the member states of the UN without exception. Even so, it would not follow that the stated rights are 'human' in the relevant sense. Though the rights were binding on every existing government, since all had signed the declaration, it does not follow either that they existed independently of the declaration, or that subsequent governments who did not take part in the declaration must consider themselves bound by it.

Oswald Hanfling

It is important not to confuse the claim (1) that everyone *has* a right to X with the claim (2) that everyone *ought* to have a right to X, or the claim (3) that everyone *ought to have X*. Let us take the proposition that everyone has a right to an old-age pension. This right exists in most western countries, and the term 'right' is clearly in place here. The right owes its existence to certain legal enactments, which brought it about that one party (people of a suitable age) has a legitimate claim against another (the government) in virtue of those enacments. Now it might be claimed that the right to a pension is a universal one—that everyone has this right, even where no such undertaking has been given. But what would this mean? We might agree that (3) every old person who needs it *ought* to get a pension, that this is desirable and ought to be done wherever possible; but to speak of it as 'a right' would add nothing unless we can identify someone, or some agency, who has this duty in virtue of some undertaking or other relationship.[33] One might also agree, in accordance with (2), that people ought, as far as possible, to be *given* that right, and that agencies should be created with the duty of providing that benefit. Then the people concerned could claim what they need by way of an entitlement and not request it as a favour; and this might make the provision more regular and effective, as well as avoiding feelings of indignity on the part of recipients. But these arrangements would be justified by utilitarian considerations and not from a recognition of pre-existing rights.

According to Thomas Pogge, a commitment to human rights involves one in recognizing that human persons have certain basic needs, and that these needs give rise to weighty moral demands; they are to be recognized as giving rise to human rights. But a mere 'commitment to human rights' does not entail that the satisfaction of basic needs is a human right. One may be committed to human rights—to respecting them and supporting their enforcement—without accepting that claim. To support the claim, it would have to be shown that all those whose basic needs are not satisfied have a justified grievance against all those, however remote, who might contribute to satisfying them but do not do so.

A person with a right to X can properly demand X from others, but one is not in this position merely because one's basic needs are unsatisfied. And those who are willing to help such people can properly deny that they have a *right* to be helped. Suppose a drug company agrees to supply expensive drugs to a third-world country

[33] Cf. Onora O'Neill, *Towards Justice and Virtue* (CUP, 1996), ch. 5.

at half-price. 'So', we say to the company's manager, 'you accept that those people have a right to the reduction.' The response might be: 'No, I don't. We do it because their need is great, and not because they have a right to the reduction.' One might also describe this as an act of charity. To donate money out of charity (and also *to* charities) is reasonable because the recipients need help but not because they have a right to it. The expression 'a right' might of course be used here, and this might be effective in persuading people to donate; but this would be using 'a right' in a diluted sense. This is not to say that the reasons for providing what is needed must be less urgent than in cases where a right clearly exists; it is merely to warn against confusing one kind of moral reasoning with another.[34]

A similar caution is appropriate for the use of 'duty'. It is often said that we have a *duty* to relieve the hardship of people in remote countries with whom we have no relationship, by giving money or other means. From this it would follow that people who do not do this are guilty of failing to do their duty. But is this really a duty? What is undeniable is that many people *feel* it to be a duty; but that is not sufficient for claiming that it *is* a duty—in contrast to cases where the existence of a duty is undeniable. But here again, this is not to deny that the relief of hardship in those cases is a reasonable and worthy activity.

A confusion is also liable to occur when speaking of 'human rights advocates'. In a newspaper we read that in a particular society men have certain rights over women—rights that are contrary to western ideas of right and wrong. Their exercise of these rights is criticized by 'human rights advocates', who claim that they 'have no right' to treat their women as they do. But what does this mean? The fact is that they do have that right; they have it, let us supposed, by way of tradition. If such a man is challenged to say what gives him those rights, he can properly reply that they are part of the tradition to which he belongs. Whether those rights ought to be endorsed is what is really at issue in such debates. And this question is not to be answered merely by denying, in the name of 'human rights', that the men have them—nor, of course, by pointing out that they do have them.

---

[34] Cf. Melden, op. cit. 'The fact that a stranger needs my help does not in itself establish that he has a right to it; and granted that I ought to give him help it is not always or even generally true that I ought to do so because I am under an obligation to him. The fact that my help will benefit him is reason enough ...' (17).

Oswald Hanfling

Rights have an essential and distinct role in moral reasoning, but they are not always sufficient or even appropriate for deciding moral questions. And this includes questions about what rights ought to be accorded, endorsed, respected or revoked; and what should happen when there is a conflict between rights, or between rights and other moral considerations.

Suppose that in a particular society wives may not leave the house without their husbands' permission, this being in accordance with tradition. Would this be an infringement of their right of non-interference? Suppose, first, that the women are content with this arrangement. In that case there is no interference and no cause for resentment. They would still *have* the right of non-interference, but it would not be applicable to this case. Suppose, on the other hand, that they do resent the arrangement, but the latter is defended by reference to tradition and perhaps other reasons. In that case, again, they would still *have* the right of non-interference, but, as with other rights, its exercise would be subject to competing rights and other moral considerations.

I have argued that a right cannot be human in the proper 'independent' sense, if its existence depends on the making or signing of a declaration. If a right is human in that sense, then the purpose of declaring it can only be to draw attention to its existence as part of the human condition and prior to any declaration. This seems to have been the view of those who wrote 'We hold these rights to be self-evident ...'. But where are such rights to be found? If A has promised something to B, then B has a right to receive what A has promised; this is self-evident; and the same is true of promises and declarations made by governments. But are there also self-evident rights that do not depend on particular undertakings, relationships or situations?

The rights of non-interference that I have reviewed appear to be human rights in this sense. The same is true of the right against unreasonable punishment and the right to be treated with respect. These rights are of course flouted by many governments. But could such governments deny that their citizens have them? What they usually deny in such cases is that the rights are being violated and not that people have them. Or they may claim that the violations are justified by special circumstances. When governments make such denials or claims, is this merely because they want to humour the moral preferences of dominant countries? Not necessarily: there is also the fact that people who suffer rights violations have a *reasonable* grievance against those who inflict them; and this cannot be denied, without absurdity, by the latter.

Such rights are *imprescriptible* in both senses of the word: they can be neither bestowed ('prescribed') nor revoked.[35] A right that is bestowed by, say, a legal enactment, can be taken away by the same means; but this is not so with human rights. It is true that such rights can be, and often are, violated, and in such cases we may say that the victims have been 'deprived of their rights'. But this is wrong if it means that they no longer have them—as might be the case with merely legal rights that have been abolished. When people are, say, imprisoned for exercising the human right of free expression, this does not mean that they no longer have that right. Their right is being violated, but this could not be so if they did not have the right.

Reservations about the right of liberty

Rights, including human rights, leave us with problems that cannot be addressed by reference to rights themselves. This is true particularly of the right of liberty. In the writings of Mill and others this right is associated with the enlargement of choice for individuals. But that association is not as straightforward as it may seem, for enjoyment of the right of liberty is compatible with a life in which choice is largely constrained by custom and tradition.

Suppose someone lives in a society in which choices that most of us regard as matters of personal preference are foreclosed by tradition. That person may be living, nevertheless, in accordance with his personal preferences; for these might not go beyond what is regarded as proper in his tradition. Possibilities of a contrary kind may simply not occur to him. Moreover, he might prefer the life of tradition even if such possibilities did occur to him. According to Mill, 'he who does anything because it is the custom makes no choice'.[36] But a person may *choose* to live in accordance with custom, and he may indeed object to interference with that preference as a denial of his rights. In recent history there have been instances in which 'human rights activists' have tried to emancipate people from customary practices, especially when these are contrary to standards of modern western life; but the people

---

[35] Bentham, in his famous remark about 'nonsense upon stilts', took 'imprescriptible' in the negative sense: that such rights cannot be revoked; but the word also has, or had, the positive sense of 'being able to be prescribed'.

[36] 'On Liberty' in *Utilitarianism* (ed. M. Warnock, Collins 1962), 187.

concerned, or others on their behalf, have resisted these efforts by claiming a right to live in accordance with their traditions. And this right cannot properly be denied, for the right to choose must include the choice of a life of traditional constraints in preference to one of greater liberty.

The preference for such a life is not peculiar, moreover, to people of highly traditional cultures; it is also widespread in Western countries in which the ties of tradition have been loosened or destroyed to a large extent. Sartre spoke in this connection of being 'condemned to be free'. In one of his novels he described the predicament of a man who, having espoused a life of maximum freedom, wishes he could subject himself to the principles and duties of the Communist Party. 'The Party', his communist friend tells him, 'doesn't need you ... But you need the Party ... You renounced everything in order to free ... Take one step further, renounce your own freedom'.[37] One might think that people who have thrown off the constraints of tradition and custom in favour of greater personal choice would lead happier lives. But we have become used to observing that this is not always so. A person who has greater freedom of choice may wish himself back in a world in which this was not so; or if he still inhabits such a world, he may resent attempts to interfere with his existing way of life.

An extreme case of voluntary constraint is that of selling oneself into slavery. This practice, as Mill observed, is not permitted in 'most civilized countries', where such transactions would be considered 'null and void'. The reasons for this he took to be obvious: 'by selling himself for a slave, he abdicates his liberty and foregoes any future use of it beyond that single act'; and 'the principle of freedom cannot require that he should be free not to be free' (235–6). This sounds as if there were something self-defeating about such an act, but that is not really so. A man may make this decision without being under any confusion about what he is doing or about the value of liberty. The right of liberty is a right of non-interference, and it is overridden if we compel someone to remain free in spite of his wishes. It is true that he might later regret his decision; but the same is true of many of our decisions, including some that are irreversible. It is also true that there may be social reasons for outlawing such practices. But these would be reasons for overriding the principle of liberty and would not be drawn from the principle itself, as Mill implies.

---

[37] *The Age of Reason*, (Penguin), 118.

A different kind of reservation about the right of liberty concerns the desires on which we act. The right of liberty is the right to behave as we desire. But how do we come to have the desires we have? To some extent they belong to our nature as human beings and indeed animals. But to a large extent they have been moulded by practical possibilities. Let us consider how this works from early childhood. What we experience in this 'original position' is that while we are free to do what we want to some extent, there are also occasions when this is not so, owing either to physical obstacles or to interference by our elders. In due course we learn to distinguish kinds of behaviour in which obstruction is likely from those in which it is not; and then our desires become adapted to these realities. We may still wish we could do the 'naughty' things—'desire' to do them in that sense—but these are now idle desires, not connected with intention and action. In this way our desires are brought into harmony, to a large extent, with what is possible for us. We are able to do what we want because, to a large extent, we have learned to want only what we are able to do.

Consider some of the choices that one may reasonably expect to be able to exercise in our society, such as those of voting, opening one's own business, applying for a course at a university, travelling to other countries. For a person living in our society it would not be unreasonable to want to do such things; and he might have a justified grievance against anyone who tried to prevent him. But what if they were forbidden by the government? Then he could not reasonably expect to engage in them without interference. And then his desires might come to adjust themselves accordingly. And in a society in which expectations are kept to a minimum by control of education and the media, such desires might never arise in the first place. Yet the liberty of those people to do what they want might be no less, perhaps even greater, than in a society, such as ours, in which new expectations and choices proliferate. And the same is true of societies in which expectations, and hence desires, have long been circumscribed by custom.[38]

---

[38] Callicles, in Plato's *Gorgias*, tells us that a man 'should encourage his appetites to be as strong as possible' and then 'be able by means of his courage and intelligence to satisfy them in all their intensity by providing them with whatever they happen to desire.' Socrates succeeds in making fun of Callicles's position, but the opposite extreme is also not endorsed in the dialogue. Given the question 'Then the view that those who have no wants are happy is wrong?', Callicles is allowed to reply: 'Of course; at that rate stones and corpses would be supremely happy.' (492a-e)

Oswald Hanfling

Let us consider the case of slavery in this light. What is wrong with slavery? Here one might think of the sufferings that have been inflicted on slaves such those on the American plantations. And the deprivation of liberty—taking away accustomed liberties—was certainly among these. But let us imagine a population of slaves who are not ill-treated and who have never known liberty; who have been brought up to regard their condition as normal, and to whom thoughts of liberation, or of resentment against their condition, would not occur. The principle of liberty—of being able to do what one desires—would not necessarily be infringed in such a society. And the same would be true of a world in which, as Aristotle believed,[39] some people are slaves by nature.

When considering populations for whom the range of reasonable expectations is much narrower than ours, it is tempting to conclude that their lives are inferior to ours in respect of liberty; but this would be a mistake. This is not to say that we must condone the situation of those people. We might object to it on grounds of 'human flourishing'—ideas, such as those also expressed by Aristotle, about realizing human potential, etc. On the other hand, ideas about human flourishing might also be invoked *against* the enlargement of choices. In any case, the right to do what we choose cannot be used in favour of such enlargement.

Confusions about this are liable to arise with some recent uses of 'liberation'. An example is that of 'women's liberation', which implies that women are not, or were not, as free as men to do what they wanted. This was indeed so to considerable extent, as we learn from the testimony of many women and other evidence. To a large extent, however, the change in the lives of women has not been one of greater freedom to do what they desired, but the inculcation of new desires which could hardly have occurred to most of them. And the same has been true of other social changes that have been brought about by reformers. To the statement that one is satisfied with life as it is, that one does not want the advantages in question, such reformers are apt to reply that one *ought not* to be satisfied; that it would be better if one desired things that one had not

---

[39] *Politics* 1252a34. See also Michael Levin, 'Natural Subordination', *Philosophy* 1997; and D.H.M. Brook, 'Dogs and Slaves', *PAS* 1987–8.

desired. Now there may be good reasons for advocating such changes, but the right to do what one desires could not be among them.[40]

In the cases just considered the inculcation of new desires is done for paternalistic reasons, but in other cases it is done from motives of profit or political advantage; and here a major influence, especially since in an age of mass media, has been that of advertising. The economies of modern western countries are driven to a large extent by the satisfaction of desires that did not exist and, in the case of new kinds of products, could not have existed, prior to the information and, more importantly, persuasion, with which we are inundated by advertisers. By these means the scope of our desires is vastly enlarged and so, for many people, are the means of satisfying them; while, on the other side, there is a corresponding enlargement of the scope for disappointment and envy. Whether these changes have, on the whole, been for the better is certainly open to question. And to this question again the principle of liberty, which applies to existing desires, provides no answer.[41]

[40] Some Boy Scouts were asked by the Scoutmaster to report on their 'good deed for the day'. One boy said he had helped an old lady to cross the road, and was commended for doing so. A second boy reported that he had also helped the old lady to cross the road, for which he was also commended. But when the third and fourth boys reported likewise, the Scoutmaster was moved to ask whether it really took so many to help an old lady to cross the road. 'The trouble was', replied one of the boys, 'she didn't want to cross the road.'

[41] I am grateful for comments on previous drafts from Peter Cave, David Cockburn, Laurence Goldstein, Peter Hacker, John Kekes, and John Tasioulas.

Prerogatives to Depart from Equality[1]

MICHAEL OTSUKA

I.

Should egalitarian justice be qualified by an agent-relative prerogative to act on a preference for—and thereby in a manner that gives rise to or preserves a greater than equal share of the goods of life for—oneself, one's family, loved ones, or friends as compared with strangers?[2] Although many would reply that the answer to this question must be 'yes', I shall argue here that the case for such a prerogative to depart from equality is much less far-reaching than one might think.[3] I have in mind a prerogative to depart from a specific form of equality: namely, equality of opportunity for such advantages as resources or welfare. I mean to refer to the strong form of equal opportunity elaborated and defended by Richard

[1] This is a revised version of the text of a lecture for the 2004–05 Royal Institute of Philosophy Lecture Series on political philosophy which was delivered on 12 November 2004. Versions of this lecture were also delivered at University College Cork, the Oxford Political Thought conference, and the University of Reading. I thank the members of these audiences for their comments. I also thank G. A. Cohen, Magda Egoumenides, Simon Hampson, Alon Harel, Annabelle Lever, Michael G. F. Martin, Véronique Munoz-Dardé, Thomas Porter, Hillel Steiner, Peter Vallentyne, Andrew Williams, and Jonathan Wolff for their comments.
[2] For the purposes of this discussion, I set to one side prerogatives to advance projects or follow through on commitments which one regards as of fundamental importance but whose importance is unrelated to one's own welfare or the welfare of those close to oneself. These cases give rise to an interesting and interestingly different set of problems for egalitarians.
[3] In speaking of a prerogative to depart from equality, I invoke a concept that bears obvious affinities to the now-familiar notion of an agent-relative prerogative to refrain from maximizing an impartial good such as utility. On the latter, see Samuel Scheffler, *The Rejection of Consequentialism* (Oxford: Oxford University Press, 1982), and Thomas Nagel, *The View from Nowhere* (New York: Oxford University Press, 1986), ch. 9.

Michael Otsuka

Arneson[4] and G. A. Cohen[5] whereby, roughly speaking, two people have equal opportunity for advantage if they face the same choices and will end up at the same level of advantage if they make the same choices.[6]

In order to maintain clear focus on the question I have just posed, I shall assume in the remarks that follow that equality is fully compatible with the leading of a decent life. Prerogatives to raise oneself or one's loved ones beyond equality might seem compelling when equality is inconsistent with having enough in absolute terms to lead a decent life. But this is to say that one might have a prerogative to escape from or protect oneself against insufficiency—and also, I should add, a prerogative to escape the full demands of act-utilitarianism when one would have to sacrifice a decent life in order to maximize utility.[7] It is not to establish a prerogative to depart from equality when equality is compatible with sufficiency.

Even when one restricts oneself to cases in which a departure from equality is not also an escape from or protection against insufficiency, one must guard against being misled by the

[4] See Richard Arneson, 'Equality and Equal Opportunity for Welfare', *Philosophical Studies* **56**, No. 1 (May 1989), 77–93.

[5] See G. A. Cohen, 'On the Currency of Egalitarian Justice', *Ethics* **99**, No. 4 (July 1989), 906–944.

[6] Here I state a sufficient condition rather than a necessary and sufficient condition of equality of opportunity for advantage. It is not a necessary condition for at least two reasons, one of which is that people who do not face the same choices might nevertheless face choice sets which are equally valuable in terms of their opportunity for advantage. A second reason is that people who face the same choices and end up with different levels of advantage will nevertheless enjoy equality of opportunity for advantage if these choices involve gambles of a certain type. It would take some effort to spell out a set of necessary and sufficient conditions of equality of opportunity for advantage, but it is not necessary to expend this effort for present purposes.

[7] In cases of extreme scarcity where survival is at stake, might one have an agent-relative prerogative simply to grab those resources which are necessary for one's own survival or that of one's loved ones rather than to draw lots with one's competitors? I believe that such grabbing might be excusable, given the high cost of not grabbing, but that it would not be justifiable. In other words, one ought to draw lots, though we might understand if someone could not bring himself to do the right thing in such extreme circumstances. See Michael Otsuka, *Libertarianism without Inequality* (Oxford: Oxford University Press, 2003), ch. 4, for a relevant discussion of the morality of the killing of innocents in self-defence.

competing pulls of different 'metrics' of equality. Some cases which at first glance appear to involve a justifiable prerogative to depart altogether from equality might instead be explained by the fact that the assumed metric of equality is inadequate insofar as it does not fully capture our implicit even if not explicitly acknowledged egalitarian convictions—and hence departure from this metric might be justified, not by virtue of a prerogative to depart from equality, but in the name of a wider or different metric of equality which better captures our egalitarian intuitions.

Let me explain what I mean by showing how one of David Estlund's alleged examples of a prerogative-justified departure from equality may suffer this defect. Here is his example:

> *Paul and Pauline* are married with two children. He earns $30,000 per year happily running a restaurant. Pauline earns about the same working as an accountant. She does not hate her work, but she wants very much to go to design school and to produce her own line of fashionable children's clothing. She is very talented at both business and design, and would likely succeed. Paul, who is already very happy in his work, dreams of becoming a doctor in a poor area, something he is well capable of. He does not care to make more money than now, except for the fact it would take quite a bit more money to allow him to become a doctor *and* to allow Pauline to become a clothing maker. With this in mind he is not willing (or, better, he and Pauline are not willing for him) to become a doctor for less than $100,000 per year. This amount is much more than is required to maintain the present quality of life of him and his family when he is a doctor (which would have its burdens), but nothing less would allow Pauline to pursue her project too.[8]

This example is set in a just society as measured by the egalitarian standard of John Rawls' difference principle, which condemns all inequalities in wealth and income that do not maximally benefit the

---

[8] David Estlund, 'Liberalism, Equality, and Fraternity in Cohen's Critique of Rawls', *Journal of Political Philosophy* **6**, No. 1 (March 1998), 99–112, at 104. In this article, Estlund does not himself affirm that Paul has a justified prerogative to benefit Pauline in this case. Rather, he merely endorses the conditional claim that if one shares G. A. Cohen's commitment to a prerogative to pursue one's self-interest to some reasonable extent, then one ought also to affirm Paul's prerogative to benefit Pauline in this case. See ibid., 101.

least well off.[9] Since the example is meant to provide an illustration of a prerogative to depart from the impartial demands of egalitarian justice, let us suppose that $30,000 is an average income in this society and that granting people such as Paul the opportunity to earn far in excess of the average in order to benefit their loved ones would give rise to inequalities in income that do not maximally benefit the least well off. Given the Rawlsian context, Estlund assumes the primary goods of wealth and income, and not welfare, to be the relevant measure of equality. But, as I shall demonstrate below, we must nevertheless pay close attention to how Paul and Pauline fare in the space of welfare. For simplicity, let us suppose that, in his current job running a restaurant for average pay, Paul's opportunity for welfare is at the average level for a member of his society. Moreover, let us suppose that Paul would reap no increase in his own opportunity for welfare were he to become a high-earning doctor. All such benefits from his change of profession would accrue to Pauline. Insofar as her prospects are concerned, we need to draw a distinction between two possible elaborations of Estlund's example: in the first, Pauline's becoming a clothing maker would move her from below-average to average opportunity for welfare; in the second, Pauline's becoming a clothing maker would move her from average to above-average opportunity for welfare.[10]

Does Paul have an equality-departing prerogative to earn $100,000 in order to benefit Pauline?

In the first of the two elaborations of Estlund's example which I have just distinguished,[11] we might be sympathetic to Paul's case for earning $100,000. But here Paul's increase in income would entirely serve to redress Pauline's less-than-equal share of the goods of life as measured by her opportunity for welfare. So here an implicit commitment to welfare egalitarianism might fully explain

[9] See John Rawls, *A Theory of Justice* (Cambridge, Massachusetts: Harvard University Press, 1971), 75–83 and *passim*.

[10] Here I draw a distinction which is inspired by a distinction which G. A. Cohen has drawn in a different context between the 'special burden' and 'standard' cases of talented individuals who are motivated to work in a matter which benefits the least well off only if they are paid an above-average income for this work. See Cohen, 'Incentives, Inequality, and Community', *The Tanner Lectures on Human Values*, XIII, Grethe B. Peterson (ed.) (Salt Lake City: University of Utah Press, 1992), 263–329, at 296–299.

[11] Where Pauline's becoming a clothing maker would move her from below-average to average opportunity for welfare.

our sympathy. If it does, the example does not lend support to the claim that we have a prerogative to depart from equality. Even if we maintain that Paul is permitted to benefit Pauline rather than donate his extra income to a stranger whose opportunity for welfare is even lower than Pauline's, we do not thereby embrace a prerogative to *depart* from a welfarist version of equality. This is because the permission in question is not a prerogative to raise Pauline above her welfare-egalitarian entitlement, since she will not end up with a greater-than-equal share of opportunity for welfare. Moreover, Paul's benefit to Pauline is a move in the direction of greater equality of opportunity for welfare even if not as significant a move in that direction as his giving to a worse off stranger would be.

Let us turn now to my second elaboration of Estlund's example.[12] If we are justified in believing that Paul is permitted to earn $100,000 in these circumstances, that would provide confirmation of the proposition that we have a prerogative to depart from equality. But Paul's case for earning such a high income is not, I think, very strong here. What's so compelling about the thought that people are allowed to confer advantages on their loved ones that move them beyond equality of opportunity for welfare? Egalitarians would be unsympathetic to Paul's case for earning a high income in a different scenario in which this would finance *his own* move from equal to greater-than-equal opportunity for welfare. The fact that the motive in Estlund's example is other-directed rather than self-directed might make us more sympathetic to Paul's case for earning $100,000, but does it radically distinguish it from the self-directed case?

One might try to distinguish the self-directed from the other-directed case by arguing that the latter involves a natural manifestation of Paul's love for another— and why should we stand in the way of people's expression of their love for others in a manner which benefits the beloved, even if the benefit moves the beloved beyond the level of equal opportunity for welfare? When we suppose that Pauline's opportunity for welfare is already at the average level, does it absurdly follow from egalitarianism that Paul is not permitted under any such circumstances to manifest his love for Pauline in a manner which benefits her? Well, one might be willing to grant Paul a prerogative if, rather than reaping a high income in order to confer this premium for his talent on

---

[12] Where Pauline's becoming a clothing maker would move her from average to above-average opportunity for welfare.

Pauline, he remained at a more modest, egalitarian income, a sizable chunk of which he transferred to Pauline, thereby sacrificing his average level of opportunity for welfare so that she could reap a benefit which moves her above the average level of opportunity for welfare.[13] This would be a moving and admirable sacrifice in the name of love which some egalitarians might be tempted to permit even though it disrupts equality, and I shall discuss another example of this sort below.[14] But one's sympathy for Paul should be much fainter if he's prepared to raise Pauline's level of opportunity for welfare above the average only on condition that his remains at the average level.

II.

In this section, I shall argue that egalitarians should not endorse an agent-relative prerogative in a just society to own a greater-than-equal share of material resources that gives rise to greater-than-equal opportunity for advantage. In order to guard against the problem of competing egalitarian metrics which I have flagged in the previous section, I shall confine myself in this section to cases in which welfarist and resourcist metrics do not diverge in the distributions they recommend.

I shall begin by noting some contexts in which it would be incoherent for a government that is distributing resources to distribute them unequally out of respect for an agent-relative prerogative. Suppose that all land and other natural resources are unowned and that the government is trying to bring about a just distribution of land between two individuals named Alpha and Beta who take no interest in one another's welfare. Their capacities, including their productive talents, are equal, and they derive equal

---

[13] Given the stipulations of Estlund's example, this would not be enough to allow Pauline to quit her job as an accountant and become a full-time clothing maker, but perhaps it would benefit Pauline in somewhat less dramatic fashion by enabling her to take time off from work to enrol in a few design school classes and engage in a bit of freelance but poorly remunerated clothing design.

[14] See my discussion of the second of two examples in Section II below involving Alpha, Beta, and Gamma.

welfare per unit of resource consumed.[15] Suppose also that, if the government divides the land into two equal-sized plots, each could grow more than enough food to live comfortably. The government could, however, divide the land unequally so that, for example, one of the two is able to grow enough in order to feast luxuriously, whereas the other is left just above the threshold of sufficiency. Now it would make no sense for the government to give the one person more land than the other on the grounds that this is licensed by the one person's agent-relative prerogative to favour his own interests over those of strangers.

Even if we consider a case which is identical to the above except for the fact that there is no government, but rather simply two mutually disinterested individuals who confront unowned land in a state of nature, there is still no case for agent-relative prerogatives in the matter of the distribution of land. The one person does not have an agent-relative prerogative to acquire more than half of the available land for himself even if he leaves enough for the other to maintain a living just above the threshold of sufficiency. Rather it is clear that the one person ought to leave, not just enough land for the other, but also as good, where 'as good' consists here of a plot of land which is as large as the one that he has acquired.

Should we reach a different conclusion regarding the justifiability of prerogatives to acquire a greater-than-equal share of resources when we introduce the non-market giving of resources by those who are not mutually disinterested but rather moved by a concern for others? I think not. Let us modify the case of Alpha and Beta by introducing a third person into this state of nature: Alpha's brother Gamma, whose capacities and ability to derive welfare from resources are equal to Alpha's and Beta's. Suppose that Gamma acquires one-third of the land available but that Alpha acquires more than one-third, thus leaving Beta with less than one-third to acquire. It should be clear that Alpha would not have an agent-relative prerogative to acquire more than one-third of the available land even if he did so, not for his own gain, but in order to transfer all of this extra benefit to his beloved brother

[15] For the sake of simplicity, I shall assume in this example and the ones that immediately follow that the individuals in question live on an isolated island and that farmable land of uniform quality and its fruits are the only resources available to them. But my points generalize to cases involving a fuller range of resources.

Gamma. The fact that Alpha's motivation to engage in inegalitarian acquisition is other-directed rather than self-directed does not serve to justify an agent-relative prerogative to depart from equality.

The appeal of equality-disrupting prerogatives may seem stronger in cases involving the non-market giving of a portion of one's own equal initial share of resources to others for whom one has a special concern. Suppose that Alpha, Beta, and Gamma each initially acquire equal-sized plots of land in a state of nature. Yet Alpha subsequently makes the sacrifice of giving his brother Gamma the majority of his initially equal share. As the result of such giving, Gamma's share of resources would end up greater than Beta's. This case differs from the previous one insofar as inequality arises in spite of an initial equal distribution of land, whereas in the previous case inequalities arise through an initial acquisition of unequal parcels of land.

Though egalitarians might be sympathetic to a prerogative to give in this last case, it should be noted that this case is not so different from Nozick's famous Wilt Chamberlain example involving inequality-generating exchanges among the unequally talented which arise from a baseline of an equal division of resources.[16] In both cases, some are willing to transfer a portion of their equal share to somebody else, thereby giving rise to inequality. Egalitarians are not inclined to affirm a prerogative to depart from equality in the Wilt Chamberlain case. Egalitarians would endorse the taxing away of Wilt's earnings which are surplus to equality when his greater talent is unchosen by him because purely the result of his greater genetic endowment. They would also endorse Wilt's taxation when his greater talent is unchosen by him because purely the result of the choices of his parents to lavish their money on him to send him to an especially good private training camp in his youth.[17] If we assume that Wilt's parents' wealth was cleanly generated against a background of equality of opportunity for advantage, this case is relevantly similar to the case of Alpha, Beta, and Gamma which I presented in the previous paragraph. In both cases, inequality is the consequence of the choices of others to

[16] Robert Nozick, *Anarchy, State, and Utopia* (New York: Basic Books, 1974), 160–164.

[17] Egalitarians would endorse such taxation even when we ignore any inegalitarian advantage apart from higher earning power which greater talent confers. For simplicity, I shall assume that Wilt's greater talent confers no advantage apart from greater earning power.

transfer some of their equal share to another. The difference between the two cases is that Wilt's unequal wealth is the result of the combination of familial gift (i.e., paying for his training) and subsequent market transactions, whereas Gamma's unequal wealth is the result of familial gift alone. This difference, however, is insufficient to justify a prerogative to depart from equality in the latter case, given that it is unjustified in the former case involving Wilt.

III.

In the last section, I argued that egalitarians should not endorse any prerogative in a just society to own a greater-than-equal share of material resources that gives rise to greater-than-equal opportunity for advantage. In this section, I shall consider cases in which inequalities in opportunity for advantage arise solely through the welfare-affecting choices of individuals to associate with one another and not through any inequality in the distribution of resources. I shall suppose that it is possible, in these cases, to counteract these inequalities through a compensatory unequal distribution of resources. Although some of these cases—namely those involving inequalities arising from highly personal forms of association—may appear to provide compelling examples of cases in which we have a prerogative to depart from equality, I shall argue that even here the case for prerogatives to depart from equality is illusory.

These cases all presuppose the following background of an island whose resources are of uniform quality and unowned at the outset. In the absence of any association with one another, any two people with the same resource holdings will also enjoy the same opportunity for welfare. Moreover, the mental and physical capacities of individuals are equal and people derive the same amount of welfare per unit of resource consumed. But if any of them form an association, they thereby make it the case that, for any given level of resources per capita, they will be better off in terms of opportunity for welfare than they would have been in the absence of this association.

Here are the first two cases. They involve a three-person island inhabited by Alpha, Beta, and Gamma:

(1) Economic Partnership: Beta and Gamma form an economic partnership from which they exclude Alpha. The partnership itself and the rewards which they receive do not involve resources, since the partnership consists of nothing more than the trading of services. For example, they provide one another with physiotherapy and acupressure in order to alleviate various ailments, or they offer one another tutorials on their differing areas of expertise.

(2) **Mutual Protection:** Beta and Gamma form a two-person mutual protective association from which they exclude Alpha. They protect one another against injury from outside invaders or natural disaster. This protection is provided without the use of resources. (This is a special case of (1).)

Each of these two cases involves the formation of an organization in order to provide a good, where the good itself is not a material resource. It is not a material resource because the good consists solely of services rendered. I shall refer to the goods created in these two cases as the goods of economic association, bearing in mind that the economy in question is entirely service-based.

If equality is to be realized, then Beta and Gamma would, on account of their exclusion of Alpha from their association, be required to leave Alpha with a greater share of resources in order to compensate him for the fact that, for any given equal level of resources per capita, they will be better off in terms of opportunity for welfare than Alpha. I do not believe that any legitimate prerogative stands in the way of realizing equality here.

It follows from what I have argued elsewhere that it would not violate anyone's self-ownership if Alpha were entitled to a greater share of resources as compensation for his lack of opportunity to acquire the goods of economic association.[18] Nor for the same reason would such entitlement violate people's rights to associate with mutually consenting others on terms of their own choosing, which is an implication of their several rights of self-ownership. Rights to associate would be violated if Beta and Gamma were required to associate equally with Alpha as a condition of their associating with one another. But they would not be violated by a transfer of resources to Alpha to compensate him for losing out on the benefits of the goods of economic association.

I would reach the same conclusions with respect to a third example which presupposes the same background as the first two except for the fact that now there are a number of other people in addition to Alpha, Beta, and Gamma. In this case:

---

[18] I shall say more about the relation between self-ownership and prerogatives in the next section.

(3) Political Society: Beta, Gamma, and these numerous others form a political society from which they exclude Alpha.

This example adds to (2) whatever else it takes, in addition to the collectivization of one's natural right to punish, to form a political society.

But now consider the following fourth and fifth forms of highly personal association:

(4) Friendship: Beta and Gamma form a friendship, but they do not befriend Alpha.

(5) Love: Beta and Gamma fall blissfully in love with one another, and neither falls in love with Alpha.

In these fourth and fifth cases, as in the previous three, Beta and Gamma (along with the others in the third case) would frustrate equality by virtue of their exclusion of Alpha if they did not allow Alpha a greater share of resources in order to counteract the inequalities in opportunity for welfare which arise from Alpha's exclusion. I acknowledge that even previously highly sympathetic readers might be reluctant to follow their egalitarian impulses this far. Many would maintain that it is absurd to suppose that resources should be allocated to compensate people for welfare deficiencies that arise on account of their being friendless or unloved even when we stipulate that their loneliness is not their fault. (Recall Nozick's account of the unlucky suitor who, despite his best efforts and through no fault of his, is unloved because of the non-unjust choices of others.[19] Or Nozick's case of universally unappealing Z who, as the result of the choices of A through Y and A' through Y', is stuck with nobody else to marry but universally unappealing Z'.[20]) One might be willing to acknowledge that people are entitled to treatment or other forms of compensation for mental or physical illnesses such as depression or hypertension which arise from such loneliness. But it is much harder to accept the claim that resources should be allocated simply in order to eliminate inequalities in opportunity for welfare that arise from others' choices of friends or lovers. Perhaps a prerogative to depart from equality gains a firm foothold here.

Some egalitarians would be inclined to draw the different conclusion that the above cases involving love or friendship simply show that equality of opportunity for welfare is an untenable

[19] *Anarchy, State, and Utopia*, op. cit. note 16, 237.
[20] Ibid., 263.

doctrine which should be abandoned as a component of advantage in favour of a form of equality which encompasses only resources and capacities. These egalitarians would maintain that prerogatives to befriend or fall in love with others without having to compensate the friendless or lovelorn for their lesser opportunity for welfare are not prerogatives *to depart from equality* for the following reason: equality, when properly understood, is not concerned with differences in opportunity for welfare but only with differences in resources or physical or mental capacities.

I do not think, however, that it is credible for an egalitarian to ignore welfare completely, as a consideration of cases involving discomfort or pain reveals. Suppose, for example, that the only material resource available for use by each of two individuals who are stranded on a desert island is an unowned blanket that can be divided into portions of any size.[21] If the blanket did not exist, both would freeze to death. One of these individuals is, through no fault of his, twice as large as the other. If the blanket is divided into equally large portions, then the smaller of the two will have enough to enjoy the luxury of being able to wrap the blanket around himself twice, whereas the larger of the two will suffer the (non-life-or-limb-threatening) discomfort of partial exposure to the cold because he will be able to cover only a portion of his body. The blanket could, however, be divided into unequal portions that enable each to cover his entire body once, thereby leaving them equally comfortable. (But neither is as comfortable as he would have been if he had a greater share of the blanket.) Intuitively, it would be unfair for the smaller person to acquire half of the blanket rather than that lesser portion which would leave him as comfortable as the other. One needs to admit welfare into the scope of one's egalitarian metric in order to capture this intuition.

Might an egalitarian who admits opportunity for welfare into his metric draw a legitimate moral distinction between different sources of lesser opportunity for welfare? Suppose he proposes to exclude from the scope of egalitarianism those lesser opportunities for welfare which are purely a matter of one's lesser opportunities for human association and have nothing to do with inequalities in one's resource holdings or one's efficiency in converting resources into welfare. This would serve to distinguish the blanket case from the cases of the friendless and lovelorn. Such a distinction, however, seems *ad hoc*. In any event, drawing the line here would

---

[21] This example is borrowed from *Libertarianism without Inequality*, op. cit. note 7, 26.

leave too much outside of the scope of equality, since one doesn't want to immunize all non-material benefits of economic and political associations (such as those in cases (1)–(3)) from the scope of equality.

Some egalitarians might try to distinguish inequalities arising from lack of love or friendship from other sources of inequality by pointing to the special practical difficulties which would arise in remedying the plight of the friendless and lovelorn. Compensation by means of extra resources for the lonely and unloved might be especially insulting, humiliating, or otherwise ineffective or counterproductive. It would also be intrusive or impossible to determine how well or badly people fare as the direct result of their social and love lives.[22]

These practical difficulties are very real, but they do not fully, and therefore do not adequately, explain the egalitarian's reluctance to address inequalities which are the direct result of differential access to the love or friendship of others. For let us suppose that we somehow know, by non-intrusive means, how well off Beta and Gamma are as the direct result of their relationships of love or friendship. Perhaps Beta and Gamma are, to the annoyance of onlookers, happy to broadcast this fact through veridical and highly informative public displays of affection. Suppose furthermore that friendless and unloved Alpha's level of unhappiness is fully transparent and that he is perfectly happy to submit a claim for cash compensation which will allow him to purchase expensive holidays and luxury goods which would provide him with an opportunity for welfare equivalent to Beta's and Gamma's. Even after practical difficulties have been stipulated away in this fashion, many egalitarians will nevertheless remain reluctant to embrace the claim that egalitarian justice demands the compensation just described.

Is the best explanation of this reluctance that they embrace a prerogative to depart from equality in matters concerning love and friendship? I think not. A better explanation is that they are moved by a belief in the inappropriateness of addressing one form of disadvantage (lack of love or friendship) by means of a very

[22] See Jonathan Wolff, 'Fairness, Respect, and the Egalitarian Ethos', *Philosophy and Public Affairs* **27**, No. 2 (Spring 1998), 97–122, and Elizabeth Anderson, 'What Is the Point of Equality?', *Ethics* **109**, No. 2 (January 1999), 287–337.

different form of compensating advantage (holidays and luxuries).[23] So on reflection these 'separate spheres' egalitarians would not say that inequalities in love and friendship fall beyond the scope of, because they involve a prerogative to depart from, egalitarianism. Rather, they would say that they fall within the scope of egalitarianism but need to be addressed in an appropriate manner through the provision of goods of roughly the same kind.[24] Though providing the friendless and lovelorn with meaningful companionship would be the provision of a benefit in kind, it would of course either be impossible or an injustice insofar as it is possible to frogmarch others into being their friends and lovers. But let us suppose, no doubt counterfactually, that it is possible for the state fully to redress the lesser opportunities for welfare of the lonely and unloved by subsidizing such things as singles clubs and professional matchmakers.[25] In this case neither 'separate spheres' egalitarians nor other egalitarians would have reason to endorse prerogatives on the part of those lucky in love and friendship that stand in the way of their being taxed as a matter of egalitarian justice to fund these clubs and matchmakers.

IV.

It has been a recurring theme of the previous sections that various putative examples of prerogatives to depart from equality turn out on closer inspection to be illusory. Many people are nevertheless convinced of the existence of such prerogatives. In this concluding section, I shall briefly identify two of the sources of this conviction, both of which trace to rights of ownership. I shall explain why neither grounds the sorts of prerogatives that people commonly affirm to depart from equality in a just society.

Some might press the claim that equality-departing prerogatives follow from a right of self-ownership, by which I mean a 'very stringent right of control over and use of one's mind and body that

[23] See Jonathan Wolff, 'Addressing Disadvantage and the Human Good', *Journal of Applied Philosophy* **19**, No. 3 (2002), 207–218.

[24] As the term ' "separate spheres" egalitarians' suggests, this approach bears affinities to the account of 'complex equality' that Michael Walzer provides in *Spheres of Justice* (New York: Basic Books, 1983). I should note, however, that Walzer does not claim that a norm of equality applies to each of his spheres of justice.

[25] For this supposition to hold, we will need to stipulate away practical difficulties akin to those mentioned two paragraphs ago.

bars others from intentionally using one as a means by forcing one to sacrifice life, limb, or labour, where such force operates by means of incursions or threats of incursions upon one's mind and body (including assault and battery and forcible arrest, detention, and imprisonment)'.[26] This is a right that just about everyone affirms, even those Rawls-influenced liberal egalitarians who disapprove of the word 'self-ownership'. When we consider cases that involve nothing other than sacrifices of limb or labour, the thought that one has an agent-relative prerogative not to make sacrifices to the point of equality seems fairly compelling. Well-off individuals might be morally required to render relatively non-burdensome services to those in dire need. The legal coercion of some such services via threat of imprisonment, as in the case of easy rescue laws, might also be unobjectionable. But it would typically be unjustifiable to use such means to force a well-off individual—and such an individual would typically have no moral duty—to devote his time and effort (i.e., his labour) to the enhancement of the opportunity for welfare of someone very badly off to the point at which it is no less great than his.[27] Similarly, one might be morally required to give a pint of blood in order to save a stranger's life (though legal coercion might be inappropriate here). But one would typically not be morally required to make such sacrifices to the point of equality. Nor, to take Nozick's example, would one be morally required to give one of one's two good eyes to a blind stranger in order partially to restore his sight.

We might describe these cases as ones in which one has an agent-relative prerogative not to realize equality. But any such prerogative here would simply be a consequence of one's stringent right of control over one's limbs (broadly speaking) and one's labour—i.e., one's right of self-ownership. Such a right does not, as I have argued elsewhere,[28] imply any right to earned income that would be disruptive of equality of opportunity for advantage.[29] Nor does it imply the right to give gifts in a manner which is disruptive of such equality.[30] Nor does it stand in the way of making one's access to material resources conditional on one's

---

[26] *Libertarianism without Inequality*, op. cit. note 7, 15.

[27] See ibid., ch. 1, sec. II.

[28] See ibid., ch. 1.

[29] Except in highly unusual cases such as those discussed in ibid., ch. 1, sec. II, in which there are no worldly resources and one's income consists solely of the products of one's body.

[30] See ibid., ch. 1, sec. V.

agreeing not to do things which would violate equality of opportunity for advantage.[31] Hence the right of self-ownership cannot form the grounds of an agent-relative prerogative to depart from a distribution of material resources which compensates for inequalities in opportunities for advantage.

In addition to our belief in self-ownership, we also believe (or at least many of us do) that we have moral entitlements to that which we have legally earned and been given in the actual world even though the actual world falls far short of an ideally just world. We at least implicitly regard ourselves as having moral rights of ownership that are grounded in our legal rights of ownership in holdings, where these legal rights typically encompass the right to give away, share, or consume these holdings. We regard these moral rights as stringent even though less stringent than our rights of control or ownership over our limbs or labour. It is a consequence of our belief that we have a moral entitlement to these holdings that we believe that, so long as we respect others' rights of self-ownership and their legal rights of world-ownership, we are entitled to do as we please with our riches even when we are much better off than others. And it is a consequence of this latter belief that we think we have an agent-relative prerogative to favour ourselves or those whom we care about over strangers insofar as the disposition of these riches is concerned.

If, however, the better off in the actual world really have a moral entitlement to that which they legally own, this would most plausibly be explained by the hypothesis that present legal entitlements have moral force because of the disruption to people's lives which would occur if the status quo were overturned and transformed into a justly egalitarian society. There may be limits to what one can, in the name of equality, force a person to give up which he already possesses—his already inherited wealth, for example, which he has invested in expensive projects with which he strongly identifies and which have shaped his character over the years.[32] But here we confront a problem of limited duration. Future as yet unborn generations would have no comparable claim to have greater-than-equal wealth to spend on expensive projects. It does

---

[31] See ibid., ch. 1.

[32] Cf. Bernard Williams, 'A Critique of Utilitarianism', in J. J. C. Smart and Bernard Williams, *Utilitarianism: For and Against* (Cambridge: Cambridge University Press, 1973), and 'Persons, Character, and Morality', reprinted in his *Moral Luck* (Cambridge: Cambridge University Press, 1981), ch. 1.

not follow from the explanation under review of prerogative-implying moral entitlements of people to hold onto their riches in the actual world today that there would be any analogous reason to think that people would have a prerogative to depart from equality in an ideally just society in the future.

Recall that we concluded above that it was nonsense for the government to give the one person more unowned land, and seemed unreasonable to allow one person to take more unowned land, out of deference to an agent-relative prerogative. In these thought experiments, we operated under the assumptions that the resources in question do not come with strings of ownership already attached and that any claims of ownership need to be justified against an initial presumption of non-ownership. These are surely the right sorts of assumptions to bring to our deliberations about the ideally just society, since they serve to cleanse our deliberations about ideal justice of irrelevant facts about our historically uncleanly generated and otherwise morally arbitrarily grounded actual legal rights of ownership in things. Elsewhere I have offered Lockean arguments on behalf of the claim that our theorizing about the property rights that would obtain in the ideally just society should be modelled on our theorizing about the just distribution of unowned resources.[33] One might regard the Rawlsian veil of ignorance as another means of cleansing our deliberations about justice of these irrelevancies. There are, no doubt, significant differences between the Rawlsian original position and the Lockean state of nature. The Rawlsian original position involves the selection of principles for a modern, constitutional democracy, whereas the Lockean state of nature involves our pre-political rights of ownership over a much more primitive state of the world. But I see no more reason to think that we need to add agent-relative prerogatives as an extra ingredient above and beyond our property rights over things in the more civilized Rawlsian context than in the natural Lockean context.

---

[33] See *Libertarianism without Inequality*, op. cit. note 7, ch. 1.

Casting the First Stone: Who Can, and Who Can't, Condemn the Terrorists?[1]

G. A. COHEN

'No matter what the grievance, and I'm sure that the Palestinians have some legitimate grievances, nothing can justify the deliberate targeting of innocent civilians. If they were attacking our soldiers it would be a different matter.' (Dr. Zvi Shtauber, Israeli Ambassador to the United Kingdom, BBC Radio 4, May 1, 2003).

a. Preliminaries

In April 1997 my son Gideon was dining out with his then wife-to-be in the Blue Tops restaurant in the centre of Addis Ababa. Suddenly, a hand grenade sailed into the room. The explosion killed one woman and it severely injured other people, but Gideon and Carol protected themselves by pushing their table over and crouching behind it. While Carol was physically unharmed, shrapnel hit and entered Gideon's right temple. It was removed three-and-a-half years later, after it had caused bad headaches. Not only the identity but even the inspiration of the Blue Tops terrorists remain, up to now, unknown.

One year later and one country away, in Sudan in 1998, my daughter Sarah was less anonymously menaced. For she was one mile from the Khartoum factory that was said by President Clinton to be producing chemical weapons and that was bombed by Clinton in what was presented as an appropriate response to then recent

[1] I thank Marshall Berman, Akeel Bilgrami, Paula Casal, Clare Chambers, Miriam Christofidis, Avner de-Shalit, Marcos Dracos, Jon Elster, Nir Eyal, Cécile Fabre, Diego Gambetta, Samia Hurst, Keith Hyams, Natalie Jacottet, Catriona McKinnon, John McMurtry, Avishai Margalit, David Miller, Michael Neumann, Michael Otsuka, Mark Philp, Joseph Raz, Michael Rosen, John Roemer, William Simon, Saul Smilansky, Sarah Song, Hillel Steiner, Andrew Williams, and Arnold Zuboff for illuminating comments, and Gideon and Sarah Cohen for information, and the members of the non-Bullshit Marxism group for challenging discussion.

anti-American terrorism in Africa. Whatever may have been the motive, or mix of motives, behind Clinton's action, the bombing of the pharmaceutical facility (which was merely *maybe also* a weapons factory) with Sarah nearby enabled me to identify with the victims of superpower military force more than a Western person normally might. Hundreds of miles away, I could fear for Sarah's fate under possible further Khartoum bombing.

These experiences caused me to ruminate more than I otherwise would have done on the similarities and differences between the little bombs of the underdog and the big bombs of the overdog,[2] and I thank you for allowing me to present some of that rumination to you today.

On May the 1st, 2003, Dr. Zvi Shtauber, who was then Israel's ambassador to Britain, said this on British radio:[3]

> No matter what the grievance, and I'm sure that the Palestinians have some legitimate grievances, nothing can justify the deliberate targeting of innocent civilians. If they were attacking our soldiers it would be a different matter.

Shtauber's statement made me angry, and I want to explain why it did so. I was not angry because I disagreed with what he said, and I shall not challenge the truth of what he said in this paper: I shall neither deny it nor affirm it, and everything that I shall say is intended to be consistent with the claim that the deliberate targeting of innocent civilians is never justified. Yet while I shall not deny what the ambassador said, I shall raise some questions about his right to say it, with the vehemence and indignation that

---

[2] Perhaps I should define the word 'overdog'. On September 4, 2003, just before 1.30 p.m., U.K. time, the World at One, a British news programme, interviewed a spokesperson for the British arms industry (whose name I did not catch) about the then current International Arms Fair in London. The spokesperson was asked whether he did not agree that, although arms exports made money for Britain, and British people might welcome that, they would nevertheless be happier still if the same amount of money were being made through some form of *non*-arms export. He replied more or less as follows: 'Not at all. British people are proud when they see Harriers and Tornadoes being used in far-flung places. Of course, if we were selling small arms, like Kalashnikovs, that would be a different matter'. That man was a spokesperson for overdogs.

[3] To his Today programme interviewer, John Humphrys, at 8.15 a.m., U.K. time.

he displayed, and in the posture of judgment that he struck.[4] A lot of people who think it impossible to justify terrorism nevertheless find condemnations of terrorism by some Westerners, and by some Israelis, repugnant. Yet if terrorism is impossible to justify, why can't just anybody at all condemn any terrorism whatsoever? I try to answer that question here.

There has been a certain amount of discussion in the literature about how to define the word 'terrorism'. But my topic is not the definition of the word. For my purposes, we can let terrorism be what Shtauber objected to, namely, the deliberate targeting of innocent civilians, for military and/or political purposes. If that is not what terrorism *is*, it is certainly what most people object to when they object to what they call 'terrorism'. And most people think, as Shtauber manifestly does, and as I do too, that deliberately targeting innocent civilians is, other things equal, morally worse than deliberately targeting soldiers.[5]

A final preliminary point. I shall assume throughout that terrorism, or at any rate the terrorism that concerns us here, effectively serves the terrorists' aims. If terrorism, or a given case of terrorism, is *anyhow* counterproductive, with respect to the aims of the terrorists themselves, then, for *practical* purposes, no questions of principle arise, since no sane person, or anyway nobody that I want to argue with, would say that some principle justifies *counterproductive* terrorism. But note that anybody who condemns terrorism *only* on the ground that it is counterproductive has conceded a large point of principle to the terrorists. The criticism that terror is counterproductive doesn't criticize it *as* terror.[6] More approved forms of violence are also sometimes

---

[4] Voltaire famously said, 'I disagree with what you say, but I shall defend to the death your right to say it.' I am saying something closer to 'I agree with what you say, but I shall attack your right to say it.' OK, maybe not to the *death*.

[5] You might nevertheless have wanted me to say what I think terrorism actually is. But there is, in a sense, nothing that I think terrorism is, where 'is' is the 'is' of identity: I would affirm no English sentence of the form 'Terrorism is ...' of which I would say that anybody who denies that *that* is what terrorism ('is' of identity) *is* says something false. The behaviour of the word 'terrorism' is too disorderly for us to be able to identify a range of its uses that could serve as canonical tests of proposed definitions of the term.

[6] It is, moreover, false that terrorism is never productive, as Michael Ignatieff economically shows: 'As for the futility of terrorism itself, who could say with confidence that Jewish terrorism—the assassination of

counterproductive, and Shtauber's complaint was not that a course of action that includes terrorism[7] will not succeed, or that terrorism makes it harder for Israel to agree peace terms, though he would no doubt have *added* such claims, had the distinct question of the *efficacy* of Palestinian terror been raised. Shtauber's judgment was one of principle, and it is issues of principle, not difficult questions of fact, that fall under my inspection here.

The rest of my discussion is inspired by reflection on the Israeli-Palestinian conflict, although some of it has application to the confrontation between the United States and Al-Qaeda. As a left-wing Jew whose Jewishness matters to him, I am exercised, indeed, I am agonised, in the particular way that many left-wing Jews whose Jewishness matters to them are agonised, by the Israeli-Palestinian conflict. But although what I shall say is a response to the Israeli-Palestinian conflict, I offer no conclusions about that conflict: people who agree with my observations would apply them in different ways, according to their divergent further convictions. I model certain aspects of the conflict, more particularly, some aspects of the discourse that surrounds it, for the sake of philosophical discussion. But the further significance of what I have to say will depend on the answers to controversial questions of fact and principle about which I shall say nothing. I have in mind controversial factual questions about what happened in 1948 and in 1967 and earlier, and later, and other factual questions about what the intentions of various parties to the conflict are now. I also have in mind difficult questions of principle, such as whether a people, or, at any rate, a massively abused people, has a right to a state, and, if so, at whose expense, and at how much of their expense. All that will be set aside here. What will not be set

---

Lord Moyne and then of Count Bernadotte, the bombing of the King David Hotel, followed by selective massacres in a few Palestinian villages in order to secure the flight of all Palestinians—did not succeed in dislodging the British and consolidating Jewish control of the new state? Though terror alone did not create the state of Israel—the moral legitimacy of the claim of the Holocaust survivors counted even more—terror was instrumental, and terror worked.' 'The Lessons of Terror: All War Against Civilians Is Equal', *The New York Times Book Review*, 17 February 2002.

[7] Note that the proper object of assessment is not terrorism but a course of action that includes terrorism, which covers courses that also include negotiation. Pure negotiation is not the only alternative to terror: the efficacy of the good cop/bad cop strategy is well understood.

aside—it is crucial to the case that I shall build—is that the rights and wrongs of the Israeli-Palestinian conflict are deeply controversial: that much is surely *un*controversial. If you disagree with that assessment, if, in particular, you think that the Israeli position, on all the major issues, is uncontroversially correct, then you will find it difficult to sympathize with the line of argument in this paper.

b. Who Can Criticize Whom: 'Look Who's Talking'

Before we think hard about the implications of what we are saying, we may be disposed to affirm that certain conditions of extreme injustice need not be tolerated, that people may do everything within their power to remove them, or, at any rate, that the sufferers of that extreme injustice may themselves do anything that *they* can do to remove them.[8] But we are also inclined to affirm that certain means of fighting injustice should never under any circumstances be used. Yet what can we then say when our two inclinations come together because we are asked to consider circumstances that display the contemplated conditions of extreme injustice, in which the forbidden means are the *only* means available? When we acknowledge that such circumstances are possible, we are forced to *revise* some of our convictions about what morality says.

And, in what turn out to be the convictions about morality upon which we come to settle, morality might say, to some victims: 'Sorry. Your cause is just, but you are so effectively deprived of all decent means of resistance by your oppressor that the only means of resistance that remain open to you are morally forbidden means.' Morality might say that, because that might happen to be the sad moral truth of the matter. But can just anyone at all say that on morality's behalf, *in a posture of moral admonition*? Can the oppressor herself strike that posture? Can the oppressor, whoever that may be, and I make no assumptions about who qualifies as an oppressor here, can the oppressor get away with saying: 'I am sorry.

---

[8] The implications of the proposition would make most people recoil from it. Andrew Williams spells them out: 'The view contemplated here seems to me to imply that there is an injustice so burdensome that if the only way in which I can escape it is by imposing it on others, then it is permissible for me to do so *no matter how many individuals I might have to sacrifice and how little threat they pose to me.*' (Private communication.)

G. A. Cohen

Your cause is just, but you are so effectively deprived (as it happens, by me) of all decent means of resistance that the only means open to you are morally forbidden?'

As the example of the oppressor suggests, the force, the effect, of a moral admonition varies according to who's speaking and who's listening.[9] Admonition may be sound, and in place, but some may be poorly placed to offer it. When a person replies to a critic by saying: 'Where do *you* get off criticizing *me* for *that*?', she is not denying (or, of course, affirming) the inherent soundness of the critic's criticism. She is denying her critic's right to make that criticism, in a posture of judgment. Her rejoinder achieves its effect without confronting the *content* of her critic's judgment. She

[9] The question, 'Who can say what to whom?', goes largely unexplored in contemporary moral philosophy. To be sure, if all that moral philosophy were interested in were which acts are right and which wrong, then this phenomenon *might* deserve little attention. ('*Might*': I do not myself believe that the phenomenon carries no lessons as to what is morally right, because I believe that what I call the 'interpersonal test' ('Incentives, Inequality, and Community', in *The Tanner Lectures on Human Values*, Volume XIII, Grethe Peterson (ed.) (Salt Lake City: Utah University Press, 1992), 280ff.)—which is not employed in the present paper—has non-interpersonal moral implications.) But, insofar as moral philosophy seeks to reconstruct actual moral discourse, the widespread neglect by moral philosophy of the phenomenon described in the sentence to which this footnote is attached is unjustified, since it looms very large in moral discourse.

I myself began to examine the interpersonal dimension of moral utterances in 'Incentives', and the theme was subjected to further study by Jerry Dworkin in an article called 'Morally Speaking' (in *Reasoning Practically*, E. Ullmann-Margalit (ed.) (Oxford University Press, 2000)). As I said: 'A [moral] argument will often wear a particular aspect because of who is offering it and/or to whom it is being addressed. When reasons are given for performing an action or endorsing a policy or adopting an attitude, the appropriate response by the person(s) asked so to act or approve or feel, and the reaction of variously placed observers of the interchange, may depend on who is speaking and who is listening. The form, and the explanation, of that dependence vary considerably across different kinds of case. But the general point is that there are many ways, some more interesting than others, in which an argument's persuasive value can be speaker-and/or-audience-relative, and there are many reasons of, once again, different degrees of interest, why that should be so.' (*Ibid.*, page 273: a number of illustrations of the 'general point' follow the quoted paragraph.)

I hope to say more about these matters in a paper called 'Ways of Silencing Critics', a draft of which I shall send on request.

challenges, instead, her critic's right to *sit* in judgment, and to *pass* judgment. She could not similarly challenge a critic whom she had overheard saying, to a third party: 'I of course agree that what she did was morally wrong, but I'm not myself in a position to criticize her. (It's not for me to cast the first stone.)'

Let me step back a bit. We can distinguish three ways in which a person may seek to silence, or to blunt the edge of, a critic's condemnation. First, she may seek to show that she did not, in fact, perform the action under criticism. Second, and without denying that she performed that action, she may claim that the action does not warrant moral condemnation, because there was an adequate justification for it, or at least a legitimate excuse for performing it. Third, while not denying that the action was performed, and that it is to be condemned (which is not to say: while *agreeing* that it is to be condemned), she can seek to discredit her critic's assertion of her standing as a good faith condemner of the relevant action.

I should make clear what I am not claiming, when I say that a critic may be disabled from condemning, and, therefore, in the relevant sense, may be *un*able to condemn, the agent under judgment. I do not mean that the critic cannot be speaking the truth when she condemns the agent: it is central to the interest of the phenomenon under exploration here that she might well be speaking the truth. Nor do I mean that the critic should be forbidden, under whatever sanction, to make the relevant utterance. Whether there ought to be a legal prohibition, even whether there is a moral prohibition, on the utterance, is a somewhat separate matter.[10] What I mean is that there are facts about the critic that

[10] My topic is not when it's morally permissible or obligatory to condemn, and it is not part of my view that it is always bad or wrong for someone who is not in a position to condemn to condemn. I could agree with a person who said: 'I really wasn't in a position to condemn him, but issuing that savage condemnation was the only way to rally others and/or to get him to stop, and that was more important than making sure that my speech-acts were in accord with my "standing".'

I believe that lying is in itself wrong, and that it therefore counts against an act that it is a lie, which is to say that there is something wrong with lying because of its nature, whatever its typical, or unusual-case, consequences may be. But sometimes those consequences can make it all right, or even imperative, to lie. So, similarly, here: I believe that there is something wrong with condemning unless certain presuppositions are fulfilled, but if dodgy condemning is going to save the children, then I say: 'Condemn away!' It may be better that villainous superpowers condemn one another's villainies than that they remain silent about them,

compromise her utterance considered as, what it purports to be, a *condemnation*: the focus is on that intended role, or illocutionary force,[11] of the utterance. If Shtauber had said, 'By the way, I think what the Palestinians are doing is morally horrendous', then what I shall say about his actual and differently toned utterance would not apply. It is material to the contention that I shall lay before you that Shtauber was not merely seeking to speak the moral truth, but, precisely, to condemn, and the question is: was he well placed, as a spokesperson for Israel, to engage in that particular speech-act of condemnation? Did he have the right, the requisite standing, to condemn the Palestinian terrorists, in the terms in which he did?

This *third* way of deflecting criticism, that is, by impugning the right of the critic to condemn, is of great importance in the political world, where it matters enormously who can say what to whom, credibly and sincerely: that consideration helps to determine the fate of would-be critical political interventions. The world of politics is not populated by saints with spotless track records, but by non-saints who have a better hope of deflecting criticism not by trying to justify what they themselves did, but by implicating their criticizing fellow non-saints in the same or similar charges.

We often implicitly acknowledge the force of the third form of response to criticism. When someone says 'I'm not in a position to criticize him', and cites some relevant disabling fact about herself, people do not say: 'But anyone can criticize anyone, regardless of their *own* track record'. If you, reader, are indeed disposed to say the latter, then you disagree with me at a very fundamental level. If you do not recognize a difference between expressing a negative moral belief and condemning, then I do not know how you would account for the peculiar force of the disavowal that is expressed by the words, 'I'm not in a position to criticize her'.[12]

---

because that way we learn about the villainies on both sides (and, hence, *inter alia*, how poorly placed the superpowers are to condemn each other). I think one can say: 'He has no right to condemn, but let us hope he does condemn', and maybe even 'but he ought to do so ...'.

[11] The phrase 'illocutionary force' is J. L. Austin's: see his *How to Do Things with Words* (Oxford: Oxford University Press, 1962), Lectures VII-XII.

[12] It may be worthwhile to distinguish some distinct ways of resisting the claims of this paper. You disagree with me most fundamentally if, as I have said, you deny the very existence of the sort of transgression of which I accuse Shtauber, if, that is, you deny that the capacity to engage in good-faith condemnation is relative to the record and/or posture of the

An ambiguity in the word 'criticize' may cause you to resist the distinction that I have sought to substantiate. There is certainly *a* sense of 'criticize' in which, if I express a negative moral opinion about some person, then I count as criticizing that person: the word 'criticism' can be used to name a form of opinion. But it can also be used to denote speech-acts that are, or are akin to, acts of condemnation; otherwise, so I claim, it would not make sense to say, 'I think', or, indeed, 'I *know*', 'that what he did was wrong, but I'm not in a position to criticize him'. The key point is that, when the moral capacity to criticize or condemn is undermined, the capacity to perceive and register and speak the truth is not undermined with it, from which it follows—this is, roughly speaking, the contrapositive of the key point—that being in a position to utter a well-grounded truth does not suffice for being in a good position to condemn. *Exactly* what 'I am not in a position to criticize' means I do not (yet) know: I have not to date produced an explication that specifies, with satisfying precision, and in general terms, the nature of the defect in speech-acts of condemnation that is my topic, but I am confident that the quoted words signify an *explicandum* that is eminently worth explicating.[13]

Two ways of discrediting a condemning critic's standing will concern me here. They both occur widely in moral discourse, and they occur saliently in exchanges of condemnation about terrorism, and, in particular, in exchanges between Israelis and their supporters on the one hand and Palestinians and their supporters on the other.

The first of these techniques for compromising a critic's voice was signalled in my childhood by the retort 'Look who's talking!' Shapiro might say, 'Hey, Goldstein, how come you didn't come to the club last night? All the guys were expecting you.' And Goldstein might reply: 'Look who's talking. *Twice* last week, *you* didn't show up.' Unless Shapiro could now point to some relevant difference, his power to condemn was compromised, whether or

---

would-be condemner. But you might accept that relativity thesis yet insist, against what I have said, that absolutely excluded acts *can* be condemned by anyone: Shtauber might then be immune to my critique. And he might also be thought immune to it for some other reason, even if one's standing *does* bear on one's capacity to condemn absolutely excluded acts.

[13] For some further attempts at explication, see my 'Ways of Silencing Critics': see footnote 9 above.

not the criticism he originally made of Goldstein was sound.[14] In places that are more genteel than the immigrant streets of post-war Montreal where I grew up, people do not say, 'Look who's talking', but 'That's the pot calling the kettle black'. If I, the putatively black kettle, make that reply, under criticism, to the putative black pot, I am not denying (or, necessarily, accepting) that I am tarnished. I am saying that, since the pot is even more *whatever* it is that leads it to condemn me than I am, the pot, on its own express view of the matter, should look upon on its own hue rather than on mine.[15]

And a still more elevated epithet that occurs in the contemplated range of disabling replies is more elevated still because it is in Latin. I have in mind the sentence, '*Tu quoque*', which means, 'You, too.'

When Jesus said 'judge not, that ye be not judged', and when he allowed only the sinless to cast the first stone,[16] he was invoking *tu*

[14] Yet both Goldstein and Shapiro could, of course, be condemned by the conscientious club-attender Hockenstein.

[15] This is not to deny that what the pot says is true, and in some contexts, its truth will be all that matters. If the kettle had said that it was clean, what the pot says to the kettle might pass muster. But in political contexts, in contexts of political enmity, what the pot says is often discredited *even if* it is preceded by a rosy and false self-appraisal on the part of the kettle

Compare Christopher Ricks' quip about T. S. Eliot: '... Ricks said Eliot's clearing Wyndham Lewis of having fascist sympathies was like the pot calling the kettle white. 'I was right and wrong to make the joke, which was quite a good joke,' says Ricks. 'If you follow it remorselessly it suggests Eliot was a fascist which I don't think he was. But he also wasn't in a position to clear other people of the accusation. There is too much that Eliot is associated with that is not without its links to fascism.' (Profile of Christopher Ricks by Nicholas Wroe, Guardian Newspaper Review Section, January 29, 2005, 23)

Worthy of narration here is the following joke: The rabbi has left the synagogue to do some shopping, and the *shammas*, or, if you must, the verger, is in charge. The rabbi returns unexpectedly early, and, entering the synagogue, finds the *shammas* on the floor, in prayer: 'Oh, Lord, thou art everything and I am nothing!' Says the rabbi: 'Hah! Look who says he's nothing!'

Nietzsche said it quicker: 'He who despises himself still esteems the despiser within himself.'

[16] I presume here that, despite the context of that remark, Jesus intended it as advice not only about literal but also about metaphorical stone-throwing.

quoque in an extreme form. But he was not saying that the compromised judgment would be mistaken. He was, on the contrary, implying that the judgment he was forbidding would indeed be correct, yet one that *you* are not well placed to make, because it also applies to, and against, you. 'Judge not, that ye be not judged' is extreme because it disempowers me as a critic as long as I am not *entirely* sinless. Contrast the other Jesus statement, about not pointing out the mote in my brother's eye when there is a beam in my own eye. Beams are larger than motes, so if, somewhat unrealistically, we take the beam/mote statement *au pied de la lettre*, then we may say that the beam/mote statement relaxes the Jesus view a bit, because it condemns judgment only from judges whose sins are *worse* than the sins of those whom they seek to judge.[17]

For that first type of would-be discrediting response I have three good labels: 'look who's talking', 'pot calling the kettle black', and '*tu quoque*'. For my contrasting second type I have no good vernacular or Latin tag. But I will point you in the right direction by reminding you of retorts to criticism like 'you made me do it', and 'you started it', even though those phrases don't cover all the variants of the second type. I shall name the second type 'You're involved in it yourself', but if anybody can think of a better name, then suggestions are welcome.

[17] Would Jesus have allowed you to cast a stone if you first signed up for being the next victim of stone-casting? Consider monks who flagellate each other. Why shouldn't the fact that we are all sinners mean that we should all criticize each other, rather than, as Jesus says, that no one should criticize anybody? (I thank Marshall Berman for that pregnant counter-suggestion). Compare the discussion of the 'inconsistency explanation' of *tu quoque* in my 'Ways of Silencing Critics': see footnote 9 above.

There is some further investigation of *tu quoque* in my 'Ways of Silencing Critics' (see footnote 9 above). And we should also consider what might be called *counterfactual tu quoque*: 'You'd do this, or worse, if you were in my shoes.' Can American neo-cons put their hands on their hearts and declare that if their own weapons of mass destruction were somehow immobilized, say, by computer hackers, then they would nevertheless refrain from using terrorist means against their opponents, even if they thought them effective? (I set aside the claim that they have non-counterfactually used, and nourished the use of, such means in Latin America). Can they deny that what are now terrorists might prefer to use approved weapons of mass destruction, in acceptable ways, as the United States may be presumed to have done (in discussions with terror-condemning Americans who do not condemn the United States) at Hiroshima and Nagasaki?

G. A. Cohen

In this second type of silencing response you are disabled from condemning me not because you are responsible for something *similar* or worse yourself but because you bear at least some responsibility for the *very thing* that you seek to criticize. My Nazi superior cannot condemn me for doing what he orders me on pain of death to do, even if I *should* disobey, and accept death. I return to the second type of silencing in section c.

The first type, *tu quoque*, clearly plays a large role in Palestinian responses to Israeli criticism of Palestinian terrorism, and also some role in Israeli responses to Palestinian criticism of Israelis. Was I angered by Ambassador Shtauber's statement because it is vulnerable to the 'look who's talking' reply? In part yes, not because I am confident that what Israel does is *as* bad as terrorism is, but because Israel so clearly has a case to answer under *tu quoque* that setting aside possible comparisons with Israeli behaviour, as Shtauber sought to do, is unacceptable. He was saying to us: '*Join me*[18] in condemning them regardless of whether we're just as bad, or worse, than they are', and that is not an invitation that anyone should accept.

The Israelis have a *tu quoque* case to answer, because they kill and maim many more people, and deprive many more still of their homes and livelihoods, than Palestinian terrorists do. To be sure, there are Israelis who are oppressed by that fact and who are highly critical of their own government, but who believe that that government may nevertheless credibly condemn Palestinian terrorism because terrorism is morally much worse than any violence that the Israeli government *itself* commits. In response to the claim that Israeli condemnation of Palestinian terror is silenced by the fact that Israelis kill many more Palestinians, and a lot more children, these Israelis argue that Israeli killing is not as bad as Palestinian killing.

Some of these Israelis invoke the principle of double effect, which distinguishes between killing innocent people as an unintended but foreseeable *side-effect* of *otherwise* targeted action, and killing innocent people who *are* your target, people, that is, whom you hope and intend to kill. 'Our government can condemn

---

[18] I italicize those words, because they point to a theme that occurred to me late in the course of my work on this paper, and that needs further development. In some fashion condemners invite third paries to *join* them in condemning the condemnable, but when *tu quoque* applies to condemners, there are reasons for third parties to refuse to join them.

them', these Israelis might say, 'because although our government kills *more* innocent people than they do, our government does not *aim* to kill innocent people.'

Now I myself believe in the principle of double effect, or at any rate in the judgments about cases that are meant to illustrate that principle.[19] But I also believe that the only sane form of the principle of double effect is comparative, rather than absolute. I believe, for example, that, holding everything else equal, such as, for instance, the amount of justice that there is in the motivating cause, killing two hundred innocents through foreseeable side-effect is actually *worse* than killing one innocent who is your target. It seems to me ludicrous for us to say that *you* committed an outrage when you set your sights on, and killed, *a* civilian with your petrol bomb, but that we did not commit an outrage when our bombing destroyed not only the Hamas leader that we were aiming at but also fifteen people that lived near him, because we merely *foresaw* that effect, without intending it. And we also have to take into account how careful combatants are to avoid killing civilians. It is possible not to *aim* at killing them yet to be utterly reckless of their safety, and it seems pretty clear that Israeli soldiers have become more reckless, in some cases wilfully reckless, as the conflict has deepened.[20] And worse still than (merely) reckless side-effect killing is side-effect killing that is still not aimed at, that remains 'mere' side-effect, but that is expected and welcomed, because it deters potential terrorists who care about their families and their neighbours.

So it is not at all clear that Israeli criticism of Palestinian terrorism can escape the *tu quoque* rebuke by sheltering under the doctrine of double effect. But Palestinian terrorists and their apologists also face a powerful *tu quoque* challenge.

Palestinians complain that they lack a state. They complain that their rights are denied. But how can they then justify a terror that denies the right to life of innocent others? Is not the right to life more precious still than the right to a state?

Palestinians might protest that they do not *aim* at innocents but only at Israelis who are complicit in causing their grievance. But no

---

[19] The diagnosis of those judgments, and whether or not they really support double effect, is controversial.

[20] If some amount of side-effect killing n is just as bad as some lesser amount of aimed-at killing m, then some lesser amount of side-effect killing p ($m<n<p$) where recklessness is displayed would surely be just as bad as *that* amount (m) of aimed-at killing.

defensible doctrine of complicity, however wide may be the criteria for complicity that it proposes, will cover everybody in those Tel Aviv cafés, including the children, and the non-citizens of Israel. In face of that fact, can Palestinians claim that they are *aiming* only at the *complicit* citizens in the Tel Aviv bars, and that the other deaths are side-effects? I, for one, do not find that posture credible. But how does it differ from the posture of Israeli assassination squads who blow up houses because Hamas supporters live there even when they know that innocent people who also live there will lose their homes and their livelihoods and even their lives?

In sum: I'm not sure who can point the finger at whom here, but I'm sure that it's absurd, given the uncontested facts, for either to point the finger at the other with no comment on his own glass house: and that was undoubtedly one provocation to the anger that I felt when I heard Shtauber's statement. (I should also have been angry if a Hamas leader had accused Israeli soldier-killers of a callous disregard for human life: but that isn't the example on the table.)

c. Who Can Criticize Whom: 'You're involved in it yourself'

So much for the case to answer that faces Shtauber under *tu quoque*: that case puts his right to condemn in question. But he has two further cases to answer under the contrasting 'You're involved in it yourself' challenge. Let me first say something about 'You're involved in it yourself' in general terms. After that, I'll return to Shtauber, and the two subtypes of this second type of silencing that I want to distinguish.

I said earlier that among the variants of this second way of deflecting criticism (*tu quoque* was the first) are 'You started it' and 'You made me do it': the reply has many variants, with 'It's your fault that I did it' at one kind of extreme and 'You helped me to do it' at another. And note that if it's your fault, in whole or in part, that I did it, then it can be your fault for structurally different reasons. Here's part of the relevant wide array: you ordered me to do it, you asked me to do it, you forced me to do it, you left me with no reasonable alternative, you gave me the means to do it (perhaps by selling me the arms that I needed). When such responses from a criticized agent are in place, they compromise criticism that comes from the now impugned critic, while leaving third parties entirely free to criticize that agent. The functionary who obeys Nazi orders can't be condemned for obeying those orders by the superior who issues the orders;[21] he can nevertheless be condemned by us. (When, as a child, I tried to excuse an action on the ground that someone else had *told* me to perform it, my mother, a third party, could and did reply: 'So, if they told you to jump off the Empire State Building, you would do that too?')

Note, now, how this second type of challenge, 'You're involved in it yourself', differs from 'Look who's talking'. 'Look who's talking' says: 'How can you condemn *me* when you are *yourself* responsible for something similar, or worse?'[22] In 'You're involved in it yourself' the responding criticized person need make no judgment about whether her critic has *herself* done something similar or worse. Instead, 'You're involved in it yourself' says: 'How can you condemn me when you are *yourself* responsible, or at least co-responsible, for the very thing that you are condemning?' That responsibility can run from physically forcing at one end to merely abetting at the other. 'You criticize me for robbing the bank, but why, then, did you willingly give me the number on the lock on the safe?'[23]

The general form of 'You're involved in it yourself' is this: you are implicated in the commission of *this* very act, as its co-responsible stimulus, commander, coercer, guard, assistant, or whatever (whether or not what you did was wrong, or similar to what I did, or worse than what I did).

Let me now consider Ambassador Shtauber's statement within the 'You're involved in it yourself' framework. I focus first on the concession at the opening of Shtauber's statement, the concession which says 'Your *grievance* may be just.' That concession is often heard from Israelis who speak about Palestinian terror. But I believe that there can be a problem about proceeding to condemn the terrorist means after you have expressed a willingness, in principle, to concede just grievance, when you, the critic, are the *source* of the grievance, *if* there is one. I believe that whether or not the Palestinians *have* a legitimate grievance, and whether or not those Palestinians who use terrorism in pursuit of a supposed grievance are justified in doing so, Shtauber's statement is indefensible, on *his* lips, because they are the lips of a spokesperson

---

[21] Note the present tense: I do not say that a reformed Nazi superior cannot condemn an unreformed lesser functionary for having obeyed him.

[22] On 'similar *or* worse', see 'Ways of Silencing Critics', section (1).

[23] Also worthy of exploration is how and under what circumstances your involvement imposes on you a *duty* to condemn. And there may be cases in which you have both a duty to condemn and no right to do so.

for Israel: an Israeli spokesperson is not morally qualified to make the 'no matter what the grievance' concession when it is followed by the 'nothing can justify' condemnation. For you are yourself more or less implicated in the act you seek to condemn if you caused a *legitimate* grievance to which the act is a response. And how, therefore, can you reasonably expect your condemnation of the act to be received as made in good faith, unless you address the grievance of those you condemn? How can you suppose yourself to be free to set aside the size and character of that grievance, and your putative role in causing it, and proceed to condemn the responsive terrorist act, as a third party freely might? If the Palestinian grievance is large, and Palestinians have no effective way of pursuing it save through a strategy that includes terror, then, even if it is not Israel that thus constrains their practical options, the putative Israeli responsibility for the grievance itself compromises what Shtauber says after he has made his concession.

One might mount the following objection to what I have claimed. Someone who imposes a grievance and thereby induces a violent response might not be able to complain that there was some sort of aggressive response, but could still condemn a particular response as *disproportionate*. If, in response to my callous snub, you shoot me in the foot, that your shooting is a response to my callous snub does not disable me from condemning it. And one might say that terrorism, because always wrong, is *a fortiori* always disproportionate, and therefore condemnable by anyone.

To this objection I have two replies. First, that the objection over-generalizes. For, if the grievance I impose is spectacular, one that is as absolutely condemnable as is the terrorist response to it, then the fact that the latter is morally excluded does not seem to me to show that it is, in particular, a *disproportionate* response. (Suppose, for example, the imposing of the grievance is *itself* a disproportionate response to a still previous insult: the power of *tu quoque* then joins the present different disabling fact to condemn the condemnation.)

And a further reply to the objection is that some sort of discount rate applies here. Suppose responses can be calibrated on a scale of severity which runs from 1 to 10, and, in a particular case, anything over 5 would be disproportionate, and the response under examination is 6 or 7. Then a third party can, *ex hypothesi*, condemn that response, but one might nevertheless think that it needs to be, say, 8, for the provoker *herself* to condemn it. For this further reason, I do not bow to the suggested vindication of Shtauber's right to say what he did that I sketched two paragraphs back.

But there is a second and distinct way in which Israelis might be thought implicated in the terrorism that they seek to condemn. For whoever caused a particular grievance, and whatever the weight of that grievance may be, an agent who unjustifiably constrains the practical options that are available to the putatively aggrieved is not well placed to condemn the choice of an option (in our case, terrorism) that he, the constrainer, makes particularly eligible, from the point of view of the aims of the constrained. (Recall that we have legitimately supposed—see page 115 above—that the terrorist option is a particularly good one for Palestinians).

Consider a Wild West parallel. A certain varmint is deprived of his gun, when everybody else has one, because guns are standard equipment for wild westerners. Suppose it was Cal who removed the varmint's gun. If Cal now seeks to condemn the varmint's recourse to whatever it is that is worse than a gun—maybe a hand grenade—that the varmint perforce uses instead, then Cal must either justify his removal of the varmint's gun or show that its removal, even if unjustified, didn't effectively *drive* the varmint to his alternative course. If you've got somebody up against the wall, don't complain if he kicks you in the balls, unless you are prepared to say something about your own act of putting him up against the wall. (You *can* protest when a homicidal criminal that you have disarmed tries to strangle you, but that is because disarming him was justified. After all, he made you do it.)

Let me now pursue the putative—putative is enough—parallel between Cal and the Varmint on the one hand and Israel and the Palestinians on the other. If you rule over a people who have no citizenship in your country, and whom you therefore deny civil democratic means of redress, if it is you, moreover, who disarmed them, and you who deprive them of weaponry that is effective against your soldiers, or at least ensure that they cannot get such weaponry, then *you* in particular cannot complain if they use unconventional weaponry against non-soldiers, *unless* you can justify your constraining action, or show that the constraint was not substantial enough to make their action understandable. Israelis ensure that Palestinians cannot acquire conventional means of combatting Israeli forces, and they therefore cannot complain that the Palestinians use other ones, *if* the Palestinians have a legitimate and sufficiently substantial grievance. If B claims to have a legitimate grievance, and A, who may not have caused that grievance, leaves B no effective recourse except horrible violence, or even if A makes such violence a strategically attractive recourse, then how can A in particular complain about that horrible violence, without commenting on the justifiability of his, A's, constraining B's options, and therefore on the status of B's putative grievance (again, whether or not it was A himself who *caused* that grievance)? Because other people routinely carry guns, Cal has to explain why he removed the varmint's, if he wants to condemn the varmint's use of a hand grenade. And when other peoples, Israelis, Americans, British and so forth, have 'superguns', true weapons of mass destruction, then those who deprive the Palestinian people of the capacity to acquire similar weaponry must explain why they did so if they seek to condemn the Palestinian recourse to unsimilar weaponry.

Thus, and for two reasons: *even if* it is the moral truth that one should never attack civilians, in terrorist fashion, the Israelis in particular can't condemn Palestinians for attacking civilians, *regardless* of the justice of their grievance. Even if terrorism is always wrong, Shtauber's stance in condemnation of Palestinian terror is unsustainable, in the absence of an argued case against the Palestinian grievance, not because their grievance might justify terrorism (that being excluded by the *protasis* of this sentence), but because, if the Palestinians have a legitimate grievance, then it is against an Israel that *both* created their grievance *and* restricts their practical options of response.[24] Accordingly, the question of the justice of the Palestinian grievance cannot be set aside by those who deprive them of conventional means of redress in a discussion of the particular unconventional means that they use to pursue their grievance, *especially* (but not only) if those who deprive them of conventional means are *also* the unjust causers of that grievance.

The two charges against Shtauber that belong under the 'You're involved in it yourself' heading—'You caused our grievance' and 'You forced us to use terrorist means'—do not simply lie side by

---

[24] Suppose some oppressed opponents of a state begin a campaign of liberation by attacking soldiers. But then the state gives its soldiers bulletproof armour, and, needless to say, doesn't also issue such armour to its oppressed opponents. Suppose that, as a result, the oppressed can *now* have an effect only by attacking civilians. Can they not say, tellingly, that their oppressors, in adopting the armour policy, have left them with no other recourse? *We*, the bystanders, may be able to condemn *both* co-responsible sides: the state for its armour policy, the oppressed for now attacking civilians. But how can the state condemn the oppressed, *unless* the state can impugn their grievance?

side. Though logically and practically independent, in the general case,[25] they are, in a certain manner, fused here. For consider. If the Palestinians had normal democratic sovereignty and normal civil liberty they would have a normal army which is not equipped merely to police its own people.[26] It is central to their grievance that they lack a *state*,[27] and, therefore, among other things, the approved means of violence that a state possesses. But the lack of what they would have, if they had a proper state, to wit, just such an army, contributes strongly to the explanation of their mode of pursuing their grievance. For it is only by *un*conventional means that you can pursue any grievance which includes the grievance that you lack conventional means of pursuing grievances.[28]

Let me expose and defend two conceptual claims that inform my thinking about the 'You made it a good choice' part of the case that Shtauber has to answer. Each conceptual claim is a bit surprising, but each is, so it seems to me, incontrovertibly true.

The first truth is that your having left me with no reasonable alternative does not itself entail that I was forced to do whatever it was you left me with no reasonable alternative to, if only because I might nevertheless *not have done* that thing. If you think that

[25] By that I mean that the grievance-causer need not be the options-restricter, or vice versa: I do not mean that 'You caused our grievance' is powerful even if we have many good non-terrorist options, or that 'You made terror a good recourse' is powerful even if we have no justified grievance. The force of each consideration is indeed normatively dependent on the force of the other.

[26] An army which they would of course not need to use to seek to achieve an independence that they lack!

[27] Many Israelis would claim that both the Oslo agreement and Camp David offered the Palestinians a state, but that Arafat's venality and incompetence lost it for them. Palestinians counterclaim that what was offered was both constitutionally and geographically inadequate: a set of powers that amount to less than full and rightful sovereignty, within a set of 'Bantustans' that did not satisfy the full and rightful Palestinian territorial claim. I take no stand on these matters here. But the Israeli case, even if sound, cannot be pressed against my criticism of Shtauber, since to raise that case is to embark on the enterprise of assessing the Palestinian grievance—and that is what Shtauber thought and sought to avoid.

[28] To be sure, there exist non-violent unconventional means, and they are sometimes more effective than terrorism, but recall our decision (see page 115) to face the challenge of a terrorism that is distinctively productive. In any case, Shtauber wasn't forbidding violence, just violence against non-soldiers, and violence, to similar effect, against soldiers, is harder for Palestinians to achieve.

sounds peculiar, then consider the following example. Suppose a highwayman credibly says 'Your money or your life', and thereby leaves his victim with no reasonable alternative to giving up his money. It does not follow that the victim will hand over the money: he might, instead, choose death, for example, out of defiance. *If* he hands over the money, then he does so because he is forced to, because he had no reasonable alternative. But he cannot be said to be forced to do it if he does not actually do it. Therefore having no acceptable alternative to doing something does not entail being forced to do that thing.

The second truth is that having no reasonable alternative to doing a certain thing does not entail being *justified* in doing that thing,[29] supposing that one *did* do it. Having no acceptable alternative to using terror may be a necessary condition of being justified in using terror, but it does not follow that it is a sufficient condition of being justified in using terror. For it might be true, I might be in the parlous position that, while I have no acceptable alternative to terrorism, terrorism is nevertheless *more* unacceptable than one or more of my *other* unacceptable courses. I might have to choose between disaster for me and a course so morally horrible that the only decent thing I can do is to choose disaster for me. But how can *you in particular* condemn me if I refuse to choose disaster for me, when it was you who deprived me of all acceptable alternatives, unless you can justify your having done so? If someone has no acceptable alternative, then there is a case to answer against whoever made that true. If the sad moral truth is that, although all of my alternatives to terrorism are unacceptable, my terrorism is nevertheless unjustified, then how, even so, can the person who deprived me of acceptable alternatives, and so drove me to admittedly unjustifiable terrorism, condemn that resort, without justifying the action that thus disabled me? That person must respond to my grievance that he left me with no acceptable alternative to a morally heinous and forbidden action. That my only way out is fobidden does not forbid me to reject *his* condemnation of me if I take that way out.

Shtauber supposes himself entitled to condemn terrorist means *even if* the Israelis have made a course that includes terrorism the

---

[29] I think that one reason why colossal terrorism in response to colossal injustice perplexes us is that we commonly take a person's lacking any reasonable alternative to an action A as justifying her doing A. It usually does. But not always. And realizing that helps us to think more clearly about terrorism.

best course of a sorely aggrieved people whose grievance, moreover, the Israelis themselves caused. But *if* that is actually so, then he could not condemn them. So he cannot set aside as an irrelevance the question of whether it *is* so, in his bid to condemn them.

The terrorists say: 'Your brutal occupation makes us use these methods.' The Israelis say: 'Your terrorist methods necessitate the continuation of our occupation.' And each accuses the other of worse acts than what they themselves commit. These claims raise charges of 'You're involved in it yourself' and '*Tu quoque*' that cannot be adjudicated in the absence of some view about who has what sort of justified grievance. But Shtauber affected a right to condemn that prescinded from all that controversial matter, and that, so I have sought to persuade you, is a right that he did not have.

d. Envoi

Two further remarks.

(1) I have assumed, in order to expose some lines of moral principle, that Palestinian terrorism is an effective strategy. But certain non-terrorist strategies might in fact be more effective. Suicide protests which kill only the protesters might be far more effective, because of the reaction of world opinion.[30] But Shtauber couldn't decently recommend pure suicide as an alternative, even if third parties could do so. Or suppose that the Palestinians retire their anti-Israeli armed struggle and demonstrate wholly peacefully on a mass scale against the semi-apartheid-semi-colonial status that they are coming to have under Israeli rule. Might this not, in time, produce a potent international, and Israeli, outcry against Israeli rule? Should Ambassador Shtauber recommend that Gandhian course?

(2) It has been a central claim of this paper that one consequence of the difference between an expression of moral opinion and a condemnation is that it might be true *both* that terrorism is to be condemned (moral opinion) *and* that some particular person is not

[30] But straightforward suicide is forbidden by Islam, whereas suicide that also kills infidels or other legitimate opponents is honourable martyrdom: in which case it would be religious belief, not Israeli action, that blocks this more effective and, judged non-Islamically, more acceptable course. (I owe the suicide-without-homicide suggestion, and the comment on it in this footnote, to Diego Gambetta).

in a position to condemn it. But equally, so it follows, the fact that someone is not in a position to condemn something does not imply that the thing is not to be condemned. So if some leftist thinks that the present Israeli government cannot condemn the Palestinian terror, then I might agree with him about that, but if, as some leftists seem to think, he also thinks it *follows* that the Palestinian terrorist response cannot *be* condemned, then I part company with him at that point.

Both Shtauber and the imagined leftist believe, falsely, that, if the terrorist is blameable, then Shtauber can blame him. Shtauber concludes that he can blame the terrorist. The imagined leftist concludes that the terrorist is not blameable. Both make an invalid inference.[31]

APPENDIX—Israel and me

I can explain something, quite a lot, of my attitude to Israel by taking you through some of my personal history.

Israel was founded in 1948, when I was seven years old, old enough to understand what it meant that Israel was being founded, young enough[32] to be enthralled by that in a childlike way. My parents were Stalinist communists, but the Soviet Union blessed Israel at its inception, and it was with no ambivalence at all that I walked beside my father, hand in hand, to the Montreal Forum, in the summer of 1948, upon which some 15,000 of Montreal's then probably about a hundred thousand Jews were converging, to celebrate the glorious event. Hatikvah, the Israeli national anthem, was sung in the Forum. It affected me profoundly.

We shift to 1983, my first visit to Israel, now with my son Gideon, who was then sixteen years old. We arrived just a few days after the assassination of Emil Grunzweig, who was the first Jew to be killed (the second was Yitzhak Rabin) by a Jew because assassin

---

[31] After writing this paper, I benefited from reading Tim Scanlon's 'Blame', a work in progress that distinguishes three items: blameworthiness, (the attitude of) blame, and the act of blaming. One might say that I explore above certain contrasts between the first and the third of those. I should therefore note that, as it seems to me, much of what disqualifies the act would also disqualify the attitude, and that, as it also seems to me, a major reason why the act gets disqualified, in the relevant cases, is that it expresses a disqualified attitude.

[32] The end of what the Jesuits consider to be a person's most impressionable age.

and victim held different views of the Palestinian-Israeli conflict, Grunzweig's being to the left of his assailant's. I had been invited by the Van Leer Institute to give a lecture and I was quite unaware when we arrived, I hadn't known, that Grunzweig had been an active member of that Institute.

Gideon and I were taken by taxi to our billet, an apartment near the Ramban. We were greeted in the apartment by a young man called 'Adeeb'. He gave us a note from the Director of Van Leer, which said, with real warmth, that we were most welcome, and that he greatly regretted that we were coming at such a terrible time.

We began to talk to Adeeb. I, in my ignorance, one could even say in my stupidity, did not realise that Adeeb was an Arab: his name should have told me that. Adeeb had beard stubble. He explained that he was unshaven because he was in mourning, and that Emil Grunzweig had been his best friend. It dawned on us somehow, or maybe the further conversation implied, it, that Adeeb was a Palestinian. This made the whole context of our visit that much more weighty and moving.

The next day there was in the evening an outdoor memorial meeting for Emil Grunzweig which was held near the Knesset. Gideon and I went with Adeeb. At the end of the meeting it was time to sing Hatikvah, the Israeli national anthem, which I had heard sung so joyously in 1948. I was conflicted. Had Adeeb not been beside me, I would have sung the song with my fellow Jews, and I wanted to sing it, but I also thought that I should not, because how could Adeeb fail to experience the song as celebrating the event that dispossessed his people? I decided it would nevertheless be dishonest not to sing, and I sang.

We come to 1998, in the month of June, when I was travelling in a car with my friends Dani Attas and Avner de-Shalit from Jerusalem to Haifa. We talked about the conflict all the way up to Haifa, and I was shown countless Israeli achievements, and many places that were now Arab-*rein* that had been summarily confiscated, and I learned a lot that I had not known about the treatment of Arabs within the pre-1967 borders. As we travelled up to Haifa I felt swells of pride, and of shame, sometimes about more or less the very same thing.

If I were in Israel today, and there was a demonstration by progressive Jews, and Adeeb and I were side by side at the demonstration, and Hatikvah was to be sung, I would not, I could not sing it, I could not dream of singing it.

G. A. Cohen

I have not tried to justify anything here, not any past or present attitude of mine. But I believe that my present attitude is amply justified.

Against Egalitarianism*

JOHN KEKES

Initial Doubts

It is possible that the fame of the Texas Rose Rustlers Society has not yet reached readers of these words. They may want to know then that its members prize roses that survive unattended in the wilds of Texas, having eluded the benevolent attention of gardeners. These unattended roses are not too distantly related to the 'unofficial English rose' that the poet says 'Unkempt about those hedges blows' in the proximity of The Old Vicarage at Grantchester. As all respectable societies, the Texas Rose Rustlers has by-laws stating the principles that unite its members. Here are some of them: there is more than one way of being beautiful; good climates are in the eye of the beholder; if you are attacked by disease, abandonment, or a bad chain of events, do not despair, there is always the chance that you were bred to be tough; and everyone should not smell the same. I mention these admirable principles because they offend profoundly against egalitarianism, which happens to be my target on this occasion.

Egalitarianism threatens to become the dominant political ideology of our age. Since it is unreasonable, morally unacceptable, and politically dangerous, its dominance, in my opinion, would not be a good thing. A simple statement of egalitarianism is that all human beings, and no doubt roses too, should be treated with equal concern unless there are good reasons against it.[1] This assumes that

* I am grateful for permission to use material from my book, *The Illusions of Egalitarianism* (Ithaca: Cornell University Press, 2003).

[1] 'Every nation of the world is divided into haves and have-nots ... The gap ... is enormous. Confronting these disparities, the egalitarian holds that it would be a morally better state of affairs if everyone enjoyed the same level of social and economic benefits', Richard J. Arneson, 'Equality', in Robert Goodin & Phillip Pettit, (eds.) *A Companion to Contemporary Political Philosophy*, (Oxford: Blackwell, 1993), 489. 'From the standpoint of politics, the interests of the members of the community matter, and matter equally.' Ronald Dworkin, 'In Defense of Equality', *Social Philosophy and Policy*, No. 1, (1983), 24–40, at 24. 'Everyone matters just as much as everyone else. [I]t is appalling that the most effective social systems we have been able to devise permit ... material

equal concern should be the norm and departure from it needs justification. It is a testimony to the spread of egalitarianism that this simple statement is widely regarded as a truism. But it is certainly not that, since a little thought prompts serious questions about it.

Human beings differ in character, personality, circumstances, talents and weaknesses, capacities and incapacities, virtues and vices; in moral standing, political views, religious convictions, aesthetic preferences, and personal projects; in how reasonable or unreasonable they are, how well or badly they develop native endowments, how much they benefit or harm others, how hardworking or disciplined they were in the past and are likely to be in the future; and so forth. Why should, then, the norm be equal, rather than unequal, concern?

The questions mount when it is asked, as it must be, who owes whom equal concern? Clearly, parents should not treat their own and other people's children with equal concern; we do not owe equal concern to those we love and to strangers; governments betray their elementary duty if they treat citizens and foreigners with equal concern; and a society would be self-destructive if it showed equal concern for its friends and enemies. The questions grow in number and urgency when it is asked, as it must again be, what differences would warrant unequal concern? If differences in morality, reasonability, law-abidingness, and citizenship count, then very little remains of equal concern, since there are great

---

inequalities.' Thomas Nagel, *Equality and Partiality* (New York: Oxford University Press, 1991), 64. 'Being egalitarian in some significant way relates to the need to have equal concern, at some level, for all persons involved.' Amartya Sen, *Inequality Reexamined* (Cambridge: Harvard University Press, 1992), ix. 'A basic principle of equality [is] the principle of equal consideration of interests. The essence of the principle of equal consideration of interests is that we give equal weight in our moral deliberations to the like interests of all those affected by our actions.' Peter Singer, *Practical Ethics* (Cambridge: Cambridge University Press, 1993), 2nd ed., 21. 'We want equalization of benefits ... [because] in all cases where human beings are capable of enjoying the same goods, we feel that the intrinsic value of the enjoyment is the same.... . We hold that ... *one man's well-being is as valuable as any other's*.' Gregory Vlastos, 'Justice and Equality', in *Social Justice*, Richard B. Brandt (ed.) (Englewood Cliffs, N.J.: Prentice-Hall, 1962), 50–51.

differences among people in these respects. And if such differences are not allowed to count, then how could it be justified to ignore them in how people are treated?

These questions show at the very least that the simple statement is not a truism and that egalitarianism needs a reasoned defence that answers these questions. Yet when critics ask them, they are ignored, and their questions are deplored as signs of moral insensitivity. Egalitarians simply assume that equal concern is a basic moral requirement, and to question it is to question morality. They also assume that the key to meeting this supposed requirement is to redistribute property so as to minimize its unequal distribution. The mere fact that some people have less property than others is supposed by egalitarians to make it a moral requirement to take from those who have more in order to benefit those who have less, regardless of why they have less.[2]

Egalitarians have by now bullied generations into accepting this so-called moral requirement even though it means the redistribution of property from victims of crime to criminals, from blue collar workers to illegal immigrants, from taxpayers to welfare cheats, from prudent people who had saved for retirement to spendthrifts who had not. The supposed moral requirement is to treat moral and immoral, prudent and imprudent, law-abiding and criminal people with equal concern. If as a result of immorality, imprudence, and criminality people find themselves poor, then, according to egalitarians, the government's obligation is to deprive moral, prudent, and law-abiding people of a considerable portion of their property in order to benefit the poor regardless of why they are poor.

It may be thought that so implausible a view cannot be widely held, but we have the assurance of well-known egalitarians that it is. Ronald Dworkin says that 'no government is legitimate that does not show equal concern for the fate of all those citizens over whom it claims dominion and from whom it claims allegiance.' Peter Singer claims that 'the principle that all humans are equal is now

---

[2] 'What makes a system egalitarian is the priority it gives to the claims of those.. at the bottom... .. Each individual with a more urgent claim has priority ... over each individual with a less urgent claim.' Thomas Nagel, 'Equality', in *Mortal Questions* (Cambridge: Cambridge University Press, 1979), 118. 'We can express a more general principle as follows: ... first, maximize the welfare of the worst off ... second, for equal welfare of the second worst-off ... and so on until ... the equal welfare of all the preceding.' John Rawls, *A Theory of Justice* (Cambridge: Harvard University Press, 1971), 82–83.

part of the prevailing political and ethical orthodoxy.' In Gregory Vlastos's view 'in all cases where human beings are capable of enjoying the same goods, we feel that the intrinsic value of their enjoyment is the same.' And Bernard Williams informs us that 'we believe ... that in some sense every citizen, indeed every human being ... deserves equal consideration.... . We know that most people in the past have not shared [this belief].... . But for us, it is simply there.'[3] To these egalitarians, unofficial roses are offensive: morality requires that undressed and unperfumed, everybody should smell the same.

Perhaps it is not unduly mistrustful to ask who the 'we' are who subscribe to this amazing moral requirement of equal concern. Do 'we' include Chinese peasants? The castes of India? Ex-Yugoslavians murdering each other over religious and ethnic differences? Murderous African tribes? All those men who, according to some egalitarians, are sexist? All those whites who, according to much the same egalitarians, are racist? Do Shiites regard Sunnis with equal concern? Arabs the Jews? And vice versa? Are they perhaps Republicans or conservatives who keep electing politicians who explicitly repudiate the view that 'we' hold?

These questions will no doubt be decried as unfair. What we mean by 'we', egalitarians will say, are those who think reasonably about political matters. But this cannot be right because there still are some few critics of egalitarianism left, such as Charvet, Flew, Frankfurt, Hayek, Lucas, MacIntyre, Matson, Narveson, Pojman, Raz, Sher, and myself.[4] It is beginning to look as if 'we' included

---

[3] The passages are from: Ronald Dworkin, *Sovereign Virtue: The Theory and Practice of Equality* (Cambridge: Harvard University Press, 2000), 1; Singer, *Practical Ethics*, 16; Vlastos, 'Justice and Equality', 51; Bernard Williams, 'Philosophy as a Humanistic Discipline', *Philosophy* **75**, (2000), 477–496, at 492.

[4] A partial list of such critics is: John Charvet, *A Critique of Freedom and Equality* (Cambridge: Cambridge University Press, 1981); Antony Flew, *The Politics of Procrustes* (Buffalo: Prometheus Books, 1981); Harry G. Frankfurt, 'Equality as a Moral Ideal', in *The Importance of What We Care About* (Cambridge: Cambridge University Press, 1988) and 'Equality and Respect', in *Necessity, Volition, and Love* (Cambridge: Cambridge University Press, 1999); Friedrich A. Hayek, *The Constitution of Liberty* (Chicago: University of Chicago Press, 1960); John Kekes, *The Illusions of Egalitarianism* (Ithaca: Cornell University Press, 2003); J. R. Lucas, 'Against Equality', *Philosophy* **40** (1965), 296–307 and 'Against Equality Again', *Philosophy* **42** (1967), 255–280; Alasdair MacIntyre, *After Virtue* (Notre Dame: University of Notre Dame Press, 1984); Wallace Matson,

only faithful egalitarians who form the left wing of the Democratic party in America and the democratic and not so democratic socialists of Europe.

One prevalent egalitarian response to criticism, I regret to have to say, is to abuse the critics. Richard Arneson says that 'all humans have an equal basic moral status. They possess the same fundamental rights, and the comparable interests of each person should count the same in calculations that determine social policy ... .These platitudes are virtually universally affirmed. A white supremacist or an admirer of Adolf Hitler who denies them is rightly regarded as beyond the pale of civilized dialogue.'[5] Having placed critics beyond the pale of civilized dialogue, it becomes unnecessary to meet the objections of these white supremacists and Nazis. Dworkin's response is that 'we cannot reject the egalitarian principle outright, because it is ... immoral that [the government] should show more concern for the lives of some than of others',[6] and 'a distribution of wealth that dooms some citizens to a less fulfilling life than others, no matter what choices they make, is unacceptable, and the neglect of equality in contemporary politics is therefore shameful.'[7] That makes it immoral and shameful not to equalize the property of moral, prudent, law-abiding and immoral, imprudent, and criminal people. Kymlicka's view is that 'some theories, like Nazism, deny that each person matters equally. But such theories do not merit serious consideration.'[8] Critics, therefore, are, or are like, Nazis. And according to Thomas Nagel, 'any political theory that aspires to moral decency must try to devise and justify a form of institutional life which answers to the real strength of impersonal

---

'What Rawls Calls Justice', *Occasional Review* **89**, (1978), 45–47; and 'Justice: A Funeral Oration', *Social Philosophy and Policy*, No. 1, (1983), 94–113; Jan Narveson, *Respecting Persons in Theory and Practice* (Lanham, MD: Rowman & Littlefield, 2002); Louis P. Pojman, 'A Critique of Contemporary Egalitarianism', *Faith and Philosophy* **8**, (1991), 481–504; and George Sher, *Desert* (Princeton: Princeton University Press, 1987).

[5] Richard J. Arneson, 'What, If Anything, Renders All Humans Morally Equal?', in *Singer and His Critics*, Dale Jamieson (ed.) (Oxford: Blackwell, 1999), 103.

[6] Dworkin, *Sovereign Virtue*, 130.

[7] Ronald Dworkin, 'Equality—An Exchange', *TLS* (December 1, 2000), 16.

[8] Will Kymlicka, *Liberalism, Community, and Culture* (Oxford: Clarendon Press, 1989), 40.

values' and commits one to 'egalitarian impartiality'.[9] All critics of egalitarianism then fail in moral decency. Imagine the wave of indignation if someone would dare to say such things about defenders of egalitarianism.

Egalitarians, however, offer also another response, which is even more remarkable than the preceding *ad hominem* one. Here are some examples of it. Arneson concedes that 'non-utilitarian moralities with robust substantive equality ideals cannot be made coherent.'[10] He nevertheless regards disagreement with them as beyond the pale of civilized dialogue. Brian Barry says: 'The justification of the claim of fundamental equality has been held to be impossible because it is a rock-bottom ethical premise and so cannot be derived from anything else.'[11] This is a mealy-mouthed admission that egalitarianism rests on an unjustifiable assumption. Isaiah Berlin tells us: 'Equality is one of the oldest and deepest elements in liberal thought and it is neither more nor less "natural" or "rational" than any other constituent in them [sic]. Like all human ends it cannot be defended or justified, for it is itself which justifies other acts.'[12] So egalitarianism is based on a rationally indefensible article of faith. Joel Feinberg declares that egalitarianism 'is not grounded on anything more ultimate than itself, and it is not demonstrably justifiable. It can be argued further against skeptics that a world with equal human rights is *more just* world ... a less *dangerous* world ... and one with a *more elevated and civilized* tone. If none of this convinces the skeptic, we should turn our back on him and examine more important problems.'[13] I wonder whether egalitarians would be satisfied with such a response when they question conservative or religious attitudes. Kymlicka writes that 'every plausible political theory has the same ultimate source, which is equality.... . A theory is egalitarian ... if it accepts that the interests of each member of the community matter, and matter equally.... . [I]f a theory claimed that some people were not entitled to equal consideration from the government, if it claimed that certain kinds of people just do not matter as much as others, then

[9] Nagel, *Equality and Partiality*, 20.

[10] Arneson, 'What, If Anything, Renders All Humans Morally Equal?', 126.

[11] Brian Barry, 'Equality' in *Encyclopedia of Ethics*, Lawrence C. Becker & Charlotte B. Becker (eds.) (New York: Garland, 1992), 324.

[12] Isaiah Berlin, 'Equality' in *Concepts and Categories*, Henry Hardy (ed.) (London: Hogarth, 1978), 102.

[13] Joel Feinberg, *Social Philosophy* (Englewood Cliffs, N.J.: Prentice-Hall, 1973), 94.

most people in the modern world would reject that theory immediately.'[14] This invites us to believe as an obvious truth that most people would immediately reject the view that torturers and their victims, or the scourges and benefactors of humanity do not matter equally. Kymlicka gives no reason for this breathtaking claim: it is the assumption from which he proceeds. Nagel says that he is going to explore a 'type of argument that I think is likely to succeed. It would provide a moral basis for the kind of liberal egalitarianism that seems to me plausible. I do not have such an argument.'[15] This does not stop him, however, from claiming that 'moral equality, [the] attempt to give equal weight, in essential respects, to each persons' point of view ... might even be described as the mark of an enlightened ethic.'[16] Years later he says: 'My claim is that the problem of designing institutions that do justice to the equal importance of all persons, without unacceptable demands on individuals, has not been solved', but he nevertheless 'present[s] a case for wishing to extend the reach of equality beyond what is customary in modern welfare states.'[17] Although Nagel explicitly acknowledges the lack of justification, he holds that the mark of an enlightened ethic is to deprive people of legally owned property. Imagine claiming that although one can offer no justification for it, one nevertheless holds that the mark of enlightened ethic is to deprive blacks of freedom. John Rawls concludes his discussion of 'The Basis of Equality' by saying that 'essential equality is ... equality of consideration', and goes on: 'of course none of this is literally an argument. I have not set out the premises from which this conclusion follows.'[18] Thus the absurd policy of equal concern for moral and immoral, prudent and imprudent, law-abiding and criminal people is put forward with the explicit acknowledgment that the premises from which it is supposed to follow have not been provided.

Not far below the surface of this flaunted indifference to making a reasoned case for egalitarianism is the self-righteous belief that the rejection of egalitarianism is immoral. The labels of Nazi, racist, white supremacist, sexist, Social Darwinist, reactionary,

[14] Will Kymlicka, *Contemporary Political Philosophy* (Oxford: Clarendon Press, 1990), 4–5.
[15] Nagel, *Mortal Questions*, 108.
[16] Nagel, *Mortal Questions*, 112.
[17] Nagel, *Equality and Partiality*, 5.
[18] John Rawls, *A Theory of Justice* (Cambridge: Harvard University Press, 1971), 507 and 509.

egoist, and so forth readily spring to the lips of many egalitarians by way of maligning their critics and making the justification of egalitarianism unnecessary. If their critics appealed to faith or resorted to abuse instead of reasoned argument, egalitarians would rightly judge their position as intellectually disreputable. That judgment, however, does not alter if the positions are reversed. Egalitarians should take to heart Mill's words: 'The worst offense ... which can be committed by a polemic is to stigmatize those who hold contrary opinions as bad and immoral.'[19]

Dworkin on Equality

Against this dismal background comes Dworkin's recent book, *Sovereign Virtue: The Theory and Practice of Equality*.[20] It begins thus: 'No government is legitimate that does not show equal concern for the fate of all those citizens over whom it claims dominion and from whom it claims allegiance. Equal concern is the sovereign virtue of political community—without it government is only tyranny—and when a nation's wealth is unequally distributed, as the wealth of even very prosperous nations now is, then its equal concern is suspect' (1).

It does not seem to bother Dworkin that the absurd implication of this piece of rhetoric is that in the past and present of humanity there has never been a legitimate government. Suppose, however, that we join Dworkin in condemning all governments that have ever existed and hope for political legitimacy in the future. What reason does Dworkin give for believing that it depends on equal concern? The answer is that he gives none, as he makes clear: 'I have tried to show the appeal of equality of resources, as interpreted here, only by making plainer its motivation and defending its coherence and practical force. I have not tried to defend it in what might be considered a more direct way, by deducing it from more general and abstract political principles. So the question arises whether the sort of defense could be provided ... I hope it is clear that I have not presented any such argument here' (117–8). And a little further on, he writes: 'my arguments are constructed against the background of assumptions about what equality requires in principle.... My

[19] John Stuart Mill, *On Liberty* (Indianapolis: Hackett, 1978), 51.

[20] Dworkin, *Sovereign Virtue*, op. cit., (references in the text are to the pages of this book).

arguments enforce rather than construct a basic design of justice, and that design must find support, if at all, elsewhere than in these arguments' (118).

Egalitarians may find this admission disarming. It should be remembered, however, that on the basis of the rhetoric that Dworkin calls 'argument', he urges depriving people of legally owned property and condemns opposition to it as immoral and shameful. This is specious moralizing, unsupported by reasons. That Dworkin calls it an argument, does not make it have what it sorely needs.

The core of these many pages is an account of equality of resource as the correct interpretation of equal concern. This account is presented as if it were an argument, but it is in fact a tedious elaboration of what Dworkin himself calls an egalitarian fantasy concerning the ideal distribution of resources (162–3). Such distribution must meet 'the envy test', which asks whether people are satisfied with the resources they have and do not prefer someone else's resources instead of their own. It should not escape notice how extraordinary it is to make envy the test of ideal distribution. Envy is the vice of resenting the advantages of another person. It is a vice because it tends to lead to action that deprives people of advantages they have earned by legal and moral means. The envy test is indifferent to whether people are entitled to the advantages they have; it is concerned only with whether those who lack the advantages would like to have them. And of course the answer will be, given the human propensity for envy, that they would like to have them, that they are not satisfied with what they have. Counting on this, Dworkin claims that the ideal distribution would be one that removes this dissatisfaction. It would distribute advantages evenly so that no one could be envious of anyone else's. Instead of recognizing that envy is wrong, Dworkin elevates it into a moral standard.

Having based his egalitarian fantasy on a vice, Dworkin proceeds to explain how it would work as a test for imaginary people in an imaginary situation. People on an island participate in an auction. They bid for miraculously available resources by the use of clamshells, which they possess in equal numbers. Through their bids, they express their preferences, and because all start with the same number of clamshells, no one can have an advantage that others could envy. The auction keeps going until all the people have used up their clamshells. Dworkin thinks that the auction will not, by itself, eliminate unacceptable inequalities because post-auction lives will be affected by luck. He distinguishes between brute and option luck. The contingencies of life that no one can control constitute brute luck. How people's deliberate and calculated choices, expressed by their bids, turn out is a matter of option luck. Dworkin then adds to the imagined auction the fantasy of a compulsory insurance market in which people must purchase protection against the risk of bad luck. If life goes badly, insurance payments will compensate for it. People, therefore, will not suffer from the brute luck of having been born with handicaps. Dworkin says that 'this imaginary auction [and, one may add, insurance scheme] can serve as a rough model in designing political and economic institutions for the real world in search of as much equality of resources as can be found' (14). Dworkin then uses over 100 pages imagining how the imaginary bidders and insurers in this imaginary situation are likely to proceed.

Reactions to this sustained exercise in fantasy are likely to range from admiration to exasperation. Be that as it may, the question needs to be asked how this egalitarian fantasy relates to the real world. How should individuals act if they apply the model of the auction and the insurance scheme to the allegedly immoral society in which they live? Dworkin's answer is that 'it is a complex and perhaps unanswerable question what equality of resources asks of us, as individuals, in our own society' (281). But since the fantasy was meant to help us answer that very question, and it seems that it will not do that, what is its point? It needs also to be asked why it should be supposed that if the model were applied, then the inequalities Dworkin finds immoral and shameful would be lessened? Dworkin's answer is that 'it is, of course, impossible to say in advance just what the consequences of any profound change in an economic system would be, and who would gain or lose in the long run' (105). So that if a society were crazy enough to change its economic system to reflect Dworkin's model of auction and insurance scheme, the inequalities that are anathema to Dworkin may just increase as a result. Dworkin's model is thus unsupported by reason and provides no reason to suppose that its goal could be achieved by the means it provides. It is remarkable that both the lack of reason and the impossibility of telling whether it would lead to its goal are explicitly acknowledged by Dworkin. These considerations show, I believe, that Dworkin has given no reason for accepting his version of egalitarianism. It is nevertheless worthwhile to consider it further because it illustrates problems that most versions of egalitarianism have.

The Problem of Individual Responsibility

Dworkin says that 'someone who is born with serious handicaps faces his life with what we concede to be fewer resources, just on that account, than others do. This circumstance justifies compensation, under a scheme devoted to equality of resources' (81). But people may have fewer resources as a result of contingencies that make it impossible for them to satisfy their preferences or realize their ambitions. 'The latter', Dworkin says, 'will also affect welfare, but they are not matters for compensation under our scheme' (81). The difference is between brute and option luck. The idea is that if life goes badly for people because of circumstances over which they have no control, they should be compensated; if it goes badly because they have chosen a way of life that is more vulnerable to luck than another they might have chosen, they should not be compensated. This may seem like a sensible idea, until it is asked what counts as brute as opposed to option luck.

This question splits the egalitarian ranks. Dworkin agrees with Rawls that 'the initial endowment of natural assets and the contingencies of their growth and nurture in early life are arbitrary from the moral point of view.'[21] But he disagrees when Rawls goes on to say that 'the effort a person is willing to make is influenced by his natural abilities and skills and alternatives open to him. The better endowed are more likely, other things equal, to strive conscientiously, and there seems to be no way to discount for their greater fortune.'[22] Dworkin rejects this because Rawls 'prescinds from any consideration of individual responsibility', whereas 'the hypothetical insurance approach ... makes as much turn on such responsibility as possible.' Dworkin believes that 'though we must recognize the equal objective importance of the success of a human life, one person has a special and final responsibility for that success—the person whose life it is' (5). Rawls thinks that whether inequalities are morally objectionable must be decided independently of individual responsibility; Dworkin thinks that only those inequalities are morally objectionable for which people with less property cannot be held responsible. In this disagreement, both kinds of egalitarians have a decisive objection to the other. Dworkin is right and Rawls wrong: any acceptable approach to politics must take into account people's responsibility for having or lacking property. Rawls is right and Dworkin is wrong: the choices people

[21] Rawls, *Theory of Justice*, 311–312.
[22] Ibid., 312.

make and the property they have partly depend on their natural assets and circumstances for which they cannot be held responsible.

What follows is a dilemma that egalitarians cannot resolve. If they acknowledge that people are partly responsible for the property they have, then they must agree with their critics that it is unreasonable, morally unacceptable, and politically dangerous to equalize the property of responsible and irresponsible people. If egalitarians insist that individual responsibility makes no difference to what property people should have, then they are committed to the unreasonable, morally unacceptable, and politically dangerous policy of depriving moral, prudent, and law-abiding people of their property in order to benefit others even if they are immoral, imprudent, and criminal.

Dworkin opts for the first alternative and must answer the question of how to distinguish between brute luck, which he thinks is incompatible with the assignment of responsibility, and option luck, which, according to him, is compatible with responsibility. His answer is: 'Equality of resources assumes a fundamental distinction between a person, understood to include features of personality like convictions, ambitions, tastes, and preferences, and that person's circumstances, which include the resources, talents, and capacities he commands.... . [E]quality of resources aims to make circumstances ... equal' (14). Thus, according to Dworkin, brute luck affects people's property, talents, and capacities, and for them they are not responsible. Option luck affects people's convictions, ambitions, tastes, and preferences, and for them they are responsible. The fact that people have less property, talents, and capacities 'justifies compensation ... equality of resources ... seeks to remedy ... the resulting unfairness' (81).

It follows that if people are unimaginative, lethargic, or gloomy, if they have poor memory or a displeasing appearance, if they lack a sense of humor or aesthetic appreciation, and if, as is likely, this affects the quality of their life, then they should be compensated by depriving others of their legally owned property. No reasonable person can accept this absurdity. But if some did, they would still have to contend with Rawls's point that people's convictions, ambitions, tastes, and preferences, for which, according to Dworkin, they are responsible, are decisively influenced by their property, talents, and capacities, for which they are not supposed to be responsible. So the distinction between option and brute luck collapses.

Dworkin, therefore, must choose: he can give up the idea of making equality of property depend on individual responsibility or he can accept that the distribution of property should depend, in part, on individual responsibility. The first alternative commits him to Rawls's version of egalitarianism, which he has good reason to reject. The second commits him to the anti-egalitarian position against which he so self-righteously and without good reasons inveighs.

The Problem of the Plurality of Political Values

Egalitarianism is an ideology. Its fundamental claim is that equal concern for citizens is a political value that overrides any other political value that may conflict with it. Dworkin makes clear that this is his position. 'Equal concern is the sovereign value of political community—without it the government is only tyranny.... . Equal concern is a precondition of political legitimacy—a precondition of the majority's right to enforce its laws against those who think them unwise or even unjust' (1–2). Dworkin is not alone in positing an overriding political value. Rawls, for instance, says that 'justice is the first virtue of social institutions ... laws and institutions no matter how efficient and well-arranged must be reformed or abolished if they are unjust. Each person possesses an inviolability founded on justice that even the welfare of the society as a whole cannot override.'[23] But if egalitarians are committed to some overriding political value, then they cannot also be committed to pluralism, which denies that there is any political value that ought always to override any political value that conflicts with it. Egalitarians cannot be pluralists, and pluralists cannot be egalitarians.

Dworkin is clear on this point. He says that his book is 'contrary in spirit to ... the value pluralism of Isaiah Berlin ... [who] insisted that important political values are in dramatic conflict—he particularly emphasized the conflict between liberty and equality.' Dworkin, by contrast, 'strive[s] to dissipate such conflicts and to integrate these values' (5). He defends the view that 'if we accept equal resources as the best conception of distributional equality, liberty becomes an aspect of equality rather than, as it is often thought to be, an independent political ideal potentially in conflict with it' (121). If asked how the conflict between equal property and liberty is to be dissipated, Dworkin replies: 'Any genuine contest between liberty and equality is a contest liberty must lose... .

---

[23] Rawls, *Theory of Justice*, 3.

[A]nyone who thinks liberty and equality really do conflict on some occasion must think that protecting liberty means acting in some way that does not show equal concern for all citizens. I doubt that many of us would think, after reflection, that this could ever be justified' (128). In Dworkin's scheme of things, unofficial roses have no place because their claim to smell different is overridden by the claim of 'the best conception of distributional equality'. This calls for three comments.

First, 'many of us' do think, after reflection, that on occasion liberty may override equal resources is obvious and its denial is absurd. The 'many of us' includes liberals, like Berlin, who are genuine pluralists; conservatives and Republicans who oppose policies that involve depriving people of their legally owned property in order to benefit those who own less; and political thinkers (listed in note 4) who offer reasoned arguments against egalitarianism. Dworkin's claim is no more than inflated rhetoric familiar from political speechifying, but out of place in what purports to be reasoned argument.

Second, Dworkin's 'solution' to dissipating the conflict between liberty and equality and to integrating the two values is to subordinate liberty to equality. That solution, however, is available to all parties to all conflicts because all it takes is to reaffirm their arbitrary preference for the value they favour. Dworkin, however, denies this. He says: 'we might be tempted to dogmatism: to declare our intuition that liberty is a fundamental value that must not be sacrificed to equality.... But that is hollow, and too callous. If liberty is transcendentally important we should be able to say something, at least, about why' (121). Now, as Dworkin must know, defenders of liberty are able to say something about why it is, on occasion, more important than equality: they say that liberty is a precondition of any life worth living. And that is not hollow. As to its being callous, how could it be callous to try to protect the liberty of citizens to control their legally owned property?

Dworkin's position, however, is open to the even more serious charge that the requirement he lays on his opponents, and which they certainly endeavour to meet, is one he admits that his own position fails to meet. I repeat what I have quoted earlier: 'I have tried to show the appeal of equality of resources, as interpreted here, only by making plainer its motivation and defending its coherence and practical force. I have not tried to defend it in what might be considered a more direct way, by deducing it from more general and abstract political principles. So the question arises whether the sort of defense could be provided ... I hope it is clear that I have not presented any such argument here... . [M]y arguments are constructed against the background of assumptions about what equality requires in principle... . My arguments enforce rather than construct a basic design of justice, and that design must find support, if at all, elsewhere than in these arguments' (117–8).

Third, liberty is not the only political value that may conflict with equality. Some others are civility, criminal justice, decent education, healthy environment, high culture, order, peace, prosperity, security, toleration, and so forth. Egalitarians are committed to the view that if any of these values conflicts with equality, equality should override it. They may offer as an argument for this that equality is a precondition of the moral acceptability of all of these values. But this is a bad argument. It is just false that equality is a precondition of the moral acceptability of, say, peace, prosperity, or security. A society can conform to these values and be morally better for it even if its citizens are not deprived of their legally owned property, as equality is said by Dworkin to require. Furthermore, defenders of the values that conflict with equality can claim with as great a plausibility as egalitarians that the value they favour is a precondition of the value they subordinate. If there is no prosperity, the equal distribution of property merely spreads poverty around more evenly; if the environment is unhealthy, lives will be cut short and the dead cannot enjoy their equal share of property; if crime is rampant, its victims will soon be deprived of their property, regardless of whether its distribution is equal or unequal.

Egalitarians must face the fact of the political life in contemporary democracies that pluralists recognize. There are many conflicting political values. The welfare of a society requires that these conflicts be resolved, but for this no blueprint exists. Politics is about defending the whole system of values, and this requires subordinating one of the conflicting values to the other. But which should be subordinated to which depends on complex historical, economic, sociological, religious, moral, technological, and other considerations, which are always in a state of flux. It is dangerously simple-minded to insist that one of the many political values should always override the others. Egalitarians are guilty of this charge, but they are not alone. The same charge convicts those who insist that liberty should be the overriding value. There is no political value that should always override all other conflicting values. Pluralists recognize this, and that is why they reject egalitarianism, as well as all other ideologies that insist on the overridingness of any one or any small number of values.

John Kekes

The Problem of Scope

Dworkin is emphatic that equal concern is the obligation of the *government* and it holds in respect to all *citizens*. 'No government is legitimate that does not show equal concern for the fate of all those citizens over whom it claims dominion' (1). But why *only* for citizens? A justified answer depends on there being some characteristic or cluster of characteristics that all and only citizens have. In large multi-cultural democracies, however, there are no such characteristics. Religion, ethnicity, language, education, race, history, attitudes to sex, death, marriage, child-rearing, illness, work, and so forth divide rather than unite the citizens of large Western multi-ethnic societies. Nor are all citizens taxpayers, since the poor, children, and many others pay no taxes; they are not the products of the same school system, since many are educated at home, or in private or religious schools; they are not all native born, since many are immigrants. They do have some of the same legal rights and obligations, but certainly not all, and the question is why equal concern should be among the rights shared by all and only citizens.

The temptation here is to say that people share such characteristics as the capacity for autonomy, rationality, moral agency, self-consciousness, language use, and so forth. But even if this were true, it would be of no help to egalitarians who restrict equal concern to citizens. For these capacities are supposed to be shared by all human beings, not just by the citizens of a democracy. If equal concern were justified by universally shared human capacities, then the government ought to treat everyone, not just citizens, with equal concern. And if equal concern required the redistribution of property, then the government ought to make it worldwide. That this would impoverish prosperous societies without relieving the poverty of the rest is only one of the absurdities that follows from this idea.

Furthermore, any government committed to worldwide redistribution would betray its most basic obligation, which is to protect the interests of its citizens, not of other people. It is perhaps because egalitarians recognize this that they restrict equal concern to citizens. But then Dworkin should not try to justify equal concern by saying that there is 'a natural right of men and women to equality of concern and respect, a right they possess not by virtue of birth or characteristic or merit or excellence but *simply as human beings'*,[24] Kymlicka should not say that 'the idea that *each person* matters equally is at the heart of all plausible political theories',[25] and Nagel should not say that 'the impartial attitude is, I believe, strongly egalitarian ... and takes to heart the value of *every person's* life and welfare.'[26] [Emphases added.]

Egalitarians thus face a hard choice. They can restrict equal concern to citizens or extend it to everyone. If they restrict it, they need a justification in order to avoid arbitrariness. The justification must be based on some characteristic that all and only citizens have, but egalitarians have not found it. If they extend equal concern to everyone, then they must explain how a government can have the obligation to provide the same education, health care, police protection, roads, and so forth to the citizens of other countries as it has to provide for its own. It is, of course, not difficult to avoid having to make this hard choice. One can give up the indefensible claim that a government is obliged to treat everyone with equal concern.

The case against egalitarianism is that it deprives a large majority of citizens of a sizable portion of their legally owned property. Egalitarians claim that equal concern for all citizens obliges the government to adopt this policy, but they not only fail to justify this claim, they explicitly acknowledge, as we have seen, that it cannot be justified. On the basis of this unjustified and unjustifiable claim they advocate depriving moral, prudent, and law-abiding people of their property in order to benefit others without asking whether they are immoral, imprudent, and criminal. In advocating this injustice, they obfuscate the responsibility of individuals for the lives they lead, dogmatically elevate equality into a value that overrides all other values, and arbitrarily restrict equal concern to the citizens of a democracy, while their rhetoric demands that it be extended worldwide. Egalitarianism is thus an unjust, unjustified, inconsistent, and absurd policy of discrimination. The time has come to add it to that odd collection of historically influential but indefensible beliefs which includes the divine right of kings, classless society, superiority of the white race, damnation outside the church, planned economy, and an idyllic prehistoric society which civilization has corrupted. The defenders of these prejudices were like egalitarians are in clothing their indefensible beliefs in

---

[24] Ronald Dworkin, 'Rights and Justice', in *Taking Rights Seriously* (Cambridge: Harvard University Press, 1977), 182.

[25] Kymlicka, *Contemporary Political Theory*, 5.

[26] Nagel, *Equality and Partiality*, 64–65.

moralistic fervour and excoriating their critics as immoral. But critics should not let them get away with doing by bullying what they cannot do by reasoned argument.

Last Thoughts

Nothing I have said is intended to deny that if citizens in a democracy through no fault of their own are poor, then, given the availability of resources, their society should alleviate their plight. I favour this policy, but egalitarians cannot consistently accept it. For what makes this policy right is not that inequality is morally objectionable, but that blameless fellow citizens lack the basic necessities of a decent life.

This has been argued for with great clarity by Frankfurt: 'Economic equality is not as such of particular moral importance. With respect to the distribution of economic assets, what is important from the point of view of morality is not that everyone should have the same but that each should have enough. If everyone had enough, it would be of no moral consequence whether some had more than others.'[27] It is not morally objectionable if billionaires have more than millionaires, or if people are poor as a result of immoral, imprudent, or criminal actions. There is no obligation to help those who are responsible for being poor, and certainly no obligation to force on others a policy of helping them. Magnanimous people may be generous enough to help even those who are responsible for their poverty, but such actions are beyond the call of duty. There is no justification for laying it on people as a moral requirement.

Nagel attempts to defend this requirement by an emotive appeal. He asks rhetorically: 'how could it not be an evil that some people's prospects at birth are radically inferior to others?'[28] There are three things to be said about this. First, the sentimentality of this appeal becomes apparent if it is put in terms of roses: 'how could it not be an evil that the initial prospects of some roses are radically inferior to others?' As all gardeners know, this is not an evil, but the natural state of affairs.

Second, given any population and any basis of ranking prospects, some will rank much lower than others. Lowest ranked prospects will be radically inferior to the highest ranked ones. Inveighing

[27] Frankfurt, 'Equality as a Moral Ideal',134–135.
[28] Nagel, *Equality and Partiality*, 28.

against this statistical necessity is like lamenting differences in intelligence. To call it an evil is a sentimental cheapening of the most serious condemnation morality affords. It misdirects the obligation people feel. If egalitarians would merely say that it is bad if people suffer undeserved misfortune and those who can should help them, then decent people would agree with them. But this agreement has nothing to do with equality.

Third, the emotive appeal of this question invites the thought that our society is guilty of the evil of dooming people to a life of poverty. What this often repeated charge overlooks is the historically unprecedented success of Western democracies in having only a small minority of poor citizens (about 10–15%) and an at least modestly affluent large majority (about 85–90%). The typical ratio in past societies was closer to the reverse. It calls for celebration, not condemnation, that for the first time in history we have a political system in which a large part of the population has escaped poverty. If egalitarians had a historical perspective, they would be in favour of protecting this system, rather than advocating radical changes to it with admittedly incalculable consequences.

A decent society should do what it reasonably can to alleviate the poverty of those citizens who are not responsible for being poor. This policy differs from the egalitarian one in several basic respects. First, its intended beneficiaries are only those who are poor as a result of adversity they could not avoid or overcome. The egalitarian policy is intended to benefit the poor regardless of why they are poor. Second, the aim of the policy is not to equalize property, but to alleviate poverty. The policy is intended to provide no more than the basic necessities of a decent life in a particular society. The egalitarian policy is to institute a perpetual equalizing machinery that benefits the worst off regardless of whether and why they are poor. Third, the motivation for the policy is an obligation to help fellow citizens if they are impoverished by the contingencies of life beyond their control. The motivation for the egalitarian policy is the unfounded belief that those who have less are entitled to a portion of the legally owned property of those who have more. Egalitarians are rightly concerned with the undeserved poverty of their fellow citizens, but they wrongly suppose that its appropriate expression is equal concern. Its appropriate expression is concern for those citizens who are poor through no fault of their own.

The justification of this concern is prudential. It endangers the stability of a society if a substantial number of its citizens through no fault of their own lack the basic necessities of a decent life. Reasonable people recognize that a good society is a cooperative system in which citizens participate because it provides the conditions they need to live as they wish. These conditions are lacking for people whose misfortune makes them poor. The more numerous such people are, the more the cooperative system is threatened. The justification of not allowing undeserved misfortune to deprive citizens of basic necessities is to protect the stability of the society by protecting its cooperative system. If prudence is a virtue, this justification is moral. But it is not a justification that has anything to do with the misguided egalitarian claim that everyone ought to be treated with equal concern. Reason, morality, and realistic politics require that moral and immoral, law-abiding and criminal, prudent and imprudent people should be treated differently. As the Texas Rose Rustlers rightly say, everyone does not smell the same.

Big Decisions: Opting, Converting, Drifting*

EDNA ULLMANN-MARGALIT

I. Big, Small and Medium

I want to focus on some of the limits of decision theory that are of interest to the philosophical concern with practical reasoning and rational choice. These limits should also be of interest to the social-scientists' concern with Rational Choice.

Let me start with an analogy. Classical Newtonian physics holds good and valid for middle-sized objects, but not for the phenomena of the very little, micro, sub-atomic level or the very large, macro, outer-space level: different theories, concepts and laws apply there. Similarly, I suggest that we might think of the theory of decision-making as relating to middle-sized, ordinary decisions, and to them only. There remain the two extremes, the very 'small' decisions on the one hand and the very 'big' decisions on the other. These may pose a challenge to the ordinary decision theory and may consequently require a separate treatment.

By 'small' decisions, I have in mind cases where we are strictly indifferent with regard to the alternatives before us, where our preferences over the alternatives are completely symmetrical. Every time I pick a bottle of Coke or a can of Campbell soup from the shelves of the supermarket, I have made a small decision in this sense. To the extent that we take choosing to be choosing for a reason, and choosing for a reason to presuppose preferences, it looks like we have to conclude that in such cases rational choice is precluded. As Leibniz put it in his Theodicy, 'In things which are absolutely indifferent there can be no choice ... since choice must have some reason or principle.'

I have elsewhere dealt with such cases of choice without preference, referring to them as instances of picking rather than

* I am indebted to Avishai Margalit, Pasquale Pasquino and Cass Sunstein for helpful discussions and detailed comments on earlier drafts. I have also greatly profited from Eric Dickson's commentary and from the general discussion at the conference on Epistemologies of Rational Choice, NYU, December 3–4, 2004.

choosing.[1] My present topic however is not the picking end of the scale but its other end, that of big decisions. More precisely, I am interested in a somewhat narrower subset of decisions within the large class of what might strike us as 'big' decisions. These will be, roughly, decisions that are personal and transformative, decisions that one takes at major crossroads of one's life. I exclude from this discussion the big decisions one may take in virtue of one's official position or institutional role, which primarily affect the lives of others; for example, a statesman's decision to go to war or to drop an A-bomb.

II. Big Decisions Characterized

I shall consider a decision 'big' in the sense I am here concerned to explore if it exhibits the following four characteristics:

- it is transformative, or 'core affecting';
- it is irrevocable;
- it is taken in full awareness;
- the choice not made casts a lingering shadow.

I shall refer to decisions exhibiting these characteristics as cases of *opting*. Decisions such as whether to marry, to migrate, or to leave the corporate world in order to become an artist, might be examples. Whether or not these cases do indeed qualify as cases of opting is a question I shall leave for later. First, I need to spell out the characteristic features in more detail.

The first feature of a case of opting is that it is a *big* decision in that it is likely to transform one's future self in a significant way. When facing an opting situation one stands at a critical juncture in one's life. The choice one makes alters one's life project and inner core. Now the expressions 'future self', 'life project', and 'inner core', may be helpfully suggestive but they are too broad and vague. For the notion of opting to be useful, I shall have to be more precise. So let us think of cases of opting as cases in which the choice one makes is likely to change one's beliefs and desires (or 'utilities'); that is, to change one's cognitive and evaluative systems. Inasmuch as our beliefs and desires shape the core of what we are

---

[1] Edna Ullmann-Margalit and Sidney Morgenbesser, 'Picking and Choosing', *Social Research* Vol. 44, No. 4, (1977). I should like to dedicate this essay to Sidney's memory, who passed away August 1, 2004.

as rational decision makers, we may say that one emerges from an opting situation a different person.

To be sure, there is a sense in which every choice changes us somewhat. The accumulation of these incremental changes makes us change, sometimes even transform, as life goes on and as we grow older. But what I am here calling attention to are the instances in which there is a point of sharp discontinuity. In these instances a person's inner core of beliefs and desires does not simply gradually evolve but undergoes, instead, an abrupt transformation.

Note that sometimes a critical juncture, a point of discontinuity and transformation may occur not as an instance of opting. I am thinking here of results of external happenings. Think of the possible transformative effect on one's life of an accident, the death of someone close, the collapse of the stock market, a draft to serve in a war, and so on. Such cases do not concern us here.

The second characteristic feature of opting situations is their irrevocability: they are points of no return. Again, in a strict, literal sense, every decision is irreversible; 'what's done cannot be undone'.[2] We can apologize for words but they cannot be literally unsaid, we can lower the arm we raised but we cannot un-raise it, a move we make we can retract but not un-make. Yet we treat a great many of our deeds, in a rather straightforward sense, as not irreversible: we compensate, return, or retreat. Various devices are available to us for restoring the situation to the way it was prior to our action or at any rate to a state of affairs sufficiently similar, close or equivalent to it. To be sure, the restoration may be costly in terms of time, money, effort or emotional outlay, but restoration it nevertheless is. So when I say that opting situations constitute points of no return I intend to mark these cases as different. When one opts, one is embarking upon a road that is one way only, leaving burning bridges behind. A reversal in the ordinary sense is impossible.

The next item on the list of characteristic features of opting situations is the element of awareness. It is constitutive of the opting situation that the person facing it is conscious of its being an opting situation. That is, not only is it, as a matter of fact, a critical juncture and a point of no return, but the person concerned also perceives it as such. We may put this more precisely in terms of two epistemic conditions: in an opting situation the person believes (a) that he or she must make a genuine choice between viable alternatives, and (b) that the decision they are called upon to make

---

[2] Shakespeare, *Macbeth*, Act 5, Scene 1.

is 'big'—transformative and irrevocable. The significance of this stipulation will be seen shortly. When either of its clauses is dropped one gets instances which are no longer ones of opting but rather ones of *converting* (when (a) is dropped) or of *drifting* (when (b) is dropped). But this is already jumping ahead.

The fourth and last feature is perhaps only a derivative of the first three. Yet it deserves separate treatment. It concerns the shadow presence of the rejected option; the ghost of the Road Not Taken.

Let me explain. In an ordinary choice situation there is a set of alternatives from which the person chooses one. Upon his or her decision, the non-chosen members of this set ordinarily cease to exist as far as the decision makers are concerned. In the case of opting, however, the rejected, un-opted-for option characteristically maintains a sort of lingering presence. In other words, I suggest that what is of significance to the opting person's account of his or her own life is not only the option they have taken, but also the one they have rejected: the person one did not marry, the country one did not emigrate to, the career one did not pursue. The rejected option enters in an essential way into the person's description of his or her life. The shadow presence maintained by the rejected option may constitute a yardstick by which this person evaluates the worth, success or meaning of his or her life.

III. Big Decisions Illustrated

Having described the opting situation, we must now ask, are there instances of opting situations? I mentioned earlier decisions such as whether to marry or to migrate. Think, for example, of the decision whether to have children or to quit one's job as a Director General of a high-tech company to become a Buddhist monk. Or, think of a young talented person who faces a choice between a career as a concert pianist and as a nuclear physicist.

Consider some famous cases. King Edward VIII made the agonizing decision to leave the throne 'for the sake of the woman he loved'. The early socialist Zionist pioneers in the 1920s left everything behind—home, family, religion—and came to Palestine in order to become the New Jews of their ideals. Many defected from the East-bloc countries to the West before 1989. The Biblical Ruth chose to tie her fate with that of her mother-in-law Naomi, who was returning from Moab to her native land and people in Bethlehem.

So, are these cases examples of opting? I offer them at this point as tentative illustrations of the concept. They indicate the flavour of the big decisions here under consideration—options thrust upon us in the name of love, duty or talent, of political or religious convictions, of optimistic idealism or the depth of despair.

A couple of points may be extracted from the suggested examples as they stand. First, in contrast to ordinary decision situations, opting situations are extraordinary. It is possible to go through life with only few opting occasions, even with none at all. While extraordinary, however, opting instances need not be thought of as abnormal, perverse or pathological. Anyone interested in human decision-making cannot therefore be justified in ignoring them, thinking that they lie outside the realm of 'normal' decision-making.

Second, a distinction may be called for between what can be termed opting (A, B) and opting (Yes, No). In an opting (A, B) situation one faces a decision between two new life options. In an opting (Yes, No) situation the choice is between the Yes, that is the new life option, and the No, that is the continuation of one's life in its present path (which may nevertheless not be quite what it was before, owing to the shadow presence of the Yes option).

IV. Opting vs. Converting

Why were the examples offered tentatively? What stands in the way of a clear-cut determination whether a given case is a case of opting?

To approach an answer to these questions, consider two further instances. When Tolstoy made his final move to live as a peasant among his fellow Russian peasants, was he opting? When the Apostles left their families and possessions behind to join Jesus of Nazareth, were they opting? I suggest that there is a thin but significant line dividing the cases of opting as here conceived, from cases of *conversion experiences*.

The Conversion experience is familiar to us—from literature, from history, and from life.[3] Like cases of opting, converting can be

---

[3] Although one tends to associate conversion primarily with religious conversions, the term is by no means restricted to this phenomenon. There is, first, what Starbuck terms counter-conversion, where one converts away from religion. Also, '[I]t may be from moral scrupulosity into freedom and license; or it may be produced by the irruption into the

about a life-transforming, core-affecting, often irrevocable move. Also, instances of conversion are often dramatic. In converting, like in opting, one is aware that one is about to change one's life in a significant way. But in the conversion experiences I here call attention to it is not the case that one believes that one must make a genuine decision between two viable alternatives. From the point of view of the convert, he or she has no choice in the matter; typically, they would have a strong sense of compulsion, of there being no other way.

Another feature distinguishing converting from opting has to do with the nature of the shadow presence of the rejected option. Cases of conversion are opting (Yes, No) cases, the rejected option being the continuation on the path of one's previous life. Typically, the person who has undergone conversion rejects his or her previous life not just in a technical sense, because they now adopt a new form of life, but also normatively. Converts view their previous lives in a negative light; they evaluate them as wicked or sinful.

I have mentioned two points of difference between converting and opting: the perception of the juncture point as something other than a genuine decision situation; and the negative evaluation of one's previous life. We can readily see that both of these points are perspective oriented. They have to do with the way the people concerned see their situation. In other words, from the point of view of an outside spectator there can in fact be much similarity between cases of opting and of converting, even though from the point of view of the actors they are quite dissimilar.

This explains why I was tentative about the examples. Whether a given instance is one resulting from a big decision—'opting'—or from a conversion experience is a question that cannot be settled by a mere labeling of the act, say, as an act of defection or immigration (etc.). We need to know more. Some opting-seeming situations, including marriage, might be converting situations instead. Conversely, some converting-seeming situations might be cases of opting: 'conversion' to, and away from, communism may be cases

---

individual's life of some new stimulus or passion, such as love, ambition, cupidity, revenge or patriotic devotion.' (William James, *The Varieties of Religious Experience*, Collin: The Fontana Library, 1960 (1901–2), 181. See also James's case histories of some non-religious conversions, 183–185.) Pertinent too are conversions into, and away from, communism.

in point (Whittaker Chambers, Arthur Koestler).[4] As for Tolstoy or the Apostles, upon a closer look they are indeed likelier to turn out converts than opters.

An evocative image for the difference between an opting situation and a conversion experience is provided by the contrast between Paul of Tarsus on the road (to Damascus) and Heracles on the crossroad (between Vice and Virtue). St. Paul's powerful conversion serves as my paradigm of what I refer to as a conversion experience. It occurs when he goes to the city of Damascus to arrest Christians and bring them to punishment in Jerusalem. As he drew near to the city '... suddenly there shined round about him a light from heaven: and he fell to the earth, and heard a voice ...', (*Acts* ix, 3–9). Eventually he repents of his sins, is baptized and arises to walk in the 'newness of life'. There is no decision in Paul's case: blinded by the light of the compelling new truth, he feels ordered into his transformed life. He regards his old self is an enemy of his new.

Heracles, in contrast, is described as 'debating with himself which of the two paths he should pursue, the path of virtue or of vice'. Two women personify for him the two options. Each of them tries to entice him—and the language is one of decision throughout. Vice speaks first: 'I see you, Heracles, in doubt and difficulty what path of life to choose; make me your friend and I will lead you to the pleasantest road and easiest.' Then Virtue speaks: '... I entertain good hope that if you choose the path which leads to me, you shall ...' Heracles is portrayed as facing a genuine choice and he knows that it is a one way road; there will be no way back.[5]

Note however that cases of formal or technical religious conversion need not be cases of a conversion experience as delineated here. At times, they may count as quite 'normal' decisions, and occasionally as cases of big decisions of the opting variety. What I have in mind for example are the numerous instances of Jews who have converted to Christianity in order to

---

[4] Whittaker Chambers, *Witness* (Regnery Publishing, 1952); Arthur Koestler's essay in *The God That Failed*, R. H. Crossman (ed.) (1951) and his three-volume autobiography, *Arrow in the Blue* (1952), *The Invisible Writing* (1954), and *Janus: A Summing Up* (1978).

[5] Xenophon, *Memorabilia* (Book II, ch. 1, 21–34). The plot is based upon a lost parable of Prodicus of Ceos (a Sophist contemporary of Socrates), *The Choice of Heracles*. In his *Memorabilia*, Xenophon has Socrates relate a paraphrase of the lost parable to Arisrtippus. (J. S. Bach bases his secular Cantata BWV 213, 'Herkules auf dem Scheidewege', on this material.)

remove an obstacle from the path of their chosen career (like Heinrich Heine or Gustav Mahler), or in order to open up doors for their children (like Abraham Mendelssohn, Felix's father). The point then is that not every case of an exchange of one religion for another is a case of a conversion experience in the sense here employed, so dramatically illustrated by St. Paul (or Ratisbonne).

Pascal's argument known as the Wager is an interesting case in point. It is an argument designed to convince non-believers to choose the Catholic faith through a deliberative-calculative process of decision-making, not by relying on being swept by a conversion experience.

V. The Rationality of Big Decisions

I have alluded to a contrast between deliberation-related opting on the one hand and a conversion experience on the other. What is behind this contrast?

In the case of opting, there is deliberation and there is an expectation that reason prevail. I shall presently examine this expectation and question it. In the case of a conversion experience, in contrast, there is no such expectation. The phenomenon of opting is supposed to be continuous with the realm of human decision-making or practical deliberation. A conversion experience, in contrast, lies outside this realm.

In saying that opting is expected to be guided by reasons what is meant is that opters are expected to arrive at their decision in much the same way that they arrive at their ordinary, 'smaller' decisions. This in turn means that cases of opting are supposed to be open to rational-choice explanations. An ideal explanation of an action as an expression of rational choice strives to show that the action is the best way of satisfying the full set of the person's desires, given his or her set of beliefs formed on the basis of the (optimal amount of) evidence at their disposal. In addition, the further standard requirement is added that the person's sets of beliefs and of desires be internally consistent.[6]

To return to the question of the rationality of opting cases: opters are expected not only to act rationally but even super-rationally, as it were. They are expected to be more rational about

[6] I follow here the formulation of Jon Elster in 'The Nature and Scope of Rational-Choice Explanation', in *The Philosophy of Donald Davidson: Perspectives on Actions and Events*, E. Lepore and B. McLaughlin (eds.) (Oxford: Basil Blackwell, 1985).

their opting decisions than about their ordinary decisions, simply because there is so much more at stake. This means that one would expect the opters to take extra time and care in amassing relevant information as their evidence base, to exercise extra caution in assessing the alternatives open to them—including their probabilities—and in bringing their own set of desires (valuations, inclinations, aspirations) to bear upon them, and so on. In short, one would expect an act of opting to be an exemplary candidate for the ideal rational-choice explanations just delineated.

Is this really the case? How rational are opters, and how rational ought they to be?

These are two distinct questions. The first question is empirical, the second normative. Of the first, I have little to say. There is some evidence that the attitude of people toward their big decisions is quite the opposite of the one that we might expect. That is to say, evidence seems to suggest that people are in fact more casual and cavalier in the way they handle their big decisions than in the way they handle their ordinary decisions.[7]

The normative question, how rational ought opters to be, goes to the heart of the matter. Let me begin with an (empirical) observation about how people tend to react to this question. It appears that the idea that one ought to be rational about one's big life decisions strikes some people as troublesome, even wrong. There is a view that with big decisions one ought to be guided by one's instincts, to go 'by one's gut'. The demand for cost-benefit analysis or a decisional balance sheet in the sphere of big decisions seems to some people to belittle these decisions in some sense and to detract from their significance.[8] On this view, it is only the

---

[7] Regarding the ways people handle their big financial decisions, for example their retirement plans, see Cass R. Sunstein and Richard H. Thaler, 'Libertarian Paternalism Is Not An Oxymoron'. AEI-Brookings Joint Center Working Paper No. 03–2; U. Chicago, Public Law Working Paper No. 43; U. Chicago Law & Economics, Olin Working Paper No. 185.

[8] For a well-known taxonomy of decision strategies for coping under stress, time pressure, and risk see Janis, I. L. & Mann, L.: *Decision Making: A Psychological Analysis of Conflict, Choice and Commitment* (Free Press, MacMillan, 1977); it includes a decisional balance sheet.

In 'Feeling and Thinking' (*American Psychologist*, 1980, footnote 6), R. B. Zajonc underlines the role of affect in decision-making. He describes how, in trying to decide whether to accept a position at another universtiy, Phoebe Ellsworth said, 'I get half way through my Irv Janis balance sheet and say: Oh, hell, it's not coming out right! Have to find a way to get some

temperamental, intuitive leap, a 'naked act of decision' as it were, that does justice to the weight of the decision.[9]

Economists, on the other hand, care little about the phenomenology of peoples' attitudes to their decisions. Theirs is a world-view of revealed preferences, and as long as people exhibit consistency in their choices it does not much matter, from the standpoint of rationality, whether the choice was intuitive or resulted from a calculative deliberation. As we shall see, however, it is the notion of consistency that is challenged by the cases of big decisions of the opting variety.

Let us consider people who face opting situations and who want to opt rationally. We suppose that they are conscientious, fully informed and well aware of all the relevant aspects, external as well as internal, of the decision before them. We suppose that they want to choose that option which they believe more fully satisfies their comprehensive, internally consistent desires, given the consistent set of their beliefs—including of course their present beliefs about their own future states in each of the options open to them.

Think for example of a high-tech executive who, craving spirituality, considers opting for a life as a Buddhist monk. We imagine him to want the isolation, simplicity, peace of mind and closeness to nature that (he believes) characterize the life of Buddhist monks. He will seek every piece of information relevant to his decision—about the lives of Buddhist monks, about the process of becoming one, etc. He may even be able to assess his

---

pluses over on the other side!' (I am indebted to Thomas Schelling for this quote.) A recent report of four studies on consumer choice indicates that it is not always advantageous to engage in thorough deliberation before choosing. The scientists' new advice for anyone who is struggling to make a difficult decision is, Stop thinking about it and, when the time comes to decide, go with what feels right. See: Ap Dijksterhuis, Maarten W. Bos, Loran F. Nordgren, Rick B. van Baaren, 'On Making the Right Choice: The Deliberation-Without-Attention Effect', *Science* **17** (February) Vol. 311, No. 5763, 2006 1005-1007.

[9] Consider 'A Psychological Tip', a poem by Piet Hein, from *Grooks* (Cogpenhagen: Borgens Forlag, 1982), 38: 'Whenever you're called on to make up you mind / And you're hapmered by not having any, / The best way to solve the dilemma, you'll find / Is simply by spinning a penny. / No—not so that chance shall decide the affair / While you're passively standing there moping / But the moment the penny is up in the air, / You suddenly know what you're hoping.' (I am indebted to Thomas Schelling for this quote too.)

probability of success in achieving the transition and becoming the person he wants to be. As we picture him, he has, in addition to his beliefs and desires, second-order preferences as well, about the sort of person he wants to be. Being materialistic, he may prefer to have ascetic and spiritual preferences; being sex-minded, he may prefer to be a person who prefers abstention.

Now we want to consider what it means for this person to make an optimal choice, relative to his present beliefs and desires. Whose ends is he aiming to promote? Is the opter trying to promote the ends of Old Person or of New Person? The reason for casting doubt about the nature of the optimizing is that, once he opts, Old Person undergoes a personality transformation: there is no continuity in his personality identity and so there is also a problem about his being consistent in his choices.[10]

New Person is now, by hypothesis, a transformed person. Opting transforms the sets of one's core beliefs and desires. A significant personality shift takes place in our opter, a shift that alters his cognitive as well as evaluative systems. New Person's new sets of beliefs and desires may well be internally consistent but the point about the transformation is that inconsistency now exists between New Person's system of beliefs and desires, taken as a whole, and Old Person's system taken as a whole. I am not questioning his ability to actually make a choice, or his ability subsequently to assess himself as happy (or unhappy) with his choice. The question I am raising is whether it is possible to assess the rationality of his choice, given that this choice straddles two discontinuous personalities with two different rationality bases.

So: rational action is relative to the person's beliefs and desires, and the person's beliefs and desires constitute the basis against which the rationality of that person's actions is assessed. Therefore, the transformation our opter undergoes affects his or her rationality

---

[10] I was told of a person who hesitated to have children because he did not want to become the 'boring type' that all his friends became after they had children. Finally, he did decide to have a child and, with time, he did adopt the boring characteristics of his parent friends—but he was happy! I suppose second order preferences are crucial to the way we are to make sense of this story. As Old Person, he did not approve of the personality he knew he would become if he has children: his preferences were not to have New Person's preferences. As New Person, however, not only did he acquire the predicted new set of preferences, he also seems to have approved of himself having them. How are we to assess the question whether he opted 'right'? Who is asking? Who is answering, and on whose behalf?

base. The opting juncture is a point of discontinuity, or break, in the opters' biography and personality and so the basis for assessing what is rational for them to do beyond this point is different from the basis for the rationality assessment of their actions prior to that point. The personality-transforming opting situation is one in which the old 'rationality base' is replaced by a new. And yet, the rationality of decision-making and of choice is predicated on the continuity of personality identity over time.[11]

Can we not describe this situation within the familiar framework of decision under uncertainty? In a sense we can, but we have to be clearer about the uncertainly that is involved here. In the opting situation it is not the future states of the world or their probabilities that one does not know but rather one's future personality. Opting is a gamble on one's future self as a transformed assessor of results and assigner of probabilities. Cases of opting involve the opting persons' explicit or implicit second-order preference for a radical change in their set of first-order preferences. These are cases, in other words, in which people have second-order preferences over their future selves: they want to transform themselves. Given the discontinuity in the opting person's set of preferences, can one make sense of such a decision from a rational-choice perspective? If acting rationally is optimizing, can one opt optimally?

VI. Opting Reasonably

From what I said so far, one should not conclude that when it comes to opting people are intrinsically irrational: it is not even clear what it would mean to say this. In order to be irrational about something there must also be a rational way of going about it, and the rational way of going about opting is what I am here questioning. A satisfying post-opting life is no indication of the rationality, or otherwise, of the big decision involved.

'Acting rationally' need not mean optimizing; it can also mean acing reasonably. What would it take for one to opt reasonably?

Consider a strategy people may employ in an attempt to opt reasonably: they may attempt to cut down, as it were, the opting

---

[11] The best known philosophical discussion of the connection between rationality and the idea of stability of personal identity over time is Derek Parfit, *Reasons and Persons* (Oxford University Press, 1986), chapter XIV. However, he speaks of personal identity whereas I prefer to speak of personality identity.

situation into a series of ordinary 'middle-sized' decision situations. In practice, this means breaking up the big step into several steps, none of which is a dramatic leap and each of which is reversible. Small steps can be helpful. In particular, by taking small consecutive steps we can assure the continuity of our personality identity over time.

Thus, if the big decision you face is whether to marry this man or not, you may try to arrange for the two of you to live together for a while so that you can get a foretaste of your future life—and of your future self—as his wife. Or if the offer of an academic position in a country you have never been to is to you an opting situation, you may try to negotiate first for a term of teaching there, and subsequently perhaps for a year's stay in that place with your family. When the time comes for you to make your final decision, you are likely no longer to consider the last step in this series of steps as an instance of opting.[12]

That is to say, a way of resolving an opting situation is by consciously attempting to neutralize two of the characteristics that make it an instance of opting, namely, that it is a point of discontinuity in one's life, and that it involves a point of no return. These two characteristics also account for the heavy psychological burden that the opting situation imposes. Not all instances of opting may lend themselves to the application of the strategy of cutting down the opting situation to ordinary-decision size. Some cases really call for leaping across an abyss: such a jump cannot be done in small steps. But where this strategy is available I believe that it is natural, as well as reasonable, to resort to it.

VII. Opting vs. Drifting

I shall now further enrich the vocabulary of big decisions by introducing the notion of *drifting*. One will be said to drift when making one's big decisions conscious of their being decisions but not of their being big. A drifting person carries on with the business of his or her life, making incremental, stepwise decisions only. It is only in retrospect that it can be seen how a particular

---

[12] For more on the small-step strategy see Edna Ullmann-Margalit and Cass R. Sunstein, 'Second-Order Decisions', *Ethics* **110** (October 1999), 5–31. (Reprinted in: Cass R. Sunstein, *Behavioral Law and Economics*, Cambridge University Press, 2000, chapter 7, 187–298.)

series of such incremental steps—or in particular one step among them—had been all-important in transforming the future shape of their life and of their personality.

Consider this observation by Janis and Mann: 'Important life decisions are sometimes incremental in nature, the end product of a series of small decisions that progressively commit the person to one particular course of action. A stepwise increase in commitment can end up locking the person into a career or marriage without his ever having made a definite decision about it.'[13] Janis and Mann also report a study indicating that, 'the careers of law-breakers are often arrived at in the same stepwise, drifting fashion, without any single stage at which the offenders decide they are going to pursue a life of crime' (*ibid.*) I think that the brief, ambiguous love affair of Fontane's Effie Briest with the Polish officer Major von Krampas is an instance of drifting, with catastrophic consequences. In contrast, Anna Karenina's liaison is surely not a case of drifting, but I leave open the question whether or not she was an opter.

It is possible that from an outside-spectator's point of view the real nature of the actor's decisions is clear. It is possible for a person to proceed as a drifter while an informed spectator would judge that the person's situation is one of opting. When this happens, I think that we can view the actor as engaged in self-deception. The actor may be ignoring aspects of his or her decision situation, which reveal it for what it is: a first commitment leading down a core-transforming, irreversible road.

By now, I have identified a number of techniques for extricating ourselves from an opting situation. One is the mechanism of resolving an opting problem by dissolving it, or by 'cutting it down' to ordinary-decision size—the small-step strategy. Another is the phenomenon of self-deception, which we may regard as a mechanism for resolving an opting problem by pretending that it was an ordinary-size decision (or a series of such). Yet another way to extricate ourselves from an opting problem is by subtly arranging it to appear to us as if it were a case of conversion. That is, we may be channeling our mental energies to make one of these alternatives appear as a compelling and inevitable *force majeur.*

I speculate that we find pure, unmitigated opting situations difficult to deal with. We find it difficult to look them straight in the eye, as it were. The speculation also is that we may in fact be badly equipped to deal with opting situations. Infrequent,

---

[13] Janis, I. L. & Mann, L. *Decision Making: A Psychological Analysis of Conflict, Choice and Commitment*, 1977 (see note 8 above), 35.

exceptional and all-encompassing as they are, we can hardly draw on our own past experience or on the experience of others in resolving them.[14] We recognize, as theorists, that big decisions test the limits of rational decision theory while we try, as practitioners, to extricate ourselves from them as best we can.

VIII. Opting, Picking and the Absurd

I started with a distinction between the realm of decisions without preferences—picking, and the realm of 'big' decisions—opting. I want to close with a suggestion that at the deepest level of choice, picking and opting meet.

One chooses for reasons; one picks when reasons cannot prevail. This happens when the alternatives are entirely symmetrical (or incommensurate). But reasons also fail to prevail when we come to the very end of the chain of reasons, when we run out of reasons altogether. If you choose to do X for reason A and, asked to justify A, you cite B and then you give C as your reason for B and so on, you eventually reach the very bottom, the substratum of all your reasons. If reasons are forever from within a system or a framework (Wittgenstein: from within a 'language game'), the choice of the framework itself cannot be justified by appeal to reasons.

You cannot justify deduction, because there is no way to do it non-deductively. The choice to be moral cannot be justified by appeal to moral reasons. These fundamental choices, then, cannot really be choices; so are they instances of picking? These are after all the biggest, in the sense of weightiest, decisions we may ever have to make.

I believe that a similar intuition underlies Kant's position about the free yet ultimately inscrutable act of choice ('*Wilkuer*') to adhere to the maxim of the universal moral law.[15] I also believe that an intuition like this underlies the understanding of the absurd in

---

[14] Marrying may be an infrequent experience in the lives of each one of us but, seen globally, it is a frequent event: most people marry, at least once. Big decisions may therefore be discussed very differently—from an institutional rather than from a personal perspective. It is possible, for example, to think of incentives and institutional designs that could encourage people to make their big decisions come out in a particualr way, for example to reinforce their decision to follow the path of Mother Theresa or to become a legal service lawyer instead of a corporate lawyer.

[15] See Paul Guyer, *Kant and the Experience of Freedom* (New York: Cambridge university Press, 1996 (1993)), 362–4.

the writings of Karl Schmidt and of the Existentialist thinkers, notably Heidegger and Sartre. At bottom, we make our most fundamental choices of the canons of morality, logic and rationality in total freedom and without appeal to reasons. They embody acts that this literature variously describes as nihilist, absurd, or leaps (of faith). The Existentialist thinkers hold that as mature adults we can step outside ourselves as it were, to find the Archimedian point from which to make the brute act of unreasoned choice of a way of life. It may be, then, that the notions of picking and opting finally meet, on the level of these profound existential decisions.

The Epistemology of Unjust War

HILARY PUTNAM

My friend Steven Wagner, a philosopher I very much admire, recently wrote me that he finds 'Just War Theory' in its present form wholly untenable. With his permission, I shall quote part of what he wrote:

> Here's what I meant about just war theory (JWT) and ontology. The formulations of JWT effectively identify three distinct objects: a population, a nation, and the high-level decisionmakers in the government. Therefore, even if JWT is invoked in the cause of peace, it surrenders the larger battle by buying into an authoritarian political ontology. So it's an irremediably spoiled tool for justice.

> A philosopher can easily work out epistemological costs of this ontological sin. Here, though, is a cost that is related to but does not immediately come out of the pernicious ontology.

> JWT imposes requirements of justified belief: regarding the outcomes of alternative courses of military in/action. Applying elementary considerations about evidence, we argue that the relevant beliefs can be justified *only* if their source is a professional agency strictly independent of the decision-making sector and disinterested relative to the outcomes.

> These clauses need more careful formulation. E.g., 'professional' will imply membership standards no less rigorous (and applicable to the subject matter) than those governing, say, physicians and philosophy professors. 'Disinterested' must mean *at least* 'no more interested than is the population in general'.E.g., if the professionals stand to gain from a war, then no more so than the run of the people. So, e.g., the agency must be strongly separate from the military, the war industries, etc.,...

> But in no nation, ever, has such an agency existed. Not even at distant approximation. Therefore, by the standards of JWT no nation has ever made war with good reason... Q.E.D.

Now I am not prepared to go as far as Wagner, as will soon appear. For one thing, as a student of American Pragmatism, I am not

prepared to say that only judgments made by a body that is
'disinterested relative to the outcomes' are justified. (Even the
judgment that I have been aggressed against when I have just been
hit on the nose is not normally made by such a body, but it is clearly
justified.)[1]

With respect to Wagner's more political (as opposed to
epistemological) reasons, I would agree that decisions in our
imperfect approximations to democratic polities are frequently,
indeed normally, made by bodies influenced by all sorts of special
interests, but I still think that we live in what *are* approximations to
democracies. (I suspect that it is because Wagner would find this
idea naïve that he would require a body 'strictly independent of the
decision-making sector' to review a government decision to go to
war before he would be willing to call it justified; indeed, I suspect
it is not only decisions to go to war that he would regard as
epistemologically suspect when made by a 'hierarchical' government.) Nevertheless, I would not quote Wagner's letter if I did not
think it contained an important idea.

The idea that I take from Wagner's reflections is that instead of
thinking about a positive list of conditions for 'just war' we might
instead think of epistemic conditions for justified belief that resort
to war is called for. This idea appeals to me because it generalizes
an argument against certain wars that I first heard from my
colleague at Harvard (whose life was tragically cut short by a stroke
back in 1987), Roderick Firth. To be precise, I heard Firth's
argument during the Vietnam War, and I have reflected on it and
have had, sadly, occasion to use it, very often since he died. Firth's
argument does not depend on suspicion of the representative
character of what we call democratically elected governments, as
(or so it seems to me) Wagner's does, nor does it follow from Firth's
argument that 'no nation has ever made war with good reason'.

But like Wagner's more radical argument, it avoids appealing to
either a grand metaphysical story or a grand ethical theory. In

---

[1] Steve Wagner will remind me, I know, that he only requires that the
agency which is the 'source of the beliefs' concerning the justice of war
(the Epistemic Bureau?) be 'no more interested than is the population in
general'. While I would agree that an agency which decides on war
shouldn't do so *because* it stands to gain from a war 'more so than the run
of the people', I do not think that apart from the case of material gain,
there is any general rule as how 'interested' deciders are allowed to be.
Moreover, I do not agree that that epistemic justification requires an
agency separate from the government—unless that 'agency' be simply civil
society as a whole.

essence both Wagner and Firth suggest that the fruitful question is the epistemological question about justified war rather than the metaphysical question about the 'nature' of 'just war'.[2] And even a partial answer to the epistemological question is important if it identifies a class of cases in which we are definitely *not* epistemically justified in going to war (or, to put it less abstractly, in killing and maiming people as an instrument of state policy). Rather than seek an ontology of just war, these philosophers are saying, let us seek an epistemology of unjust war. But it is time for me to say what Firth's argument was.

Firth's argument

Firth's argument was that, even if we assume (as he himself, as a Quaker, did not) that war is justified under certain circumstances, those circumstances must be very special to override the clear moral presumption against inflicting suffering on such a large scale. What Firth claimed—this is the content of what I shall call *Firth's Principles*—was that mere probabilities (e.g., game-theoretic reasoning) are not enough.[3] One must *know*, not just have some opinions by members of a particular administration, that

(1) The Bad Thing that the war one is thinking of waging is supposed to prevent really *will* happen if one doesn't wage it; and
(2) The Bad Thing will actually be prevented (and not simply replaced by a different equally Bad Thing) if one does wage war.

I want to explain and discuss Firth's argument in a concrete context. That context is not today's, but it is immediately relevant to today's situation because it brought it about: I am speaking of the context of the decision on the part of the American government

---

[2] In contrast to this epistemological approach, traditional Just War Theory begins by requiring that the war be declared by a rightful authority. To interpret this, would require the *whole* of political philosophy! And even then, wars which are not declared by an 'authority' (e.g., wars which start with spontaneous popular resistance) are not even envisaged, as Wagner pointed out in his letter to me.

[3] This kind of argument is called an 'anti-Utilitarian argument' by moral philosophers.

Hilary Putnam

(one supported by the British government, as you all know) to wage a 'preemptive war' against the then government of Iraq, headed by the dictator Saddam Hussein.

I want us to think ourselves back to the time when the decision to destroy the Iraqi army and institute 'regime change' was arrived at. And although President Bush and Prime Minister Blair said at the time that the one overriding reason that justified 'preemptive war' was the 'weapons of mass destruction' that Saddam Hussein's allegedly possessed, and we all know now that *this* 'reason' was a mistake based on a mixture of faulty intelligence and wishful thinking, that—the mistake about 'WMDs'—is *not* going to be the only matter that I focus on. I am equally interested in the question as to whether the decision to employ all the means of modern war, including, as we now know, napalm bombs[4] would have been justified even if the intelligence had been correct (including, however, the intelligence, which was also available from UN inspectors, that Saddam's regime was far from ready for war, not because it lacked aggressive desires, but because it was successfully kept off balance by the whole series of U.N. actions after the Gulf War of 1990).[5]

---

[4] Authentic footage taken by 'embedded reporters' of the 'coalition forces' using napalm bombs is included in Michael Moore's 'Fahrenheit 911'.

[5] This was Secretary of State Colin Powell's estimate on February 4, 2001, when in the course of press remarks with Foreign Secretary of Egypt Amre Moussa he reported that 'We had a good discussion, the Foreign Minister and I and the President and I, had a good discussion about the nature of the sanctions—the fact that the sanctions exist—not for the purpose of hurting the Iraqi people, but for the purpose of keeping in check Saddam Hussein's ambitions toward developing weapons of mass destruction. We should constantly be reviewing our policies, constantly be looking at those sanctions to make sure that they are directed toward that purpose. That purpose is every bit as important now as it was ten years ago when we began it. And frankly they have worked.' Three years later, on March 22, 2004, CNN carried the following story: 'WASHINGTON (CNN) The United Nations' top two weapons experts said Sunday that the invasion of Iraq a year ago was not justified by the evidence in hand at the time. 'I think it's clear that in March, when the invasion took place, the evidence that had been brought forward was rapidly falling apart', Hans Blix, who oversaw the agency's investigation into whether Iraq had chemical and biological weapons, said on CNN's 'Late Edition with Wolf Blitzer.' Blix described the evidence Secretary of State Colin Powell presented to the U.N. Security Council in February 2003 as 'shaky', and said he related his opinion to U.S. officials, including national security

As I am sure you all remember, at the time I am talking about there were serious *moral* disagreements about the decision to invade Iraq (in addition, of course, to the empirical disagreements about the likely results of the invasion). What could a philosopher, of all people, possibly say *as a philosopher* about this sort of deep moral disagreement? At the time, I believed—and still believe—that Firth's argument was the most useful one for a philosopher to make.

Firth made his argument during the Vietnam War. Since some of you were not born during the Vietnam War, and many of you may have been children at that time let me briefly recall the situation. I am describing it, because that was the situation in which Firth made his argument—I am *not* analogizing the present situation to America's or the United Kingdom's at that time, since obviously the Vietcong and the North Vietnamese were no direct threat to America, which was, indeed, over 10, 000 miles away, while terrorism is certainly a direct threat to any government and any people the terrorists choose to single out for attack. Or rather, I am analogizing it only in the respect that Firth's Principles are ones that I believe apply to both situations. America employed very harsh measures in an attempt to defeat the Vietcong and their North Vietnamese allies. (The most horrific was the dropping of napalm bombs—a weapon our nations have also used in Iraq—but the action which originally turned me into a protester against the war, when I learned about it from the writings of the journalist David Halberstam, was the destruction of the rice crop of the *South* Vietnamese peasants to keep it out of the hands of the Viet Cong. These harsh measures, which—everyone admitted—caused immense suffering to millions of Vietnames people, were supposed to be necessary to prevent a Bad Thing. The Bad Thing was described using the metaphor of a 'row of dominos'. It was claimed that if South Vietnam fell to the communists, so would Laos and

---

adviser Condoleezza Rice.

'I think they chose to ignore us', Blix said. In the same story, Mohamed ElBaradei, director general of the International Atomic Energy Agency, is quoted as speaking to CNN from IAEA headquarters in Vienna, Austria, saying: 'Well, Wolf [Blitzer], I think I'd like to, for a moment, say that, to me, what's important from Iraq is what we learn from Iraq. We learned from Iraq that an inspection takes time, that we should be patient, that an inspection can, in fact, work.'

Cambodia (which did fall) and then the Philippines and Indonesia would fall (which didn't happen) and finally Japan would fall to the communists.

Firth argued that in the case of the Vietnam War, we did not actually *know* either that The Bad Thing (the fall of the dominos) that the war was supposed to prevent really *would* happen if we didn't wage it or that The Bad Thing would actually be prevented if we did wage war; and, of course, he was right. What I want to claim is that this is the test that American citizens and British subjects should have applied in considering whether the invasion of Iraq was morally permissible. Taking the 'Bad Thing' to be increased terrorism, the growth of extremist Islamism, and the consequent weakening of the security of our nations and the 'free world', what Firth's Principles tell us is that what we (and morally concerned human beings everywhere, for that matter) should have asked are exactly the sorts of questions that Firth posed:

(1) Did we actually *know* that the Bad Things that preemptive war and 'regime change'[6] were supposed to prevent really would have happened if we desisted from them and tried other means, especially ones which are approved by the international community as a whole, or at least by the industrial democracies?

(2) Did we actually *know* that the terrorist acts and the growth of extremist Islamism that we wished to prevent—the Bad Things in the present case—wouldn't continue and even increase if we invaded Iraq and used military force to bring about 'regime change'?

Did we, for example, know that (as President Bush alleged) that Iraq is a sponsor of al-Qaeda?[7] Or that invasion will not *bring it about* that it becomes a seedbed of international terrorism on a huge scale?

---

[6] Of course, Firth spoke of war in general, since this was the time of the Vietnam war, but I have substituted 'preemptive war and regime change' since that is the application I am making of his (more general) principle.

[7] [The Miami Herald, March 3, 2004]: 'WASHINGTON—The Bush administration's assertion that Iraqi leader Saddam Hussein had ties to al-Qaeda—one of the administration's central arguments for a preemptive war—appears to have been based on even less solid intelligence than the administration's claims that Iraq had hidden stocks of chemical and biological weapons.

I don't deny for one moment that one can offer arguments on both sides for the necessity of the problematic measures. But that is the problem that Firth's Principles highlight. 'One can offer arguments on both sides.' To me it seemed clear even at the time that there is an enormous difference between saying we *know* that invasion is necessary and effective and 'arguments on both sides'. I am a 'Firthian' here: if we don't *know*, then what we are doing is immoral. That is the philosophical question I invite us to think about, and what I shall say from here on is, I am all too well aware, only the beginning of such a discussion.

But first, to ward off a misunderstanding

Quite a few months ago, a Republican friend of mine (yes, I do have some Republican friends) said to me in a tone of awe, 'You were the only person I knew who opposed the war because you thought it wouldn't work.' While I am not one to turn down complements, even undeserved ones, this particular complement involved a misunderstanding which I must ward off if the whole philosophical point of this lecture is not to be missed. My friend heard me as making a *empirical estimate*—one, which to his surprise, had turned out to be correct—as to the future course of events in Iraq. In effect, he was complementing me for political savvy that I don't pretend to possess. My point, like Firth's, and like Wagner's hermaneutic of suspicion, was an epistemic one. I did not deny (at the time the war started, anyway) that the rosy estimates of the Bush and Blair administrations *might* turn out to be right; my estimate was that they were not epistimically justified. And killing and maiming people on grounds that are not epistimically sound is *morally wrong*, not just practically unwise. To me this seems self-evident, as it did to Firth, but I have discussed Firth's argument with enough people to know that it is far from being generally accepted. In the rest of the present lecture I shall,

---

Nearly a year after U.S. and British troops invaded Iraq, no evidence has turned up to verify allegations of Hussein's links with al-Qaeda, and several key parts of the administration's case have either proved false or seem increasingly doubtful.

Senior U.S. officials now say there never was any evidence that Hussein's secular police state and Osama bin Laden's Islamic terrorism network were in league. At most, there were occasional meetings.'

accordingly, discuss objections to Firth's argument—both ones I have heard from others, and one which have simply occurred to me.

The sceptical objection to 'one must know'

Both of Firth's Principles employ the notion of *knowledge*. According to the principles, justification of war requires that we *know* that the Bad Things won't happen if we resort to war (resort to maiming and killing) and that we *know* that the Bad Things won't continue (or be replaced by even worse Bad Things)[8] if we do resort to war. One of the most common objections that I have encountered to Firth's Principles is simply that in matters like war and the Bad Things that a war is supposed to prevent, *knowledge* properly so-called is simply impossible.[9] The conclusion that is drawn is that ordinary probable reasoning, faulty as it is, is what we must rely on.

As is well known,[10] I am a 'fallibilist' in epistemology, but this argument seems to me a misuse of fallibilism. One lesson that, I have long insisted, we should all have learned from the so-called 'classical Pragmatists', that is Peirce, James and Dewey, is that *fallibilism does not entail scepticism*. Sceptics have always pointed to (or more often simply imagined) cases in which some judgment turns out to be false—Descartes famously imagined that he was not sitting in a chair in front of a fireplace, but only dreaming that he was—and gone on to conclude (or, in Descartes' case, to worry) that we possess *no* empirical knowledge at all. But, as Peirce insisted, *real* doubt, as opposed to paper doubt, requires a context-specific *reason for doubting*—a reason with practical bearing—and the general fact that we are not infallible is, in any normal context, not such a reason. I know that I am in the United Kingdom, *and* I

---

[8] This is the version I heard from Firth, rather than the more specific version I gave above. (Cf. the previous note.)

[9] However, I often hear this sceptical objection from people who, in other contexts, claim to have an amazing amount of political 'knowledge'!

[10] For an overview of the role of fallibilism in my philosophy, see Yemima Ben-Menahem's *Hilary Putnam* (Cambridge, 2005) here, especially the chapter by Yemima Ben-Benahem herself ('Putnam on Skepticism') and the chapter by Alex Mueller and Arthur Fine ('Realism, Beyond Miracles').

know that human beings are sometimes mistaken about which country they are in, and there is no contradiction between these two claims.[11]

Coming to the case at hand, that there was no evidence of a connection between al-Qaeda (an extreme Islamist group if there ever was one) and the secular Baathist regime of Saddam Hussein, is something we knew or should have known. That there was no good evidence that Saddam Hussein's regime was in a position to make aggressive war in the near future, or would be in such a position if the UN continued its inspections, fly-overs, etc., is also something we knew or should have known. There is such a thing as empirical *knowledge* in such matters.

However, lest this become a lecture on Pragmatist epistemology, let me *give* the word 'knowledge' to the sceptics. It is still possible to make Firth's essential point without using it. The essential point is that when it comes to the decision to use killing and maiming as instruments of state policy, the persons who make that decision must, if they are morally alive at all, accept the onus of an especially high burden of proof. There needs to be a 'fire break' between ordinary policies of building roads, raising or lowering taxes (within normal limits, anyway), etc., and policies which involve killing and maiming—at least if all talk about the value of human life is not to be exposed as sheer hypocrisy.

(Steven Wagner will remind me that it often *is* sheer hypocrisy, in the mouths of the rich and powerful. But it is one thing to acknowledge this painful fact, and another to *accept* it as the way the world must be, and I urge that we resist such acceptance, even when it is presented as 'worldly wisdom'. Indeed there is much more worldly wisdom in Firth's Principles than in the *Realpolitik* of any of the world's present leaders.)

At this point, some of you may be reminded of a famous notion of Ronald Dworkin's, the notion of 'rights as trumps'.[12] By this he meant that considerations of utility (in particular, considerations of wealth maximization) must not be allowed to 'trump',i.e., override, the moral rights of individuals. For example, the benefits that a majority might gain from discriminatory behaviour against a

---

[11] However, Barry Stroud has defended Cartesian scepticism (or at least held out the possibility that it is correct) in *The Significance of Philosophical Skepticism* (Oxford, 1984). I criticize Stroud's defence in 'Skepticism, Stroud and the Contextuality of Knowledge', in *Philosophical Explorations* **4**, No. 1 (2001), 2–16.

[12] *Taking Rights Seriously* (Duckworth and Harvard, 1977), 153.

minority cannot justify the violation of the inherent moral right of the members of the minority to be treated as free and equal citizens. Moral rights may have to be overriden in real emergencies, Dworkin recognizes, but such overriding requires strong moral justification, not just cost-benefits analysis.

There is good reason for you to be so reminded. For the right not to be maimed, killed, not to have one's children and other relatives maimed or killed, not to have one's house destroyed over one's head and the like are *prima facie* moral rights in Dworkin's sense— indeed, if they are not recognized as such, I repeat, talk of 'human rights' is meaningless hypocrisy. Thus Firth's argument can be regarded as an epistemological refinement of the idea of 'rights as trumps'. No general scepticism about the possibility of political 'knowledge' should be allowed to efface or conceal the fact that what is being appealed to by both Dworkin and Firth are fundamental ideas of what our ideals of human equality and dignity require of us.

Am I forgetting, then, that the very human rights I am appealing to were violated repeatedly and on a large scale by Saddam Hussein and his regime? Not at all. That was, in the sense of Firth's Principles, indeed a Bad Thing, and bringing that Bad Thing to an end was one of the goals that the war was intended to achieve (although not even the Bush—or the Blair—administration claims that it is right for our countries to invade any and all countries which have dictatorial regimes, regardless of whether they pose any threat to ourselves or our allies). But remember, according to Firth's Principle (2), to justify the decision to invade, it is not enough that we knew that the violation of human rights in Iraq would continue if Saddam were left in power; we needed to know that the result of the invasion would not, in the end, be an equally bad regime. And can we honestly claim to know *that* even today? Indeed, even if Iraq ends up with an elected government accepted by at least the Shi'ite majority of the country, do we know (or even have any basis for a reliable estimate of probability, for that matter) that *that* government won't, once the coalition forces leave, turn Iraq into an Iranian-style theocracy? Even to raise the questions that Firth's Principles require us to address reveals the weakness of the justifications that were accepted by our regimes as justifying the invasion of another nation.

Exceptions to Firth's Principles

Firth's Principles do have exceptions however. When I talked to students about my reasons for opposing the Vietnam War, I often explained Firth's Principles, and applied them to the case of that war. Sooner or later an ingenious student would think of a conceivable situation in which Firth's Principles gave the wrong result. The fact that these conceivable situations frequently had no relevant similarity to the Vietnam War was itself irrelevant in the eyes of the ingenious student: only an appeal to an *exceptionless* moral principle was felt to have any weight. And if there is no such thing as an *exceptionless* moral principle (or an exceptionless moral principle which applies to cases more complicated than murdering someone who has not injured you or anyone else simply for monetary gain)? In that case, perhaps these students thought that there is no such thing as an objective moral judgment, relativism and/or subjectivism are right.

But that is not the way good moral thinking works. Good moral thinking, as Kant said, requires 'mother wit' (or 'healthy human understanding'), and there is no algorithm for healthy human understanding.[13] There *are* rules of judgment which can help us: Kant famously listed three:[14] (1) Think for yourself; (2) Think from the standpoint of humanity in general; and (3) Be sure your thinking is consistent. (The last, he said, is the hardest!) But who is to decide how to apply these rules in any specific case?

The answer, as the great moralists have always said, is *Each one of us is*. Total scepticism about the normative is self-refuting, and half-scepticism is a 'cop-out'. Each responsible human being has to decide the hard moral questions in the light of their own best judgment.

Still, even if the fact that Firth's Principles have exceptions means that they cannot be followed blindly—moral judgment has to be complex because the world is complex and life is complex—those Principles are still a valuable guide. But to see their limits, let me now turn to some of the most common exceptions.

The most common exception, I believe, is to Firth's Principle (2), the principle that requires one to know that waging war will

[13] See Juliet Floyd's 'Heautonomy and the Critique of Sound Judgment: Kant on Reflective Judgment and Systematicity', in *Kant's Aesthetics*, Herman Parret (ed.) (Walter de Gruyter,) 1998, for an excellent discussion of this aspect of Kant's thinking.

[14] Immanuel Kant, *Critique of Judgment*, ##39–40.

prevent the Bad Thing (and not cause a Worse Thing to happen) in order to justify waging a war. The exception I am thinking of is simply that when one's country is directly attacked by an aggressor, one may be justified in fighting back *even if* the resistance has no certainty of succeeding. In 1939, Poland's decision to use its army to resist the German *Wehrmacht* was, I believe, the right and honourable course even though Poland knew that the assistance it hoped for from France and Britain might not come in time. I will not argue this here, because I expect that this is something all of us who are not absolute pacifists agree on.[15] But *ex hypothesi* this exception does not apply to 'preemptive war'—that's what makes such a war 'preemptive' and not simply 'defensive'.

A related (and much more often cited) exception or possible exception to Principle (2) is the subject of the often appealed to *1939 analogy*. After all, I have heard people say, when Britain declared on war on Germany in 1939, Firth's Principle (2) was violated; Britain did not know that the Bad Thing would be prevented if it waged war. Indeed, as the recent best-selling biography of the unhappy Lord Londonderry reminds us, there were voices raised in Britain who opposed the war on that ground, or partly on that ground (though not, by 1939, Londonderry himself).

I believe, nonetheless (and I hope you believe), that Britain's decision to declare war in 1939 was an admirable one, even more so in view of the fact that the odds appeared to be against success. A full discussion of why it was a justifiable decision would, I believe, require—or at least deserve—a whole book. Here I can only touch on a few of the principal considerations.

First, the 'defensive war' exception to Firth's Principle (2) must not be confined to defence of one's own territory if one has entered into binding treaties of mutual defence with other states. Indeed, to limit the idea of just war to defence of one's own territory narrowly construed would be to reject the whole idea of mutual defence and collective defence, an idea which it is vital to strengthen, as the European Community has recognized, and as Kant long ago urged in *Perpetual Peace*. In the case of 1939, Britain was bound by such a treaty to come to the aid of Poland (and, earlier, of Czechoslovakia, although it regrettably failed to stand by *that*

[15] In his *Lectures on History*, Hegel argued—plausibly, I think—that the willingness of citizens to give their lives for the defence of the nation's territory is one of the preconditions for the existence of the modern nation state.

obligation). But beyond the narrow legal fact of the treaties, there is the fact that a Geman victory would, as Churchill saw in 1939, mean that the civilization of Europe would become a fascist and racist one. After the invasion of Russia and the attack on the United States at Pearl Harbor, what, indeed, turned out to be at stake was whether not just Europe but Europe and Asia, at the very least, would suffer the fate in question.

But the Bush doctrine of 'preemptive war' is *not* justifiable on similar grounds. Saddam's regime, bad as it was, was not a real threat to the free world, and, provided one had continued to inspect and monitor and take other such measures as the United Nations was already doing, it was hardly likely to become one in the coming decade at least.[16] A rush to war was hardly called for on defensive grounds, which is why the international community (with the exception of the Blair government) refused to support it. Today Bush's supporters defend the war as part of a 'war on terror'. But 'war on terror' is a confused concept.

It is confused because, unlike a state, 'terror' has no fixed boundaries, no fixed population, no fixed army, and there is no such thing as a 'surrender' (or, for that matter, a 'peace agreement'). Like 'The War on Drugs', the 'War on terror' is a metaphor to provide an open-ended licence to the government to do whatever it wants in a particular area.

In practice, the Bush administration has identified the 'war on terror' with a war on 'state sponsored terror'. But this too is problematic. Any degree of tolerance of or assistance to terrorist organizations might count as 'sponsorship'; and since all the radical Islamic states (and some non-Islamic states, e.g., North Korea) do tolerate and or assist terrorist organizations, in principle, the idea of a war on 'state sponsored terror' could be used to justify war (simultaneously or *seriatum*) with a large number of states (including some of our 'allies', such as Saudi Arabia). Some Neo-Conservatives indeed welcome this, saying that the 'war on terrror' should have been called a 'war on radical islamism'. But in the light of Firth's Principles one must ask: do we actually know that, say, al-Qaeda, was either created by or depends for its continued existence upon particular states? Do we know that a crusade against such a significant number of Islamic states would not inflame the whole Islamic world, even the part which is now living under moderate regimes?

[16] See the statements by Colin Powell, Hans Blix, and Mohamed ElBaradei cited in note 5.

I do not deny that some regimes may, even in the near future, really begin to develop weapons of mass destruction, and that at some point military action might have to be taken, although occupying more Islamic states hardly seems wise or likely to be effective. And in any case, the volatile character of the Islamic world is clearly related to poverty and underdevelopment which the current policies of the G7 nations and the world bank may be aggravating rather than alleviating.

Another function of 'war on' talk is, of course, to make it seem that anything *other* than a military response is Munich-style 'appeasement'. But talk of avoiding 'appeasment' is a way of ignoring the fact that we are not fighting a power-mad dictator but a hydra-headed movement with complex roots. To say, as I am sure Firth would have, that we, together with the United Nations and together with other democratic nations, should try to pressure 'extremist' nations not to develop nuclear weapons or provide material support to terrorism and, at the same time, begin to address some of the root causes of violence in the Third World, and not simply send in the armed forces to 'smash the terrorists', is not 'appeasement' but elementary morality and common sense.

Exceptions to Principle (1)

But, it may be objected, 'You have only considered objections to Principle (2). What about Principle (1)?'

Yes, there are cases when Principle (1) should be overridden. If the Bad Thing is terrible enough, in some cases just knowing that there is a significant probability that the Bad Thing will happen if one does not act militarily may justify war. But at this point I think I should reconsider my criticism of Steve Wagner's position.

Recall that, as I quoted him saying at the outset, Wagner holds that 'the relevant beliefs can be justified *only* if their source is a professional agency strictly independent of the decision-making sector and disinterested relative to the outcomes.' And I said initially that I do not think that we need to require that the relevant beliefs be vetted by an agency independent of the decision-making sector. But when the beliefs on the basis of which we are asked to maim and kill other human beings are beliefs about *probabilities*, then I would ask that those beliefs be ones that reasonable and well-informed judges in other democratic countries also regard as sound. Where Wagner wants an impartial 'agency' to survey beliefs on which warfare is based because he is afraid those beliefs will be disguised justifications for imperialism, I want the 'agency' of well-informed people everywhere to support such morally momentous decisions because I am afraid they will be ideologically based, that is, based on what is ultimately *fantasy*—whether that fantasy does or does not serve this or that economic interest. If Wagner will accept this as a friendly amendment to his view, we may not be so far apart!

Conclusion

The present situation is one of occupation rather than war, and I do not—no more than anyone else, apparently—have any clear principle to suggest as to how to bring that occupation to an acceptable end. That we can't simply 'pack up and leave' is I think clear. I myself am inclined to think that the best outcome (one suggested some months ago by Peter Galbraith)[17] would be one that led to a federation (even if it wasn't called that) of three largely autonomous communities—the Shi'ite, the Sunni, and the Kurdish —in Iraq. But that is only an opinion.

So why do I ask us to reexamine the justification of the decision to wage war *now*?

My reason is not just the abstract importance of Firth's Principles, although I think they do have enormous importance (as does Dworkin's idea of 'rights as trumps'). That we stop treating killing and maiming one another as just 'policies' subject to a cost-benefit analysis is vital if respect for human rights and international law is ever to have so much as a *chance* to take hold and grow. (In *Perpetual Peace*, Kant estimated in would take 400 years!) But speaking as an American, I am also concerned because 'Neo-Conservative' voices in the Administration are reported to have urged and still be urging further 'preemptive wars'. If that is right, then no 'philosophical problem' is more urgent than the problem of thinking wisely and morally about the justification of war. I urge that Firth's Principles are the place at which we should start that thinking.

---

[17] Peter W. Galbraith, 'How to Get Out of Iraq', *The New York Review of Books*, Vol. 51, No. 8, (May 13, 2004).

High Culture, Low Politics

ROBERT GRANT

My theme at its most general is the relation between culture and power; at its most specific, the relation between a particular type of culture, so-called high culture, and two types of power, namely governmental power, and the related but more diffuse power prevailing in society at large.

So-called 'high' politics are often (and better) called statesmanship, and are typically, though not invariably, international in scope. By the 'low' politics of my title I mean, not democracy specifically, but what politicians engage in at the domestic level, where popularity matters most. Democratic or not, most politics are perforce pretty low, and are justified only because they are preferable to despotism,[1] which in its pure form signifies the absence of politics. Yet most real-life despotisms concede something to the political spirit, since they profit from their subjects' consent, endeavour to cultivate it, and are foolish if they think to dispense with it entirely. In politics proper, however, consent (like consensus)[2] must be sought; in fact, wherever avowed and conflicting interests prefer to resolve matters through

---

[1] See Bernard Crick, *In Defence of Politics*, 1962 (London: Continuum, 2000).

[2] Consent and consensus, though they overlap, are not identical. Consent means tacitly or overtly according to someone or something else a right of command, and thus acknowledging one's duty of obedience to a superior *authority*. Consensus, on the other hand, is sought and achieved (or not) between political *equals*. It involves tacit or overt agreement as to the tolerability of given political arrangements, or the desirability of a course of collective action from within them, and the recognition that agreement is preferable to unconditional self-assertion. It does not require one to dissemble or renounce one's interests, only to constrain one's pursuit of them, with the object (as often as not) of safeguarding the most important rather than staking all of them on the hazard of force. Each may *consent* to an authority individually; but he is more likely to do so, and the arrangement is more likely to hold, when the desirability of everyone's doing so is a matter of *consensus*. Consensus is typically arrived at by a less explicit process than consent, being more a matter of the 'invisible hand', the aggregate result of very many spontaneous acts of mutual accommodation. Cf. also note 4 below.

negotiation and agreement rather than through force, there we have something like politics. The conditions for consent will usually be ascertained through representative institutions. Their business is to transmit public opinion to the rulers, if those are separate from the representatives, or to act on it, where the representatives are themselves the rulers.

Despite not being democracies, nor (occasionally) even having any electoral mechanisms, some states—Hong Kong under British rule, say, some traditional non-European monarchies—nevertheless have institutions officially designated as representative. Here the representatives may claim, or be required, to represent the views of all subjects, and can in principle do so. This is not to say that they will. But they could certainly not do so if they were held narrowly accountable to an agency with its own interests to advance: to a political party, say, or even (obviously) to the whole electorate where the franchise is restricted.

In democracies, however, where the rulers are drawn from the representatives, and where both are accountable to an electorate based on universal suffrage, the ineluctable dynamics of mass persuasion and explicit consent make it necessary for the politicians to appeal to the majority's tastes and values and to dissemble their own, should those differ. Alternatively, they may be obliged to appeal to the tastes and values of some minority which holds the balance of power (the religious parties in Israel, for example) or is otherwise thought, like the British mass media, to wield disproportionate influence over electoral outcomes ('it was the *Sun* wot won it').

No doubt politicians and their publics can sometimes honestly agree on matters of taste and value. This is more likely under a restricted franchise, since, perhaps paradoxically, even in a mass democracy the political class is itself mostly drawn from a restricted category, namely (and incredible though it may seem) an educational élite. Between it and its constituency there may be a cultural gap which can be bridged only by hypocrisy and pretence. Politicians are an educational élite because political skills require, if not the very highest level of education and intelligence, then certainly one well above the average.[3] But the condition of their

---

[3] It goes without saying that very high intelligence and education may inhibit a person's political effectiveness, since the latter often requires a certain ethical and intellectual coarseness, unscrupulousness and even self-delusion. See Michael Oakeshott, 'The Claims of Politics' (1939) in *Religion, Politics and the Moral Life*, Timothy Fuller (ed.) (New Haven:

exercising those skills is that they should be seen, or at least profess, to support the values, tastes, beliefs and aspirations of their constituents, which, though by no means homogeneous, by definition tend towards the average. This would be fine if those things—culture, in short, and particularly the element in it of value—did not vary between educational classes. But if the variation in core values between educational or any other classes were so wide as to be unbridgeable, then any society in that situation would be ungovernable, or governable only by force.[4]

Now, it will be agreed either that this cultural gap is a bad thing, or that democracy is, so far as it necessitates the systematic pretence that no such gap exists. For not only is it bad for our rulers to be forced to pretend to believe things which they do not, but, once their dishonesty is detected, their rule loses whatever democratic legitimacy it possessed, and so too does democracy. The obvious answer, that we are still free to elect rulers who will be genuinely representative of us, founders upon the facts—if facts they be—that electorates expect political competence in their rulers (and will punish incompetence), that political competence is not equally distributed but depends upon above-average education, and that above-average education may foster values which not only differ from the average person's but are sometimes also hostile to them. Nobody, not even the average voter, wants a government of honest populist bunglers and half-wits, however nearly their values accord with his own. Unless his situation is desperate, he no more wants to

---

Yale University Press, 1993). Matthew Arnold, on the other hand, saw high culture as a positive brake on political crudity, one reinforced not only by its deliberate self-distancing from day-to-day politics, but also by its indirect link to them through the process of 'establishment'. See my 'Arnold's Cultural Politics', in Robert Grant, *The Politics of Sex and Other Essays* (Basingstoke: Macmillan, 2000), 127–30.

[4] 'What maintains a great number of citizens under the same government is much less the reasoned will to live united than the instinctive and in a way involuntary accord resulting from similarity of sentiments and resemblance of opinions.'

'I shall never agree that men form a society by the sole fact that they recognize the same head and obey the same laws; there is a society only when men consider a great number of objects under the same aspect; when on a great number of subjects they have the same opinions; when, finally, the same facts give rise in them to the same opinions and the same thoughts.' (Tocqueville, *Democracy in America*, tr. and ed. H.C. Mansfield and D. Winthrop [Chicago UP: Chicago, 2000], 358 [I, 2, x].)

be governed by people as ignorant (of government) as himself, than he wants to teach himself or doctor himself if he can find people better qualified to do it.

The best solution to this problem is for élites to be allowed, if they wish, to differ from the majority in their aesthetic tastes and preferences, so long as they retain a community of ethical values with them. If ethical values are the cultural component least dependent on educational attainments,[5] then it is possible after all to imagine an educationally diverse and indeed stratified society which is nevertheless still unified by shared, deeply-held beliefs. And it can be imagined, because it has actually existed. Some of us remember it, much of it survives, and that which survives is what still holds us together. Further, both we and the law habitually regard individuals as equally responsible for their actions at any intellectual level above the grossly subnormal. In so doing we accord them a basic, initial, but equal minimum of ethical respect. That minimum, and the disposition to accord it to everyone, in itself constitutes a shared value and a social bond. And everyday experience does seem to confirm that people's moral status and capacities are independent of their educational and intellectual accomplishments. You do not require intelligence in order to be good, though goodness demands that you exercise what intelligence you have. And it is certain that intelligence alone never made anyone good, though it has often been of the greatest assistance to the wicked in carrying out their designs, as in the case of Shakespeare's Iago, and in persuading so many twentieth-century intellectuals that their designs were virtuous, despite the tens of millions of corpses which those left in their wake.

What I have been driving at so far is that culture and power, though distinct, are mutually dependent and not finally separable. But it will be as well to clear up some possible misapprehensions. It is commonly thought by liberals that 'power' is necessarily malign. Doubtless we are influenced by Lord Acton's dictum that all power corrupts, and absolute power corrupts absolutely. Some left-wing thinkers, such as Michel Foucault, have professed to detect the operations of this malignant power everywhere, and especially where it seems to be least in evidence and maximally diffused, namely, in liberal societies.

---

[5] I mean on academic education. No one will deny that ethical competence (or goodness), whatever part nature plays in it, is also hugely dependent on moral education.

But the fact of the matter is this. In a way, Foucault was right: power *is* everywhere. Every social order, *qua* order, involves power of some kind. If Hobbes is right, the thing most to be feared is the *lack* of order, viz. anarchy, or lawless power. And lawless power can be constrained only by a greater. Power can be oppressive, true; but it is also what delivers us from oppression and protects us against it. You do not, if you are sensible, sit down to reason with gangsters, or appeal to their better nature. (They would not be gangsters if they had one.) You call in the SWAT team, and either swat them on the spot like flies, or haul them before the courts, establish their guilt, and then swat them less drastically at leisure. Hedge official power about with legal formalities and liberal safeguards as you please (and as you should, except in emergencies), it is still power.

In matters of social organization power is ineliminable, just like sovereignty. Voluntarily to renounce it here is simply to bestow it elsewhere, and thus still to be party to, and responsible for, whatever is done with it—which is fine, but only if what is done is good. Whether power is benign or malign depends upon who exercises it, whom they exercise it upon, whether or not they do so legitimately, and the manner in which, and end to which, it is exercised. Either in states or between individuals, naked, unaccountable power is bad, and just for that reason needs to be contained. Anything that can contain it, whilst remaining accountable itself, is 'good' power. But even 'good' power is power, and to deal with 'bad' power it may need, particularly in emergencies, to be concentrated.

Overall, to be perceived and accepted as legitimate, power requires consent and more, which is to say, cultural endorsement (or consensus). It may therefore be said that in conferring legitimacy culture is itself a form of power, though this of course raises further problems, such as how cultural power, like any other, is to be made accountable, or at least constrained. All I have space to say here is that once culture has poured itself into stable institutions which are seen as representative of it, in taking their shape it has already subordinated itself to their moderating influence, which is to say, to its own inner tendency towards permanence. If you doubt this, consider which of the following better satisfies our deepest instincts in the matter of justice: so-called summary justice, or the rule of law?

It is plausible to say that the legitimacy of a social order and of the power which maintains it depends on the endorsement of the common culture, which the resulting government exists to express and to protect. In fact, in the case of a democracy one could say as much and hope for instant agreement: universal franchise, common culture, general legitimacy, end of story. But what of so-called high culture? How does it fit into the political landscape, especially when that is democratic?

A democracy does not have to be liberal, and might not be were it not, as in our case, the heir of a pre-existing liberal tradition. But our democracy *is* liberal, and even if it accords no special privileges to high culture (partly because high culture is already perceived, and sometimes resented, as a kind of privilege) it will continue to tolerate it and people's pursuit of it, just as it tolerates almost everything else.

But one of the things about high culture is that, in the eyes of its most vociferous proponents, it is not content merely to be tolerated. It claims some kind of official recognition, status and even influence. It is not 'just a matter of taste', any more than taste is. There are those, writes the poet Wordsworth in his Preface to the *Lyrical Ballads*,[6] 'who speak of what they do not understand; who talk of poetry as of a matter of amusement and idle pleasure; who will converse with us as gravely about a *taste* for poetry, as they express it, as if it were a thing as indifferent as a taste for rope-dancing, or Frontignac, or sherry.'

For Wordsworth, Poetry is a placeholder for what would now be meant by 'high culture', even though high culture then was less self-consciously 'high' than now. That is because, although Wordsworth complains about a rash of fashionable novels and 'stupid German tragedies', there were fewer alternatives to it. If culture—books, music and the rest—was what you wanted, high culture was largely what you got. (This was partly owing to the prohibitive cost of print, so that only the rich, who were then generally speaking the best educated, could easily afford books and journals. A Jane Austen novel cost a guinea (£1.05), the modern equivalent being about 100 times that sum. Most fiction readers will have had recourse to circulating libraries.) And Poetry (with which Wordsworth brackets imaginative fiction generally) is emphatically a serious business: it is, he goes on, 'the most philosophic of all writing ... its object is truth, not individual and local, but general, and operative; not standing upon external testimony, but carried alive into the heart by passion ... Poetry is the image of man and nature ... The Poet writes under one restriction only, namely, the necessity of giving immediate pleasure to a human Being possessed of that information which may be

---

[6] 2nd edition, 1800.

expected from him, not as a lawyer, a physician, a mariner, an astronomer or a natural philosopher, but as a Man.'

Poetry gives pleasure, to be sure, but it is pleasure of a very exalted kind, the consequence, not the goal, of its operation. Poetry as Wordsworth conceives of it is not mere entertainment, aesthetic titillation, relaxation or escape. It appeals to men not in their narrowly vocational capacities, but as whole persons. It speaks, that is, to the complete human condition, and for that reason is the vehicle of truth: not the partial, material truths of science (which Wordsworth is far from despising), but ultimate truth, 'the image of man and nature'. For this reason it is best couched in the unadorned language of 'common life'.

All this has several unsurprising consequences. One, that poetry (as I have said, effectively a metonym for high culture) has ethical force. It addresses the whole man, his humanity, to which his ethical being is central, and the truths it embodies are not only imaginative but moral. Secondly, and for the same reason, it is universal in its reference, because humanity is everywhere much the same. To adapt an expression from Wordsworth's own 'Tintern Abbey', it 'sees into the heart of things'. It addresses, as it bodies forth, not only the whole man, but all men. In short, no matter what the social composition may be of its main contemporary audience (to wit, the reading classes), it is ideally classless. Thirdly, it is not only a repository of human truth, it is by the same token an agent of individual culture or moral and intellectual education, what the Germans (their stupid tragedies apart) were then beginning to call *Bildung*. Finally and consequently, it is the prototype of liberal education, that is to say, of that education which initiates one into experience simply for its own sake. Wordsworth himself thought little of formal education (he could afford to, having plenty of it), and, after a brilliantly auspicious start at Cambridge, eventually graduated with only a pass degree. Like Rousseau, he thought nature the best teacher, and the only one dedicated to the whole person. Nevertheless, when in 1854 John Henry Newman, the great Victorian champion of the university, claimed for liberal education that 'it does not make physicians, or surgeons, or engineers, soldiers, or bankers, or merchants, but it makes *men*',[7] he was recalling Wordsworth's distinction, just

---

[7] From *My Campaign in Ireland*, quoted in H. Tristram (ed.), *The Idea of a Liberal Education: a Selection from the Works of Newman* (London: Harrap, 1952), 32. (Full text: *My Campaign in Ireland*, W.P. Neville (ed.) [Aberdeen: A. King & Co., 1896], 315.)

quoted, between professional knowledge and the more general, holistic understanding required of the reader of poetry. There is a similar passage in the opening chapter of Rousseau's *Emile*.

There are many reasons for the internal fragmentation of high culture—the split, among others, between traditionalist and avant-gardist—that occurred in the twentieth century and persists today. The *ex*ternal demarcation between high-, middle- and lowbrow cultures dates only from the early 1900s. Its origins, however, lie back in the Continental culture wars of the previous century, whose opening shots were fired as early as 1830, in Stendhal's *Le Rouge et le Noir*. The campaign was subsequently carried forward by Robert Schumann in Germany and Gustave Flaubert in France against the increasing cultural influence, as they saw it, of the bourgeois 'Philistines' (originally German student slang for townspeople). Had the bourgeois been content simply and discreetly to enrich both himself and us, he would have presented no problem. But, like all others with substantial economic interests to defend, he demands political representation (which is to say, power). And again like everyone else who can afford it, he demands a share of the common cultural space in which to display, and to contemplate, his self-image. Why he finds himself resented may be not so much over any fundamental difference of values with the rest of society, nor even others' envy, but simply because both political power and cultural space are finite, so that, however deprived he was before, the more there is for him the less there is for us. Like any other rising class, the bourgeois puts the rest of us in the shade, including those, such as the working class, who have yet to stake their claims. The split within high culture seems to be an internalization of this originally outwardly-directed struggle, with traditionalism being cast in the unenviable role of the hated 'bourgeois'.[8]

But I shall come back to that. For the moment let us assume that high culture is more or less homogeneous. Perhaps there have always been splits in it, especially in France, where, since the seventeenth century, it was so heavily bound by neoclassical conventions as perpetually to lay itself open to violent, scandalous and eventually successful internal challenges (in 1829–30 de Vigny's translation of *Othello* and Hugo's *Hernani* both caused

---

[8] Under 'Philistine' the *OED* cites *Quarterly Review*, April 1899, 438: ' "Philistinism", after all, stands for two great habits, decency and order.' Yet this traditionalist Tory journal was anything but Philistine itself, being resolutely high-minded and intellectual.

riots). The vision of high culture and liberal education that we derive from Newman and Matthew Arnold, however, is one of internal consistency and a serene, almost complacent unanimity. The object of liberal education is to initiate us into high culture, and the assumption is that the product, an educated or cultivated person—or in Newman's incautious phrase, a gentleman—will be more or less standardized. In Arnold's *Culture and Anarchy* (1869), Culture speaks with a single voice, sometimes even in the inverted commas of direct speech. It tells us what and how we should think. And what is more, it speaks with an authority which is its own, and not that of government. It follows that it may criticize the government, and that in doing so it may, like an unofficial opposition, even benefit the government, by telling it truths it would be unlikely to hear from its own supporters or even their rivals.[9]

I said earlier that culture generally may be regarded as a form of power, since, through consent, it is what confers political legitimacy. What power, if any, may *high* culture be supposed to possess? And, should it have any, is this power conferred by high culture's actual content, is it a by-product of the competencies necessary to acquire high culture, or is it simply a function of the social status possessed willy-nilly by cultivated or educated people?

Let us start at the beginning. High culture is inconceivable without literacy. Further, where there is no penalty for excessive literacy, as there was in the Nazi concentration camps and in Pol Pot's Cambodia, where wearing spectacles was a death sentence, literacy is advantageous to its owner more or less proportionately to the degree in which it is possessed. If you are literate you can get a better paid job, and you are also better equipped to do battle with the bureaucracy inseparable from the workings of a modern society. So even very modest levels of culture, so long as they involve literacy, are advantageous compared with their lack. And advantage in the sense I intend means power: not necessarily political power, but the ability to get more of what you want, be it material, cultural, good or bad.

---

[9] It was for this reason that dissidents enjoyed a precarious, capricious semi-toleration (within limits) during the latter days of Eastern European communism. The authorities desperately needed the external critical perspective on current problems that the dissidents, but neither themselves nor Marxism (in which they had ceased to believe), could supply.

Robert Grant

All forms of useful knowledge, like all forms of useful skill, are advantageous, because others without them will pay one to employ them on their behalf. Furthermore, they confer prestige—which is to say, status, which is also to say, power, if only of the kind just mentioned—in proportion to their difficulty. A really good motor mechanic or computer technician is not only sought after, but admired, even by his educational superiors, and perhaps particularly by them, since he forces them to recognize that education is not everything, and that on his own patch he is much *their* superior. A Philistine who sees no point in useless knowledge will nevertheless respect the learning of a doctor or a lawyer, and even the latter's cultural acquisitions, because he knows that a due, sincere, uncalculating deference will secure his services more willingly.

And it seems that even useless or gratuitous knowledge, such as we associate with liberal education, may have practically advantageous side-effects. The labour of acquiring it will have involved the prior acquisition of unambiguously useful skills, beginning with literacy and numeracy and so on upwards. Purely academic disciplines may equip their learners with abilities employable in practical pursuits. It has been observed at least since the twelfth century that a liberal education enables a man to turn his hand to almost anything if he wishes (though he may not). In the purely practical sense, philosophy is about the most useless thing on earth; as Wittgenstein said, it 'leaves everything as it is'. Yet a degree in it is highly prized in the graduate job market, whereas a degree in media studies will get you nowhere, least of all in the media. The same is true of classics as of philosophy, though this is nowadays because the subject is difficult, and therefore an index of intellectual competence, rather than for the splendid reasons reputedly given by the Dean of Christ Church, Oxford, Thomas Gaisford, in a Christmas sermon in the 1830s, to the effect that 'the study of Greek literature ... not only elevates above the vulgar herd but leads not infrequently to positions of considerable emolument'.[10]

Adapted specifically to aesthetics, the Dean's words have been to all outward appearances empirically justified at enormous length by the late French sociologist Pierre Bourdieu in his book of 1979, *Distinction*. In a deliberate, ironical echo of Kant, this work is

---

[10] Sources are various and purely anecdotal, as a web search will confirm.

subtitled *A Social Critique of the Judgment of Taste*.[11] Since even without his statistics the fact is obvious, Bourdieu shows without difficulty that, apart from the odd (and significant) hiccup, there are more or less straightforward correlations between socio-economic class, educational level and aesthetic preferences.[12] The thesis resembles but also amplifies that of our old friends and Marxist stalwarts Samuel Bowles and Herbert Gintis, in their *Schooling in Capitalist America* (1976),[13] a text still given pride of place in countless first-year undergraduate courses.

Bowles and Gintis's supposedly world-shattering discovery was this, that education is a means by which the class system, and inequality generally, reproduces itself. In other words—and totally unsurprisingly—if you are educated middle-class parents your children are more than likely to turn out educated and middle-class too. (As they also are if, though uneducated yourselves, you still value education—from which the 'class' status follows—from the outside.)[14] Without referring at all to Bowles and Gintis—presumably he hadn't read them—Bourdieu goes a stage further, by adding the aesthetic dimension.

Veblen had theorized a relation between taste and class a full 80 years earlier, in *The Theory of the Leisure Class* (1899), but more impressionistically. Bourdieu's point is backed, not only by the data from thousands of questionnaires, by copiously-quoted interviews, magazine articles and advertisements, but also by minute, acutely sensitive observations of the everyday social surface and its symbolic strategies and manoeuvrings. Some insights are almost worthy of Proust, whom Bourdieu often cites (as he does Erving Goffman, author of the 1959 classic *The Presentation of Self in*

[11] Bourdieu, op. cit., tr. R. Nice (London: Routledge & Kegan Paul, 1984).

[12] As there are almost bound to be, in an integrated politico-educational system as self-consciously, designedly and unapologetically élitist as the French.

[13] New York: Basic Books, 1976.

[14] The dying Cockney shipping magnate in Kipling's dramatic monologue 'The Mary Gloster'—a preposterous piece, but perceptive for all that—has sent his son to 'Harrer [Harrow] an' Trinity College' (Cambridge, of course) more out of social ambition than for educational reasons. Unfortunately, whichever, education or class, is to blame, the poor boy, now 40, has been turned out a homosexual aesthete: 'For you muddled with books and pictures, an' china an' etchin's and fans, / And your rooms at College was beastly—more like a whore's than a man's.' The poem appeared in 1894, a year before before the Wilde scandal.

Everyday Life). Not only is taste a class and status marker (as we all knew), but that is its primary function and *raison d'être*. Taste opens the path to privilege and influence (if one is not already on it), and once those are attained, it then legitimizes both one's possession of them and the system which underwrites them.

One cannot but be impressed by Bourdieu's industry and ingenuity (and, ironically, his excellent taste). Much of what he says is undoubtedly true, at least as regards some taste and some people. However, to judge by the current literature, he has not attracted any serious criticism. This raises important questions about the current state of sociology, and even about the discipline itself.

The fact is that Bourdieu's account is full of holes, which he either plugs with the unthinking axioms of his profession or doesn't even notice. As with Bowles and Gintis, Marxists generally, and Durkheimians too, it is the big picture, the macroscopic view, which counts. In this perspective, agency resides with collectivities rather than with individuals. Ultimately it is classes (and other groups) which act, not their members.

Now it is true that an individual's motivation does not spring from nowhere or simply out of his own head. We are socially constituted selves, whose range of possible actions, intentions, beliefs, values and the rest are culturally bounded, so that, within a given, historic society, there are some things it is impossible that we should think, and other things that we are quite likely to think. But one would imagine that, in attempting to explain a social tendency, one might at least begin by asking the individuals concerned what *they* had supposed they were doing. The simple reason for doing so is that, unless they are acting in deliberate concert, the collective 'agent', such as a social class, which they go to compose, is speechless. A class cannot be asked anything, nor supply any reasons for its apparent 'behaviour'. Hardly surprising, you might say, since it is primarily a 'construct' of the sociological imagination. At all events, the fact that it cannot give an account of itself only makes it easier to impute motives to it from outside.

In economics the principle of unintended consequences is familiar, and has been since the satirist Bernard Mandeville first drew attention to it in the early eighteenth century. Its satirical potential derives from the fact that people refuse to recognize the demonstrable fact that their actions often produce effects precisely contrary to those they intended.[15] For them, motives are trumps, even when (as some say of foreign aid) the outcome injures those whom it was meant to benefit. What matters here, though, is that although individual actions flow from ascertainable intentions, the collective result, which may well bear the outward marks of purpose or design, in fact has none. It is precisely that, the irrelevance of the actors' intentions, which makes economics a genuine science, rather than a highly speculative, abstract, homogenizing kind of psychology. Explaining unintended social phenomena as the consequences of a hidden intention on the part of some notional macro-individual (such as a class) is really a kind of superstition, a secular analogue of natural theology.

To see unintended social phenomena as expressions of direct agency is clearly a metaphor, tolerable or even interesting in fiction, but utterly misleading in science. And Bourdieu's key categories turn out to be tendentious metaphors, promiscuously extending economic concepts to the cultural field and in so doing automatically skewing the interpretation in a given direction, so that the conclusions are predetermined by the method and terminology. Those conclusions seem to me plainly to fly in the face of immediate, readily ascertainable facts, which, despite the vast bulk and sweep of Bourdieu's book, never come up even for mention.

Bourdieu's leading quasi-economic concepts are 'social capital', 'cultural capital', 'symbolic capital', 'symbolic profit', 'consumption' and 'appropriation'. I do not propose to analyse these terms, partly because, with the exception of the last (appropriation), their meaning is fairly clear, as is their metaphorical status. People once found it merely amusing that welfare economists had to translate a familiar notion, 'job satisfaction', into the expression 'psychic income' in order to fit it into their cost-benefit calculations. Bourdieu's peculiar perversity, however, should emerge from the following rather brilliant passage, which I have abridged. The subject is the differing patterns of cultural 'consumption' of the

---

[15] This, according to Mandeville, is as true of bad intentions as of good. The subtitle of his *The Fable of the Bees* (1723) is 'Private Vices, Publick Benefits'. Whether bad motives produce good outcomes or 'good' motives bad ones, either way the virtuous cannot but be outraged. Mandeville was indicted for immorality in 1725 by a Grand Jury of Middlesex, while in France, in 1740, his book was burnt by the public hangman.

so-called 'dominated' and 'dominant' 'fractions' of the high-cultural class, that is, the paid-up (but underpaid) intelligentsia and the rich but educated bourgeois:

> For certified or apprentice intellectuals, activities such as theatre-going, visits to exhibitions or 'art' cinemas, performed with a frequency and regularity which take away any 'extra-ordinary' quality, are in a sense governed by the pursuit of maximum 'cultural profit' for minimum economic cost, which implies renunciation of all ostentatious expense and all gratifications other than those given by symbolic appropriation of the work. ('You go to the theatre to see the play, not to show off your wardrobe,' as one of them said.) They expect the symbolic profit of their practice from the work itself, from its rarity and from their discourse about it (after the show, over a drink, or in their lectures, their articles or their books), through which they will endeavour to appropriate part of its distinctive value. By contrast, for the dominant fractions a 'night out' at the theatre is an occasion for conspicuous spending. They 'dress up to go out' (which costs both time and money), they buy the most expensive seats in the most expensive theatres ... Choosing a theatre is like choosing the right shop, marked with all the signs of 'quality' and guaranteeing no 'unpleasant surprises' or 'lapses of taste'; a playwright who knows his job ... in short a goldsmith or jeweller, a past master in the 'art of construction', who has 'the tricks of the dramatist's art' at his fingertips ...[16]

And so on. The passage, like the entire book, is liberally sprinkled with inverted commas, some marking a novel or figurative usage, some ironically repeating a class cliché, and some being genuine quotations from upmarket newspaper reviews.

Bourdieu's point is that both publics, the one overtly and the other covertly, are seeking some kind of status-conferring or otherwise egoistic advantage from the cultural event they have paid to attend. This point seems not only clear, but also compelling, in the case of the moneyed 'bourgeois', especially since Bourdieu's depiction, though ironical, seems free of the ponderous, sneering, self-congratulatory malice once so popular in French intellectual circles. The point is equally clear, but much less compelling, in the other case, that of the comparatively impoverished intellectuals who have been to see (or rather, have 'consumed') a slightly different, more demanding kind of artistic product: Beckett or

[16] *Distinction*, 270.

Pinter, let us say, rather than Peter Shaffer. These people have sacrificed good money, which they can ill afford, for a particular artistic experience, But in Bourdieu's eyes that does not show (as you might think, and as they do think) their preference for artistic over material values, it merely shows that they have used a material asset to purchase a spiritual one, and that both assets represent a given quota of satisfaction or utility. In other words, aesthetic values are really no more than a sublimation of, or substitute for, material values (which include status).

Bourdieu alleges elsewhere that status, 'materialistic' though it may be, can and does attach directly, not only to aesthetic values, but also to the very *indifference* to material considerations which the financial sacrifice necessary to obtain them implies. Status attaches also to the anti-materialism of liberal education. Why the bourgeoisie support liberal education and also seek it for themselves and their offspring is, according to Bourdieu, because it elevates them above the mere wealth which enables them to purchase it, and, through the system of certification bestowed by the autonomous institutions which provide such education, supplies both them and those excluded from it with objective evidence of that same, independent cultural merit on their part. Bourdieu's manner is not notably cynical, but the overall effect is to reduce everything to the same dead level of competitive acquisition and comparative advantage.

There is nothing wrong with the things literally designated by the economic expressions 'capital', or 'profit', or even 'consumption' and 'appropriation'. But what Bourdieu calls 'cultural capital', 'symbolic profit' and the rest are not even comparable with their non-metaphorical equivalents. There is something grotesque in the idea that the prior knowledge and understanding with which one approaches a work of art are a kind of 'capital', that experiencing it is a kind of 'consumption', that experiencing it and then discussing it afterwards amounts to a 'symbolic profit' on the said cultural 'capital' (as also on the real economic cost), and that appreciating it is a form of 'symbolic appropriation'.

Bourdieu's fundamental, systematic error is to reduce quality to quantity, and intrinsic values to instrumental ones. The economy is a fact, and it is amenable to study, but everything is wrong with so-called 'economism', viz. the application of utilitarian or cost-benefit calculation to categorically different social phenomena such as art and liberal education. You can apply straightforward economics to the art *market*, as you can to vocational education. A painting is a unique object, and *can* be 'appropriated', so that if I possess it, you don't, and *vice versa*. As, but only as, a material object, it has a material value, and can be bought and sold. And it is equally not silly to see a vocational skill as a marketable commodity. The main point of (quite literally) 'investing' in a vocational education is the consequent saleability of the skill. When the skill becomes obsolete (say because of new technology), it either disappears from the market altogether or (like hand-weaving) reappears in an aestheticized form, as a craft (it can also disappear from the market but survive as a hobby).

But the value of the artistic experience embodied in the physical artwork (if it *is* a physical object, unlike a piece of music or the contents of a book) is intrinsic. The experience is neither a physical object, nor a quantity, nor saleable, nor consequently subject to ownership. Any number of cognitively-attuned people can share it. If I enjoy it, that does not leave less of it for you, so I cannot be said in any sense to have either 'consumed' or 'appropriated' it. Nor is the experience—that is to say, the work in its 'ideal' or non-physical character—necessarily cheapened by diffusion. One of Bourdieu's claims, derived in part from the 1920s defender of Modernist élitism, José Ortega y Gasset, is that the value of high culture depends upon its inaccessibility or scarcity, especially in a democratic age. Yet many artworks in the conventional high-cultural canon have universal appeal, and are often popular in origin (Dickens, Verdi). A single art form can vary between national cultures in respect of its audience's social composition. In Italy, opera has always been popular across the entire class spectrum; here it has traditionally been an élite interest, but has become hugely more popular since the establishment of subsidized provincial opera companies, so that lately (and astonishingly) more people were regularly attending operas—and spending less money on doing so—than were attending football matches.

Even more recently, however, we have seen successful attempts, in the form of so-called 'director's opera' and avant-garde 'concept' productions, to make opera inaccessible again, largely by vandalizing it, so that no normal person, let alone any educated person who loves and understands the original works, wants or can bear to see it. This feat is usually accomplished by some kind of 'deconstructionist' inversion of the original setting and stage directions. An architectural equivalent is Daniel Libeskind's proposed Spiral extension to the Victoria and Albert Museum, which, to judge by the published 'artist's impressions', will (if it is ever built, being currently 'on hold') resemble nothing so much as an old-style fairground Crazy House, with floors and walls all very amusingly cock-eyed, but unfortunately cock-eyed on the outside too. I say equivalent to deconstructionist opera, but perhaps I mean worse than it, because unlike with an opera we cannot choose whether or not to expose ourselves to it, except by avoiding South Kensington.

To return, however: no doubt high culture and its trappings *can* be converted into commodities, that is, deliberately affected, or even embraced, for whatever status-conferring properties they may chance to possess. Nietzsche characterized the German professoriate of his time—who were of course, at least in the formal sense, genuinely educated people—as just such 'culture philistines'.[17] Again, there are some who go to Glyndebourne primarily to be seen, though I am not sure that is quite the same thing. And you will find in American suburbia a superficially similar but in truth far different and much more admirable character, the 'culture vulture', invariably female and often of great intelligence, whose genuinely aesthetic instincts, for lack of a proper education and local support (such as conversation with like-minded people), have merely found no orderly outlet and are therefore all over the place. The only male culture vulture I ever encountered was a young Glasgow taxi driver. I was idly whistling Boccherini's well-known minuet (the one used in *The Ladykillers* and the Cushionflor advertisement) in the back of his cab when he identified it and went on to tell me that because he liked (he actually said *loved*) classical music he had been beaten up by his father and brothers for being a poof (his word, and he wasn't). It was recently discovered that classical music, especially Mozart, when played over the Tannoy in shopping precincts and the like, repels youthful loiterers, vandals and hooligans to such a degree that they avoid such places. We should not forget that there are those in the other, so-called excluded, classes who would also like high culture to be as inaccessible as possible, only to themselves. To them too it is a badge of status, but a status which they would rather die than claim.

There seems no reason to share Bourdieu's blanket scepticism about high culture. Some people may flaunt or counterfeit a taste for it, but that does not mean that all do, or that its sole purpose is display, or that it has a purpose at all, that is, is a means to some ulterior end, rather than being an end in itself. If high culture's scarcity were part of its value, then surely no one possessing it would wish to see it more widely diffused, or be at pains to impart it—often informally and without reward—to as many as show

---

[17] Nietzsche, *Untimely Meditations*, I, 2.

themselves receptive. There is an interesting historic contrast here with vocational skills, which the professions, the guilds and the trade unions have always sought, through controlling entry, to keep as scarce as possible, though admittedly as often to keep up standards as to keep up pay. With liberal education, pay (appropriately) has never been an issue, having always been understood as little more than the means to a barely respectable subsistence. The only limits to recruitment here are natural ones: the availability of suitably qualified teachers and of sufficiently adept students.

In sum, why should we not accept the essential disinterestedness, intrinsic value or 'in-itselfness' of high culture, and come to that, the disinterestedness of much popular culture too? Why should we not believe Bourdieu's intellectual informant, who said 'You go to the theatre to see the play, not to show off your wardrobe' (or, he implied, to show off anything else, or to benefit in any other fashion than simply by 'seeing the play')?[18] Disinterestedness, according to Kant, is the defining characteristic of contemplation, the pure aesthetic apprehension of an object, purged of all appetitive or self-regarding elements. It is the foundation of Kant's aesthetics, and Bourdieu's chief implicit target (which is finally made explicit in his Postscript). But it is too easy a target, which means that Kant is wrong, or no more than half-right. There are different sorts of disinterestedness, and to embrace or to eschew one is not necessarily to do the same to the other (or others). If genuine disinterestedness signified nothing more than Kant's thin, pure, contemplative vision—which, like his ethics, must by

---

[18] In his *The Ideology of the Aesthetic* (Oxford: Blackwell, 1990), Terry Eagleton suggests, Bourdieu-fashion, that the supposed intrinsic value of aesthetic experience, high culture, etc., to one who finds such things valuable is precisely their instrumental value in advertising to himself and others that he is socio-economically *able to afford* disinterestedness. But reasoning this tortuous (exemplifying Ricoeur's 'hermeneutics of suspicion', whereby nothing can ever be what it appears to be, let alone innocent) either leads to the madhouse, or, as here, itself invites suspicion, in that it too clearly has an instrumental value for its author (that is, both advertises his perspicacity and serves his prior agenda), and is thus far from disinterested (*tu quoque*, in short). See my 'Fetishizing the Unseen', on Marxism as itself a specimen of 'false consciousness', in Robert Grant, *Imagined Meanings: Essays on Politics, Ideology and Literature* (Basingstoke: Palgrave, 2003), 100–102.

definition exclude pleasure,[19] partiality and sympathy, those normal components of our response at least to representational art—then it could be dismissed, leaving Bourdieu to claim, as he does, that everything else can only be disguised self-interest. But disinterestedness covers more than that. We take pleasure in the good (or in good people), we are partial to and sympathize with it (or them), and so we should. But our deriving a benefit (pleasure, satisfaction) from doing so is not necessarily the reason why we do, any more than the supposed or even real social advantages conferred by high culture or a liberal education are the reason we pursue them.[20]

[19] Although Kant actually says that aesthetic judgment *does* involve 'pleasure', that this is pleasure only in a highly abstract, formalist and attenuated sense (a kind of rational satisfaction) can be seen from the following, from *The Critique of Judgment*, I, §§12–13:

'The consciousness of mere formal finality in the play of the cognitive faculties of the Subject attending a representation whereby an object is given, is the pleasure itself, because it involves a determining ground of the Subject's activity in respect of the quickening of its cognitive powers ....This pleasure is also in no way practical, neither resembling that from the pathological ground of agreeableness nor that from the intellectual ground of the represented good ...'

'Every interest vitiates the judgment of taste and robs it of its impartiality. This is especially so where instead of, like the interest of reason, making finality take the lead of the feeling of pleasure, it grounds it upon this feeling ....Taste that requires an added element of *charm* and *emotion* for its delight, not to speak of adopting this as the measure of its approval, has not yet emerged from barbarism ...'

'A judgment of taste which is uninfluenced by charm or emotion (though these may be associated with the delight in the beautiful), and whose determining ground, therefore, is simply finality of form, is a *pure judgment of taste.*' (Kant, op. cit., tr. J.C. Meredith [Oxford: Clarendon Press, 1952], 64–5).

It is not obvious how the Subject's pleasure in 'the quickening of its cognitive powers' in the act of aesthetic judgment is necessarily any more 'disinterested' or less 'pathological' than the pleasures afforded by 'charm' and 'emotion'.

[20] In Britain, at the time of writing, it seems that high culture and liberal education, or the outward appearance of them, are actually socially disadvantageous, being perceived, at least in 'official' spheres, as too 'posh'. To exaggerate only slightly, the only way a young person who (say) uses Received Pronunciation is nowadays likely to gain employment as a TV news reporter is by being black or brown, his supposed 'ethnic' disadvantage evidently being deemed to outweigh or atone for his 'poshness'.

Robert Grant

All those things we do for their own sake, as can be seen from the fact that we continue to do them even when they entail heavy political *dis*advantage, as was the case in Eastern Europe under Communism. There, although for reasons of national display musical performance (say) was cultivated assiduously enough, high culture in its creative aspect, and all genuine liberal education, were confined to the unofficial or even underground spheres, attracting severe penalties if discovered, and all this despite the provision of *ersatz* official versions of each. Here there was both a total divorce between culture and power (which made the power even more illegitimate than its origins had made it), and a notable continuity of high and common culture (which was also repressed). So much for the Marxist analysis, according to which culture is in the hands of the dominant class and is used by it to legitimize its rule. But culture cannot be 'used' in this way without degenerating into propaganda and kitsch. Only when it is autonomous can it confer legitimacy, or withhold it, as the real culture did.

Bourdieu is most plausible in his account of specifically Modernist culture; as I have said, one of his major witnesses is Ortega y Gasset. In his brilliant essay 'The Dehumanization of Art' (1925), Ortega explains the new radical Modernist aesthetic as a reaction to nineteenth century realism and sentimentalism, which he sees as foreshadowing the dominance of the democratic masses, so that the Modernists' formalism, anti-humanism and quasi-abstract aestheticism are really a kind of aristocratizing dissent, a means, Ortega explicitly says, whereby the illustrious can recognize each other and collectively distinguish themselves from the vulgar.[21] No one will deny that some remarkable works did in fact come out of this movement, but all the same it sounds exactly like the jockeying for position (together with that position's further legitimizing function) that according to Bourdieu underlies all cultural differences. And here is the moment to note that Bourdieu's structuralist ancestry leads him to concentrate on formal differences alone—that is, precisely *distinctions*—and entirely to ignore the actual substance or content of the cultural phenomena he deals with. In principle, if the function of cultural differences is simply to act as status indicators (and all that follows

---

[21] 'The new art ... helps the élite to recognize themselves and one another in the drab mass of society and to learn their mission which consists in being few and holding their own against the many.' José Ortega y Gasset, *The Dehumanization of Art and Other Essays on Art, Culture and Literature* (Princeton: Princeton UP, 1968), 7.

politically from that), it hardly matters what they are so long as they are visible. Why, from the purely functional standpoint, should high-cultural artefacts not actually be uglier and even stupider, that is, *worse*, than those of a supposedly 'lower' kind?

Of course, some Modernists, notably certain Expressionists, have actively cultivated ugliness,[22] and in any case it has always been an important weapon in the satirist's armoury. But in general, if the point of the high-cultural aesthetic is to legitimize the dominance of the class which embraces it, then it needs to have some at least superficial appeal to the dominated classes, since it is they whom works exemplifying it are meant to impress. At the same time, it must not too closely resemble the kind of things the dominated classes like and produce for themselves, or have produced for them, because then the difference is lost. What I am suggesting is that *if* Bourdieu is right about the legitimizing function of high culture—concerning which I remain agnostic—then, in order to exercise this function, it has to be recognizably *good*, independently of its function, that is, of the political uses to which, allegedly, it may also be put. In short, its value must be genuine, not merely class-determined. It must be exactly what its defenders claim it is, a good and an end in itself; one, moreover, capable of eliciting some degree of positive acknowledgment from a substantial number of those who for one reason or another remain outside it.[23] And the

---

[22] Deliberate ugliness, notably in architecture (e.g. that of the Brutalist movement), is an act of symbolic coercion. It is an assertion of *power* and *will*, not of *legitimacy*; intended not to flatter, seduce, or secure spontaneous consent, but to threaten. And it is not so much a *political* phenomenon (in the sense previously employed here), as the collective self-expression of a politically unaccountable bureaucratic and/or corporate élite. Here, as so often throughout history, the artist puts himself willingly into the service of despotism, because his masters give him a freer hand than the public would. (So long, that is, as he does not abuse his freedom by producing things that the public might actually *like*.)

[23] Unlike his surly brother Fafner, the giant Fasolt in *Das Rheingold* is moved by the goddess Freia's youthful beauty, and genuinely appreciates the gods' world of aesthetic delight which he and Freia jointly sustain, by their physical labour and immortality-conferring apples respectively. In part-contrast, the demigod Loge sarcastically consoles the Rhinemaidens for the loss of their gold—his sarcasm being aimed not at them, but at the gods—by telling them to rejoice vicariously instead in the splendour of the gods' new fortress Valhalla, whose construction (by the giants) the gold has paid for. One need not be Marxist to agree with G.B. Shaw's view that the giants, at least in part, 'represent' the working class and the gods the

same of course goes for liberal education, through which high culture is largely mediated. Might one not invert Bowles and Gintis and say that maybe *class* is a means by which *education* perpetuates itself? Liberal education is not the ideology of the bourgeois, but, like high culture, an independent good. The relation between those things and class is probably no more than this: one characteristic of the so-called bourgeois class is that more of its members recognize them as being intrinsically valuable, and therefore respect them and try to secure as much of them as they can. If doing so *also* confers wealth, power and status—which is doubtful, since a lack of culture seems to confer even more of those worldly advantages—then so be it. The side-effects of an activity are not to be confused with its goal. Nobody would claim that people pursued liberal education and high culture under the Communists *in order to* get themselves persecuted.

I come finally to the role of high culture in relation specifically to government, and particularly to that of the contemporary avant-garde. Arnold saw culture (that is, high culture) as 'the best that has been known and thought in the world'. At the same time, he saw the State, at least ideally, as the embodiment of the national 'best self'. One might say he saw the State as being in some way 'above' politics, like a constitutional monarchy or a non-executive presidency. But he is under no illusions about government. Unlike Plato, he does not think that 'the best' should rule, because he thinks that the urgencies of day-to-day politics, the inevitable fudges and compromises, and the mechanics of acquiring and retaining power, have an intellectually and morally coarsening effect, as they undoubtedly do. Culture's role, without being subversive, is essentially critical. The more like 'the best' it looks—and the easiest way to look like 'the best' is to be it—the greater will be its prestige, and the more politicians and governments will seek its implicit approval and feel themselves constrained by its example. If social esteem attaches to it, then that is a good thing, because it only increases the politicians' incentive not to lapse too far from its standards, that is, not to look Philistine. I am reminded of George Orwell's unexpected defence of

---

bourgeoisie. At all events, the point is that aesthetic value does not have to be narrowly class-bound or relativistic, and that if it were, it could not function as Bourdieu claims it does. (Which is not necessarily to agree with Bourdieu that it does so function.)

snobbery, which he says has been much underrated as a control upon certain kinds of undesirable behaviour.[24]

All that sounds utterly utopian, now that tabloid editors no longer seek admission, as they once did, to the best clubs, but instead actively flaunt their yobbish credentials, while ministers of the Crown suck up to loutish footballers and pop musicians, only to get roundly and deservedly insulted for their pains. (They have not understood the point of yob culture, which is to set itself up in opposition to all authority except its own, a fact which makes courting its approval pointless.) But what of the official endorsement given to the contemporary avant-garde, which, if only structurally, may be thought to fall into the high-cultural category?

The examples I have already given of contemporary avant-gardism, 'director's opera' and the Victoria and Albert extension, are not necessarily typical of it. Avant-gardists such as Boulez and Schnittke, whatever you think of them, are undoubtedly serious artists, and they have their British counterparts. Our governments may bestow knighthoods on Peter Maxwell Davies and Harrison Birtwistle, but I have not detected any attempt yet to appropriate them for political purposes. And needless to say, governments have no time for traditional high culture, which is perceived as élitist, though its products in fact enjoy a far wider audience than the avant-garde's. The avant-garde with which governments across Europe seek to ingratiate themselves is not the serious avant-garde, but the 'trangressive', publicity-seeking kind whose criterion of artistic excellence or validity is a work's capacity to *épater le bourgeois*, though of course this easily-shocked personage is a pure fantasy-figure, invented almost entirely for the purpose of making the artist look 'daring'. This is why architecture is so often the chosen medium for shocking the public, since it is by its nature a public art. Despite his costly education at two highly élite institutions, our Prime Minister shows no signs of ever having read a serious book, listened to a serious piece of music, or looked at a serious picture; nor of ever intending to do those things once he has the leisure. That in itself is no crime, or if it is his immediate predecessors were also guilty of it. But at least they did not think it added to their government's lustre to cultivate the young lions of BritArt, whose works show no evidence of artistic skill, and whose sole *raison d'être*, like that of yob culture, appears to lie in gestures

---

[24] 'Snobbishness, like hypocrisy, is a check upon behaviour whose value from a social point of view has been underrated', ('Raffles and Miss Blandish', 1944, final sentence).

of repudiation. No government ever increased its authority by identifying itself with, or seeking the approval of, the enemies of all authority. All that does is bring government further into disrepute, which is a bad thing, both for government and for its subjects.

Here is my advice to all democratic governments. It is of course utterly useless, maximally unlikely to be heeded, and itself a gesture of repudiation. But all is not lost if it strikes a chord in your memory:

> Whatsoever things are true, whatsoever things are honest, whatsoever things are just, whatsoever things are pure, whatsoever things are lovely, whatsoever things are of good report; if there be any virtue, and if there be any praise, think on these things.[25]

And here is some superfluous advice for the aspiring young British artist: if there be any money on offer, and if there be any notoriety to be gained, think first on these same things, and then spit on them.

[25] Philippians 4, 8 (Authorized Version).

Edmund Burke and the Anglo-American Tradition of Liberty

JOÃO CARLOS ESPADA

It is proper for more reasons than the most obvious one that I should open this talk by quoting a former President of the Royal Institute of Philosophy, Lord Quinton, whose works on political philosophy I have so much enjoyed—and learnt from.

In a chapter on political philosophy, which he contributed to the *Oxford History of Western Philosophy*, Lord Quinton says that 'the effect of the importation of Locke's doctrines in to France was much like that of alcohol in an empty stomach '.[1] In Britain, Lord Quinton adds, Locke's principles 'served to endorse a largely conservative revolution against absolutist innovation',[2] whereas in France the importation of Locke's ideas would lead to the radicalism of the French revolution. Why was this so?

I think this is a tremendously important question which has captured the imagination of several generations of Anglophiles in Europe. In this talk today I do not pretend to have an answer to this extremely important and intricate question—and one may wonder whether there is a single answer to this question. All I would like to do is to suggest a possible ingredient for a possible answer to the question. And I would like to suggest, furthermore, that perhaps the ingredient I am going to suggest and certainly the question posed by Lord Quinton are still relevant today.

My suggestion may be described as follows: Locke's principles 'served to endorse a largely conservative revolution in Britain' because they were combined with a tradition of **limited Government** which existed before Locke and which does not have to be deduced from Locke's first philosophical principles—or, for that matter, from any other particular first philosophical principles. This means, on the other hand, that the tradition of limited government may be compatible with several—but certainly not all—particular first philosophical principles. And this has tremendous consequences, as I shall try to show later.

[1] A. Quinton, 'Political Philosophy', *The Oxford Illustrated History of Western Philosophy*, Anthony Kenny (ed.) (Oxford: Oxford University Press, 1994), 327.
[2] Op. cit. note 1, 327.

For the moment I would like to suggest further that there is a British author who in my view has expressed better than any other this possibility—that is, the possibility of defending **limited government** without deducing it from first philosophical principles. And this author is Edmund Burke.

I

We all know that Edmund Burke never wanted to accept the interference of abstract modes of thought into politics—with good reasons, I think. We all know, furthermore, that he condemned in particular the idea that the duties of individuals can be exclusively or even mainly based on their will or consent. 'Duties are not voluntary', he wrote in *An Appeal from the New to the Old Whigs.* 'Duty and will', he added, 'are even contradictory terms (...) We have obligations to mankind at large, which are not in consequence of any special voluntary pact (...) On the contrary, the force of all the pacts which we enter into with any particular person or number of persons amongst mankind depends upon those prior obligations'.[3]

This view—which could hardly be described as Lockean—does not seem to be distinctive of Burke. As Professor O'Hear recalls in his book *After progress: The old Way Forward,* this view may be found, at first sight, in several, probably all, counter-revolutionary authors in continental Europe. But I would like to argue, as Professor O'Hear has also pointed out in *After Progress,* that what is distinctive of Burke is that he—unlike continental counter-revolutionaries—does not proceed to define the source of duty in Government, or even in an alliance of Church and State, or, in short, in any strictly defined political realm. Professor O'Hear goes as far as saying that Burke was himself a sort of democrat, and I shall come back to agree with his point later on. For the time being I would like to stress that Burke saw the emergence of duty from a very special sort of contract which we could perhaps describe as tacit in any civil order, in the spontaneous dealings between individuals—always rooted in their own ways of life—and between generations.

[3] E. Burke, 'Appeal from the New to the Old Whigs', *The Works of the Right Honorable Edmund Burke,* IV (Boston: Little, Brown and Company, 1866), 165–166.

Edmund Burke and the Anglo-American Tradition of Liberty

It is certainly true that Burke saw the state as playing a crucial role in this compact, but it is a great mistake, I think it is a 'great continental mistake', to infer from this that Burke's view of political arrangements is in any way similar to the views of continental counter-revolutionaries or even conservatives. Let us recall that famous passage from the *Reflections on Revolution in France*:

> Society is indeed a contract. Subordinate contracts for objects of mere occasional interest may be dissolved at pleasure; but the state ought not to be considered as nothing better than a partnership agreement in a trade of pepper and coffee, calico or tobacco, or some other such low concern, to be taken up for a little temporary interest, and to be dissolved by the fancy of the parties. It is to be looked on with other reverence; because it is not a partnership in things subservient only to the gross animal existence of a temporary and perishable nature. It is a partnership in all science, a partnership in all art, a partnership in every virtue and in all perfection. As the end of such a partnership cannot be obtained in many generations, it becomes a partnership not only between those who are living, but between those who are living, those who are dead, and those who are to be born. Each contract of each particular state is but a clause in the great primeval contract of eternal society, linking the lower with the higher natures connecting the visible and invisible world, according to a fixed compact sanctioned by the invisible oath which holds all physical and all moral natures each in their appointed place.[4]

What is this mysterious 'primeval contract of eternal society' that Burke is talking about? I would like to approach this question in three steps. First, I would like to show that this contract is not made by political design and that government itself, or politics, are bound and limited by this very primeval contract. Second, I shall emphasise that this limited government is a friend of the free market, to use this slightly misleading modern expression. My third step will consist of recalling that, for Burke, limited government is best limited when it is accountable to its subjects—and, in this sense, Burke can be seen as a democrat of

---

[4] E. Burke, 'Reflections on the Revolution in France', *The Works of the Right Honorable Edmund Burke,* III (Boston: Little, Brown, and Company, 1866), 359.

sorts, as Professor O'Hear pointed out. Then, I shall finally suggest what in my view Burke meant when he talked about the primeval contract.

Let me then, first, recall that Burke saw every attempt of government, or every political attempt, to redesign spontaneous arrangements in order to make them conform to an abstract vision—he saw this always as **an abuse of power**. In the letter to the sheriffs of Bristol, he wrote:

> I was persuaded that government was a practical thing made for the happiness of mankind and not to furnish out a *spectacle of uniformity to gratify the schemes of visionary politicians*. Our business was *to rule, not to wrangle.* [5] (Emphasis added.)

And he added in the same letter:

> As the *Sabbath* (though of divine institution) was made for man and not man for the *Sabbath*, government, in its exercise at least, ought to conform to the exigencies of the time, and the temper and the character of the people with whom it is concerned, and not always to attempt to bend the people to their theories of subjection.[6]

When Burke denounced the behaviour of the East India Company and of Warren Hastings he often paid tribute to India's old civilization:

> India is inhabited by a people for ages civilized and cultivated, cultivated by all the arts of polished life, whilst we were yet in the woods ... It has its own princes, an ancient and venerable priesthood, the depository of their laws, learning and history, the guides of the people whilst living, and their consolation in death, as well as a nobility of great antiquity and renown. (This civilisation is being devastated by British) young men—boys almost—animated by all the avarice of age, and all the impetuosity of youth.[7]

---

[5] E. Burke, 'Letter to the Sheriffs of Bristol', *The Works of the Right Honorable Edmund Burke,* II (Boston: Little, Brown and Company, 1865), 227.

[6] Op. cit. note 5, 230.

[7] E. Burke, 'Speech on Fox's India Bill', *The Writings and Speeches of Edmund Burke* V, *India Madras and Bengal, 1774–1785,* P. J. Marshall (ed.) (Oxford, 1981), 402. Quoted by J. Muller, *The Mind and the Market* (New York: Alfred A. Knopf, 2002), 126.

Edmund Burke and the Anglo-American Tradition of Liberty

Keeping the power of politics and government in due limits was always a first concern of Burke's and these limits were always, in his view, related to a certain respect for the spontaneous arrangements of particular traditions. In a curious letter to Sir Hercules Langrishe, Burke explained that there is a difference between absolute slavery and a degraded state of citizenship, where an hereditary nobility possess the exclusive rule. The latter, he explained, 'may be no bad mode of government (for those countries not blessed by British mixed government)—provided that the personal authority of individual nobles be kept in *due bounds* (...) and that the people are subjected to but *light impositions*, and are otherwise treated with attention, and *with indulgence to their humors and prejudices*'.[8] (Emphasis added.)

It was of course the indignation against unlimited political power that led Burke to attack the French revolution.

> He cannot admire the change of one piece of barbarism for another, and a worse. He cannot rejoice at the destruction of a monarchy, mitigated by manners, respectful to laws and usages, and attentive, perhaps but too attentive, to public opinion, in favour of the tyranny of a licencious, ferocious, and savage multitude without laws, manners or morals, and which, so far from respecting the general sense of mankind, insolently endeavours to alter all the principles and opinions which have hitherto guided and contained the world, and to force them into a conformity to their views and actions.[9]

This, I think, may suffice to recall that Burke has endorsed a certain type of government—I would like to call it limited government—without deducing it from Lockean first principles.

Let me now briefly recall my second point about Burke. This is that Burke's view of government was friendly towards what is now called the free market. To put it differently, Burke's limited government was very similar—in its main economic functions—to that of Locke's and was certainly very congenial to the views of Burke's friend, Adam Smith.

> But the clearest line of distinction which I could draw, whilst I had my chalk to draw any line, was this: That the state ought to confine itself to what regards the state or the creatures of the

---

[8] E. Burke, 'Letter to Sir Hercules Langrishe', *The Works of the Right Honorable Edmund Burke*, IV (Boston: Little, Brown and Company, 1866), 249.
[9] Op. cit. note 3, 78.

state: namely, the exterior establishment of its religion; its magistracy; its revenue; its military force by sea and land; the corporations that owe their existence to its fiat, in a word to everything that is *truly and properly* public, to the public peace, to the public safety, to the public order, to the public prosperity. In its preventive police it ought to be sparing of its efforts, and to employ means, rather few, unfrequent, and strong than many, and frequent, and, of course, as they multiply their puny politic race, and dwindle, small and feeble (...) My opinion is against an overdoing of any sort of administration, and more especially against this most momentous of all meddling on the part of authority, the meddling with the subsistence of the people.[10]

It is perhaps relevant to our discussion to recall that Burke's defence of the free market is seldom referred to in the continent and I would dare say it is hardly known at all. Unfortunately this has not changed significantly after the recent publication of a brilliant and short presentation of Burke's economic views by my American friend, Professor Jerry Muller, in his book *The Mind and the Market: Capitalism in Modern European Thought.* In the chapter on Burke—a real *tour de force*, I would say—Jerry Muller recalls that Burke's commitment to free trade with Ireland made him lose his parliamentary seat for Bristol. In his 'Tract on the Popery Laws', from the early 1760's, and his 'Thoughts and Details on Scarcity', written at the end of his life, in 1794, Burke argued strongly in favour of free markets for prices and wages. And Jerry Muller goes on to assert that Burke's crusade against the East India Company was based on Burke's view that the EIC 'used its military power to prevent the operation of a free market in India'.[11]

> The intrinsic flaw with the EIC of his day, as Burke saw it, was not that it was a commercial company driven by the profit motive, but that it was not a commercial company in the ordinary sense: profit was not the motivating force of the company's activities ... The EIC was impoverishing India while moving towards bankruptcy—a phenomenon hard to reconcile with the profit motive ... The problem with the East India Company, Burke believed, was that while it was nominally a commercial

---

[10] E. Burke, 'Thoughts and Details on Scarcity', *The Works of the Right Honorable Edmund Burke,* V (Boston: Little, Brown and Company, 1866), 166–167, 169.

[11] J. Muller, *The Mind and the Market* (New York: Alfred A. Knopf, 2002), 122.

company, it did not operate as a profit-making enterprise according to the laws of supply and demand ....The relations between Britain and India were not those of commerce, but of extraction based on the use of force, carried out by a nominally commercial corporation. The Indian goods that flowed into Britain, Burke showed, were not acquired through market transactions ... The EIC, in other words, was in Burke's analysis managed as vehicle for tribute. 'The main Spring of the Commercial Machine, the Principles of Profit and Loss' had been abandoned. The merchants and artisans of India were being devastated by the company's monopoly over commodities, its fixing of prices, and its use of forced labour in the textile industry.[12]

This, I think, is a powerful description of Burke's defence of free markets and free enterprise as the main tools of economic growth. Also in a recent book, another American friend of mine, the distinguished historian Professor Gertrude Himmelfarb, recalled the affinity between Burke and Adam Smith's views on economics. Burke's speech on 'Economic Reformation', Professor Himmelfarb recalls, was delivered in 1780, four years after the publication of Smith's *Wealth of Nations*:

Above all, there was the classical Smithian principle, reformulated by Burke, that commerce flourishes best when left to itself and that 'all regulations are, in their nature, restrictive of some liberty'. Fifteen years later, Burke invoked the same principle in arguing against a bill to regulate wages (in his pamphlet *Thoughts and Details on Scarcity*) ... Echoing Smith's 'invisible hand', Burke paid homage to 'the benign and wise disposer of all things, who obliges men, whether they will or not, in pursuing their own selfish interests, to connect the general good with their own individual success'.[13]

Finally, I would like to recall that Burke was a friend of representative government and, in this political sense, of government by consent. He certainly was against the so called sovereignty of the people, because he perceived it as a threat to limited government. But I would like to emphasise that, for Burke, the most secure form of limited government was government accountable to the people. Nowhere is this more clear than in his

[12] Op. cit. note 11, 121–122.
[13] G. Himmelfarb, *The Roads to Modernity* (New York: Alfred A. Knopf, 2004), 73–74.

critique of royal favouritism which he brilliantly developed in his *Thoughts on the Cause of the Present Discontents,* published in 1770. This is considered to be Burke's first great political pamphlet and also the first systematic defence of what would become modern parliamentary political parties.

This pamphlet should be read in association with the one Burke had published in the previous year, 1769, defending the Rockingham Whigs against the attacks from George Grenville. In this paper, *Observations on 'The Present State of the Nation'* Burke criticizes the inflexibility of London towards the American colonies and explains this inflexibility by two related factors: a propensity to design visionary politics based on abstract reasoning, and, second, government's lack of accountability to elected Members of Parliament.

These two ideas—lack of accountability fostering a visionary spirit of innovation—are brilliantly developed in his 1770 *Thoughts on the Cause of the Present Discontents.* Burke criticised what he called the system of 'double cabinet', or royal favouritism. He argued that the King was actually ruling the country with his personal courtiers, behind the scenes of a Parliamentary government which had only nominal power. The real problem of this system of 'double cabinet', Burke maintained, was that ministers appointed by the Crown, without direct accountability to Parliament and its constituents, were far more inclined to adopt abstract reasoning in politics and far more inclined to adopt a spirit of innovation.

> It is the nature of despotism to abhor power held by any means but its own momentary pleasure; and to annihilate all intermediate situations between boundless strength on its own part, and total debility on the part of the people. To get rid of all this intermediate and independent importance, and *to secure to the court the unlimited and uncontrolled use of its own vast influence, under the sole direction of its own private favour, has for some years past been the great object of policy* ... A scheme of perfection to be realized in a monarchy far beyond the visionary republic of Plato.[14] (Burke's emphasis.)

This means that, for Burke, accountability to the people is to be understood as an instrument to limit government and not to make it

---

[14] E. Burke, 'Thoughts on the Cause of the Present Discontents', *The Works of the Right Honorable Edmund Burke, I* (Boston: Little, Brown and Company, 1865), 446, 454.

absolute. This also means that, for Burke, accountability to the people is an instrument to limit the tendency of unaccountable government to draw visionary schemes of perfection and to get rid of intermediate balances of power: checks and balances, as the Americans would say. And it is extremely interesting to note that the American Federalist Papers deal with the same problem in a very similar Burkean way—even though their Burkean ways had been Americanised, that is to say, made more egalitarian and more democratic, but not less attached to limited government and checks and balances. This continuity of thought is particularly evident in the famous passage of Federalist No. 51:

> If men were angels, no government would be necessary. If angels were to govern men, neither external nor internal controls on government would be necessary. In framing a government which is to be administered by men over men, the great difficulty lies in this: you must first enable the government to control the governed; and in the next place oblige it to control itself. A dependence on the people is, no doubt, the primary control on the government; but experience has taught mankind the necessity of auxiliary precautions.[15] (320)

As we shall see, it was the absence of this view of limited government that led the importation of Locke's ideas into the European continent to produce the effect of alcohol in an empty stomach.

II

Let me now briefly contrast Burke with the European continent. To cut a long story short, I shall recall a very helpful observation by the late American sociologist, Professor Robert Nisbet. He said that:

> Modern philosophies of freedom have tended to emphasise either the individual's *release* from power of every kind— generally, through an appeal to natural rights—or the individual's *participation* in some single structure of authority like the General Will, which replaces all other structures.

[15] J. Madison. 'Federalist No. 51', A. Hamilton, J. Madison, J. Jay, *The Federalist Papers* (New York: Mentor Books, 1961), 322.

But from the point of view of the real, the historical roots of liberal democracy, freedom has rested neither upon release nor upon collectivization but upon the *diversification* and the decentralization of power in society. In the division of authority and the multiplication of its sources lie the most enduring conditions of freedom.[16]

Professor Nisbet was giving us three different ways of looking at liberty: as a release of individuals from power, as participation of individuals in some unitary structure of authority, or, thirdly, as decentralisation of power. I think it has become clear by now that I am suggesting that Burke's view corresponded to what Robert Nisbet called decentralization. And my argument consists of saying that Locke's ideas in the continent tended always to be understood either in the first sense (release from power), or in the second (participation in power), and almost never in the third (decentralisation of power). For this reason, Locke's ideas in the continent were never strongly combined with the idea of limited government.

This is particularly easy to describe in the case of liberty as participation, whose main promoter in the European continent was Jean-Jacques Rousseau. He certainly was opposed to Locke's ideas in several crucial ways, but he certainly was one of the greatest promoters of the idea of the Social Contract in Europe. In this sense, he can be described as a translator—a bad translator—of Locke's contractualist vision in Europe. And his translation was probably one of the most powerful forces behind despotic revolutionary government in modern Europe. In his book, *The Social Contract*, Rousseau said:

Now, as the sovereign is formed entirely of the individuals who compose it, it has not, nor could it have, any interest contrary to theirs; and so the sovereign has no need to give guarantees to the subject because it is impossible for a body to wish to hurt all of its members, and, as we shall see, it cannot hurt any particular member. The sovereign by the mere fact that it is, is always all that it ought to be.[17]

One could hardly find a clearer vision of a despotic, unlimited, unitary power which must control every particular subject and get rid of every particular intermediate institution. One could hardly

---

[16] R. Nisbet, 'The Contexts of Democracy', *The March of Freedom*, E. J. Feulner Jr. (ed.) (Washington D.C. : Heritage Books, 2003), 223.

[17] J-J. Rousseau, *The Social Contract* (London: Penguin Classics, 1968), 63.

find a better vision of unlimited government over the people and in the name of the people. As we have seen, this view of popular government is entirely the opposite of Burke's view of accountable government as a means to reinforce limited government. And needless to say, Rousseau's view of popular government is entirely the opposite of 'the republican remedies for the diseases most incident in republican government' that the American Federalist Papers tried—and, in my view, managed—to achieve.

But Rousseau was not a direct translator of Locke in Europe—even though he may have been the most powerful translator of the idea of the social contract in the continent. Locke's greatest admirer in the continent was Voltaire and his friends of *l' Encyclopédie*. For the authors of *l'Encyclopédie*, perhaps the most enthusiast (mis)readers of Locke, limited and accountable government is replaced by Enlightened government—which must be unlimited so that it can spread the lights, *les lumières*.

Several liberal anglophiles—such as Isaiah Berlin—have captured this authoritarian vein of the French champions of liberty, but with no great success. Voltaire, Diderot and their fellow *philosophes* are still perceived in the continent as the champions of liberty. My friend Gertrude Himmelfarb has just produced a new devastating account of the French Enlightenment and showed how its commitment to liberty was mainly rethorical. I wish she could have more success in Europe than the previous critics of the French Enlightenment. This is not very likely, though, namely because on the relationship between the French Enlightenment and liberty, she said:

> The idea of liberty, however, although often invoked, did not elicit anything like the passion or commitment that reason did. Nor did it inspire the *philosophes* to engage in a systematic analysis of the political and social institutions that would promote and protect liberty.[18]

Their passion for reason led the *philosophes* to endorse what they called 'enlightened despotism', this being an attempt to realise reason in the person of the enlightened monarch. Himmelfarb recalls that, after having praised Frederick of Prussia and having lived at his court, Voltaire defended Catherine of Russia because she did not accept intermediate institutions: 'Her government', he said, 'seeks to destroy anarchy, the odious prerogatives of the

---

[18] Op. cit. note 13, 158–159.

nobles, the power of the magnats, and not to establish intermediate bodies or to diminish its authority.'[19]

For the philosophers, this enlightened power is not oppressive, but the true source of liberation. It liberates precisely from what Burke described as 'the humours and prejudices' of the people and which, according to Burke, should always deserve 'light impositions', as well as 'attention and indulgence' from governments. For the *philosophes*, on the contrary, these humours and prejudices are their main enemy. They perceive them as lack of reason. And therefore they welcome and encourage the despotism of reason in order to liberate people from the yoke of their own humours and prejudices. Mercier de la Rivière explained this view with great clarity:

> Euclid is the true type of despot. The geometrical axioms which he has transmitted to us are genuine despotic laws; in them the legal and the personal despotism of the legislator are one and the same thing, a force evident and irresistible; and for that reason the despot Euclid has for centuries exercised his unchallenged sway over all enlightened peoples.[20]

This idea of the legislator as the source of enlightenment is crucial in French thought. In an article on 'The legislator', l' *Encyclopédie* explains that 'in all climates, circumstances, and governments (the legislator) must propose to change private and property interests to community interests. Legislation is more or less perfect, according to what extent it leads to this goal', (164). Getrude Himmelfarb suggests that this view of a unitary legislator which is the infallible interpreter of reason against the particular views of individuals and particular institutions permeates all French thought in the eighteenth century (with the exception of the Anglophiles like Montesquieu). It is so pervasive, she maintains, that it underpinned both the concept of the enlightened despot and of the general will:

> What the enlightened despot was to some of the *philosophes*—the supreme arbiter and legislator—the general will was to others. The concept of the general will has always, and properly so, been identified with Rousseau's *The Social Contract*, published in 1762. But Rousseau himself, seven years earlier, in his article 'Political Economy'... attributed it to Diderot's article 'Natural Law' in the same volume of the *Encyclopédie*. It is curious to find

[19] Op. cit. note 13, 163–164.
[20] Op. cit. note 13, 166.

the two articles on ostensibly different subjects making the same point, in almost the same words, about the subservience of individual wills to the general will.[21]

But Gertrude Himmelfarb extends her critique of Rousseau and the *philosophes* to the physiocrats, who have been perceived as the French counterparts of Adam Smith. In fact, Himmelfarb argues, they were akin basically on the issue of free trade. But the physiocrats had not the least inclination for limited government. She recalls the words of Walter Bagehot, who contrasted the physiocrats with Adam Smith:

> (They were) above all things anxious for a very strong government; they held to the maxim, everything *for* the people—nothing by them; they had a horror of checks and counterpoises and resistances; they wished to do everything by the *fiat* of the sovereign.[22]

'They had a horror of checks and counterpoises', Bagehot said. And indeed yes, this is the crucial point, not only about the physiocrats. Physiocrats, Rousseau, Voltaire and the French *philosophes*, they all (with the exception of Montesquieu and the so-called English school) had a horror of checks and counterpoises. This becomes even more distinctive of French thought if one looks at the enemies of the Enlightenment and of the French revolution—those who, in principle, should be closer to Edmund Burke.

Joseph de Maistre is certainly the author mostly associated with Burke as the best representative of the counter-revolutionary thought in the continent. But his affinity to Burke is, I think, extremely misleading. As Isaiah Berlin has noted, de Maistre, unlike Burke, was obsessed with power, unlimited power:

> What really fascinated Maistre is power. Power, for him, is divine. It is the source of all life, of all action. It is the paramount factor in the development of mankind, and whoever knows how to wield it acquires the right to use it; it is by that token the instrument chosen by God, at that particular moment, to work his mysterious purpose ...

> What then does society rest upon? Society is part of the vale of tears where we cannot understand the sources of things, where

---

[21] Op. cit. note 13, 167.
[22] Op. cit. note 13, 166.

> God governs us in inscrutable ways. It rests upon terror; it rests upon obedience, blind obedience to authority.[23]

This tragic vision leads de Maistre to his most famous contention: that at the center of society lies the executioner.

> Nevertheless all greatness, all power, all social order depends upon the executioner; he is the terror of human society and the tie that holds it together. Take away this incomprehensible force from the world, and at that very moment order is superseded by chaos, thrones fall, society disappears.[24]

Isaiah Berlin recalls that Saint-Simon believed that there was something in common between Maistre and the people whom he most particularly disliked, the followers of Voltaire—indeed, even Voltaire himself. And Sir Isaiah somehow agreed:

> Although they are polar opposites, both Voltaire and Maistre belong to the hard, cold, dry, lucid, tough-minded tradition of French thought. Their ideas may appear strictly to contradict one another, but the quality of mind is often exceedingly similar. Neither is guilty of any degree of softness, or vagueness or self-indulgence, nor do they tolerate these qualities in others. They stand for the dry against the moist; they are implacably opposed to everything which is turbid and misty, romantic, gushing, impressionistic.[25]

These are the words of Sir Isaiah Berlin. I would like to subscribe to them and push a little further. There is something in common not only between De Maistre and Voltaire, but also with Rousseau and, to a lesser extent, the physiocrats: *their total inability to admit the possibility of a social order which is not made by political design.* And, because they cannot admit the possibility of a social order that is not directly managed by political power, they cannot conceive that a society may work best under limited government.

III

Now, that I am reaching the final part of my argument today, I still have two questions to address: what did Burke mean by the

[23] I. Berlin, *Freedom and its Betrayal*, H. Hardy (ed.) (London: Chatto & Windus, 2002) 151, 148.

[24] Op. cit. note 23, 149.

[25] Op. cit. note 23, 150.

'primeval contract of eternal society', and my starting question, which I have borrowed from Lord Quinton, why did the importation of Locke's ideas into the continent produce the effect of alcohol in an empty stomach?

The first question really goes beyond the scope of this paper—it would entail a much more detailed discussion of Burke's thought. I think, however, that several scholars have suggested the answer, namely Lord Quinton in his book *Politics of Imperfection: The religious and secular traditions of conservative thought in England from Hooker to Oakeshott.* Similar views have been provided by Professor Himmelfarb, as well as Professors Friedrich Hayek and Michael Oakeshott.

One brief way of putting it is to quote Lord Quinton's *Politics of Imperfection.* Having identified three main features of English conservatism—traditionalism, organicism and scepticism—Lord Quinton summarises this conservative disposition, as Oakeshott would say—in the following manner:

> Man's moral imperfection, then, implies that he should be part of a society held together by traditional customs and institutions (traditionalism) and that, to the extent that he is a moral being and his society a stable and contented one, he actually is (organicism). His intellectual imperfection implies that such political knowledge as he can get is limited, practical and socially dependent (scepticism), particularly in view of the complexity of the social system (organicism) and, therefore, that politically induced change in society should be continuous and gradual (traditionalism). The two imperfections converge, from different directions, on the first, traditionalist principle, the most important of the three.[26]

This, I think, is an extremely insightful view of English conservatism, of which Burke was such an important exponent. This view has political consequences, which are my main concern today. I have referred to these political consequences under the label **limited government.** Now I draw again on Lord Quinton's *Politics of Imperfection:*

> (Conservatism) has been historically associated with the idea of strong government, a requirement theoretically sustained to some extent by the doctrine of man's moral imperfection. But

[26] A. Quinton, *The Politics of Imperfection* (London & Boston: Faber and Faber, 1978), 18.

strong government is not the same thing as absolutely comprehensive government. The gradualist and sceptical strands in conservatism combine to support an inclination to restrict government to its traditional tasks: the maintenance of legal order within the community and the defence of the community's interests against attack from outside ... (Conservative's) ideal government has to be strong since it has to control a universal impulse; but it is still very limited, it is not charged with the direct control of all the collective activities of the community. Unlike the political theorists of idealism, he neither identifies the state with society, nor absorbs society within the state.[27]

This is a fair description of the type of government Edmund Burke defended throughout his life: limited government. And because he thought that the best way to limit government was to make it accountable to its subjects, he favoured representative government within a mild and mixed regime. In this sense, as Professor O'Hear has pointed out in his *After Progress*, Burke was a democrat of sorts, that is, a democrat who ascribed to democratic politics a limited realm, similar to the limited realm he ascribed to politics. As Professor O'Hear remarked:

We *could* regard democracy as primarily a process of selecting individual rulers within a broader and pre-existing framework of authority and obedience, rather than the source and origin of political allegiance at its most basic level.[28]

Lord Quinton suggested a similar view:

Finally, the conservative is not an absolutist. Suspicious as he is of the political wisdom and moral reliability of every individual, he looks to traditional, established law and custom, a concrete and historical version of Aristotle's impersonal reason, to solve what Popper regards as the fundamental problem of politics: how to prevent bad rulers from doing harm ... The non-absolutist nature of conservatism has been obscured by forgetfulness of the earlier phases of its historical career. Its first opponent was Puritan extremism, the notion that the elect or the inspired congregation, guided by their individual interpretations of the Bible, were uniquely qualified to exercise unlimited political authority. A contrary absolutism, the doctrine of the divine right of kings, was the next position to be resisted, as it

[27] Op. cit. note 26, 20.
[28] A. O'Hear, *After Progress* (London: Bloomsbury, 1999), 41.

was exemplified in various styles by the Stuart kings and their French models and paymasters. It was in that spirit that the political career of Burke began, in opposition to the attempt at personal government of George III; but the full and more lastingly influential development of his thought was excited by the democratic totalitarianism of the French revolutionaries.[29]

I think we can now approach my final question with a certain degree of confidence and I hope my answer has by now gathered some degree of plausibility. Why did the importation of Locke's ideas into the continent produce the effect of alcohol in an empty stomach, whereas in Britain they served to endorse a largely conservative revolution against absolutist innovation?

Because, I would like to submit, Locke's ideas in the continent were re-interpreted as a radical project for the entire redesign of society—politically, socially and morally. They triggered a philosophical discussion about first principles with a view to deduce political schemes from rival first principles.

In Britain and among the English-speaking peoples, on the contrary, Locke's ideas were simply combined with the old English tradition of limited government. Rather than a project for a new society and a new morality, the English revolution of 1688 and, to a lesser extent, the American revolution of 1776 were basically, though not only, a reassertion of the rights of free Englishman to live their lives as they used to live them before—under the common protection of the laws of the land. In other words, what we now call liberal democracy has emerged in the *Anglosphere* as a natural outgrowth of existing, law-abiding and moral-abiding ways of life. For this reason, liberal democracy among the English speaking peoples has been naturally associated with an *ethos* of duty—which, as Burke pointed out, is not and should not be deduced from will. For this reason, too, liberal democracy in the *Anglosphere* has been tremendously stable. And the English-speaking peoples have always been the first to rise in defence of their cherished liberties—their way of life.

In continental Europe, by contrast, the idea of liberty has tended to be understood as an adversarial project: adversarial to all existing ways of life simply because, in a sense, they were already there; because they had not been designed by 'Reason'. This has generated a lasting instability in European politics. This adversarial attitude, combined with a widespread disregard for limited

---

[29] Op. cit. note 26, 21.

government, has led European politics to be recurrently dominated by two absolutist poles: revolutionary liberals and later revolutionary socialists, on the one hand, and counter-revolutionary conservatives, on the other. They both have aimed at using government without limits to push forward their particular, and usually sectarian, agendas. Their clash—the clash between the so-called liberal project and traditional ways of life—has been at the root of the historical weakness of European liberal democracy, when compared with liberal democracy among the English-speaking peoples. This weakness also explains why, differently from the English-speaking peoples, continental Europeans are not usually the first to rise in defence of our liberties when our liberties become at risk.

The Politics of Emotion: Liberalism and Cognitivism

SUSAN JAMES

Liberal political theorists commend a comparatively orderly form of life. It is one in which individuals and groups who care about different things, and live in different ways, nevertheless share an overriding commitment to liberty and toleration, together with an ability to resolve conflicts and disagreements in ways that do not violate these values. Both citizens and states are taken to be capable of negotiating points of contention without resorting to forms of coercion such as abuse, blackmail, brainwashing, intimidation, torture or other types of violence. In explaining what makes such a state of affairs possible, such theorists have tended to present the citizens of liberal polities as more or less rational individuals who are aware of the advantages of a pluralist, yet co-operative way of life, and understand what it takes to maintain them. Liberalism works best, they have suggested, when, and because, individuals understand its benefits, and therefore act broadly in accordance with the norms it prescribes.

Among the things that this approach was traditionally less interested in, or at any rate had less to say about, were the emotional dispositions on which pluralism depends. While arguments designed to persuade individuals of the overriding importance of mutual respect and toleration were proposed and analysed, there was relatively little investigation of the emotions that might bind people to a broadly liberal way of life. Recently, however, a number of theorists have begun to address this topic, and have started to articulate some of the key values of liberalism in more emotionally charged terms. On the one hand, there has been a revival of interest in political relationships with an obvious emotional dimension. This trend gained strength from the work done by feminist philosophers on the place of care within the polity[1], and some of their insights have subsequently been taken up in different contexts. For example, Onora O'Neill's claim that

---

[1] See for example Diemut Bubeck, *Care, Gender and Justice* (Oxford: Oxford University Prress, 1995; Virginia Held, *The Ethics of Care: Personal, Political, and Global* (Oxford University Press, 2005).

individual citizens, and especially journalists, should trust their rulers, is among other things a proposal to cultivate some emotions and minimise others,[2] and the same applies to Avishai Margalit's work on the importance of avoiding humiliation.[3] On the other hand, theorists have increasingly begun to study the role of specific affects in maintaining or undermining political institutions. Fear has been the focus of a great deal of attention,[4] and writers more or less directly indebted to Foucault have studied the disciplinary effects of a range of other affective dispositions. To add a slightly different type of example, Richard Rorty has suggested that the most all-embracing values on which liberalism depends are aversion to cruelty and a determination to alleviate suffering.[5] As Rorty sees the matter, the progress of a liberal way of life depends not just on the institutions of the state itself, but also on individuals or groups within civil society who are able to express the shortcomings of the communities to which they belong in emotionally engaging ways. This capacity is said to rest both on the ability to recognise forms of cruelty or suffering that are largely unacknowledged, and on the ability to awaken compassion, revulsion or indignation in others. For all these writers, then, the openness and harmoniousness of a polity depends on its ability to create circumstances in which particular emotional dispositions are fostered and others avoided, and its success is partly measured in these terms.

One of the strengths of these contributions is that they draw attention to psychological capacities that are often taken for granted when philosophers defend the centrality of political principles such as toleration or equality. To realise a particular standard of equality, for example, a society must be able to implement a range of egalitarian practices; and while this can sometimes be achieved by force, coercion alone is rarely sufficient. Citizens must also endorse the norms around which the practices in question are organised, as well as the conventions and ways of life in which they are expressed, and this is to some extent an emotional matter. They

[2] Onora O'Neill, *A Question of Trust: The BBC Reith Lectures 2002* (Cambridge: Cambridge University Press, 2002).

[3] Avishai Margalit, *The Decent Society* (Oxford: Oxford University Press, 1998).

[4] See for example, Brian Massumi (ed.), *The Politics of Everyday Fear* (University of Minnesota Press, 1993).

[5] Richard Rorty, *Achieving our Country. Leftist Thought in Twentieth-century America* (Cambridge Mass., 1999)

need to feel indignation when the relevant standards are violated, to admire those who go out of their way to uphold them, and to gain satisfaction from abiding by them. Establishing a norm is thus amongst other things a process of inculcating some emotional dispositions and outlawing others. For although such dispositions do not translate directly into action—people do not always act on their emotions, and their actions are in any case determined by a multitude of factors, emotional and otherwise—they nevertheless play a significant role in shaping patterns of action, and thus in creating the order in which political life consists.

While works such as those of Margalit, Honneth or Rorty have the great advantage of making this emotional aspect of politics visible, their concentration on the capacities that are needed to uphold what they identify as the key values of a morally defensible polity involves a substantial element of oversimplification. For all their sensitivity, these writers tend to overlook the fact that liberal democracies do not simply encourage positive emotional responses to a few overarching values by aiming, for example, to create citizens who feel revulsion for practices that are humiliating, and satisfaction in those that embody mutual respect. Rather, they try to get individuals to internalise an enormously complex and shifting web of emotional responses, some of them localised, in the sense of being sensitive to situation and context, and some of them contested. Once we take these considerations into account, the project of analysing the emotional capacities that underpin particular forms of pluralism becomes very much more complicated.

To appreciate the localised character of the emotional responses that might be regarded as appropriate in diverse social contexts, it is helpful to refer to the work of Luc Boltanski, who describes modern polities as divided into what he calls 'cities', each with its own justificatory norms.[6] Because the ranges of emotions that are held to be proper in the family, the market, the media, in universities, and in governmental and religious institutions do not combine into a seamless whole, internalising them is a matter of acquiring a patchwork of capacities, each suited to a different area of life. To inhabit a practice, individuals need to internalise at least some the emotional responses and expectations on which it depends, and those who fail to do so will come up against corresponding forms of coercion and disapproval. For example, a

---

[6]   Luc Boltanski and Laurent Thévenot, *De la justification: les économies de la grandeur* (Paris, 1991).

futures trader who does not gain any satisfaction from making money is likely to be something of a misfit and may ultimately be sacked, while a parent who deeply distrusts all formal education and does nothing to ensure that her children go to school may ultimately have them taken away from her. But because the norms embodied in one 'city' do not always mesh neatly with those at work in another, the emotional responses expected of citizens are extremely diverse. Some of the competitive strategies that excite admiration among futures traders would be viewed with shock and outrage if employed between friends; and forms of support and exchange that arouse feelings of approval in family contexts would be regarded as outrageously corrupt within government. Citizens are required to compartmentalise their feelings and to manage the boundaries between one city and another.

Furthermore, because pluralism licenses difference, and in some cases encourages it, both states and citizens are expected to adapt themselves to emotional conflict. Since competing descriptions of a practice or state of affairs often carry divergent and incompatible implications about the feelings it should arouse, emotional norms form an integral part of political disagreement and struggle. To adapt a case analysed by Elizabeth Spelman, a male-dominated culture may deny women a legitimate claim to express their sense of injury by characterising their anger as tantrums or hysteria, and expecting them to feel the shame or self-denigration that these labels are designed to arouse. One of the ways in which women can respond is to redescribe, and indeed re-experience their situation, in terms that vindicate their indignation by presenting it as defensible, and even admirable.[7] However, this will generate a conflict that is not just about overt behaviour, but also the emotions underlying it. It would be easy to multiply examples of situations where competing emotional norms are defended by the opposing sides in a debate or contest—by the powerful as a means of maintaining their position, by the less powerful as a means of challenging the *status quo*. As well as playing an essential part in the smooth running of a society, emotional dispositions have a vital role in political struggle.

These capacities to keep one's emotions in the right boxes, and to cope with emotional conflict in ways that are not unduly destructive, are commonplace features of society. To some extent,

[7] Elizabeth Spelman, 'Anger and Insubordination', in A. Garry & M. Pearsall, Women, Knowledge & Reality: Explorations in Femimist Philosophy (Boston & London : Unwin Hyman, 1989).

both the localisation of approved emotional norms and their contested character are unavoidable conditions of political life, and citizens everywhere are required to live with them. Nevertheless, the political challenge of finding ways to accommodate strongly contested patterns of feeling is more pressing in some circumstances than in others, and takes a particular form in liberal democracies. There are, I think, at least three reasons for this, all of which deserve to be emphasised.

First, individuals in these societies are expected to live with others whose attitudes or behaviour they find alarming, offensive or abhorrent, and to refrain from expressing their emotions in ways that are at odds with norms of equality and freedom. Except in circumstances where such emotionally-charged forms of behaviour are held to be justified, they must not be violent, discriminatory or abusive; and, regardless of the strength of their feelings, they are expected to exercise what may in some circumstances be a considerable level of emotional self-control. For example, fundamentalist Christians are required to tolerate gays, whose way of life they regard as evil and repellent, without becoming in any way persecutory; and gays are under an obligation to control their anger and frustration at such obstinate ignorance. Equally, feminists must refrain from responding to sexism in ways that are acknowledged to be cruel or oppressive, and non-feminists are required to exercise the same degree of restraint in the face of painful feminist criticism. Because this sort of emotional discipline is a condition of effective cultural pluralism, it possesses particular political significance in contemporary liberal societies.

The second and equally obvious reason is that both capitalism and democracy impose certain emotional strains. Democratic norms require minorities to be able to live peacefully under leaders who may affront their sensibilities, while keeping their opposition to policies for which they feel outrage or contempt within civil bounds. And in market societies, citizens are expected to abide by laws that license great economic and social inequalities, and to contain any feelings of envy, anger or resentment that these may generate. Here again, emotional self-control may be at a premium.

Finally, the importance that broadly liberal societies attach to the values of toleration and autonomy shapes the ways in which this kind of self-control can be achieved. In principle, a society might terrify its diverse constituent groups into co-operating with one another by ferociously punishing anyone who behaved in an intolerant fashion. Fear of punishment, so the Hobbesian argument might go, would prevent citizens from expressing their hatred or fear for one another, and would create an uneasy peace. Viewed from a liberal standpoint, however, this arrangement would not be satisfactory. If part of the aim of political societies is to promote autonomy, citizens must not be straightforwardly coerced into the ways of pluralism, but must take some of the responsibility for living tolerantly upon themselves. If they are to exist in pluralist communities, while being autonomous in the limited sense of managing this without undue coercion, they must themselves be capable of respecting norms of toleration, and of controlling the expression of emotions that run counter to them.

Liberal theorists have tended to take these capacities for granted. It is true that, viewed from one angle, this is perfectly reasonable. There are, after all, societies in which the capacity for emotional restraint on which liberty and pluralism depend, together with the emotional commitments that enable people to inhabit a variety of pluralist practices, are reasonably common. However, viewed from another angle, these purportedly liberal societies are only a limited success. For all their much-vaunted commitment to toleration, they often contain a wide range of coercive practices. Some individuals and groups regularly treat others in cruel and oppressive ways, and those who possess power do not in fact exercise the kinds of emotional self-restraint that liberal theory demands. One might think here of evidence about the brutality to be found in refugee camps, prisons and police stations, which have recently been characterised by Giorgio Agamben as states of nature within the state.[8] One might also think of the treatment of migrant workers, the institutionalisation of domestic violence, the prevalence of racism, the humiliation of the elderly, the abuse of children, the trafficking of women, of antagonism and violence towards Islamic communities, and many other cases besides. If one allows these less successful aspects of liberal democratic societies to occupy one's vision, the question of what makes it possible for people to contain the forms of rage, fear, desire or contempt that such practices express begins to seem much more pressing. By the same token, the question of how and why this issue has been largely neglected begins to seem a more central one. Although the capacity to control our feelings and use them productively is widely expected of us, this demand is tougher than we usually admit, and we are not as good at it as the self-image of liberalism suggests.

---

[8] Giorgio Agamben, *Homo Sacer: Sovereign Power and Bare Life* (Stanford, Stamford University Press, 1998).

If, as I have suggested, it is difficult to create and sustain the emotional capacities that are taken to be central to a pluralist way of life and to civilised institutions, one might expect liberal political theorists to consider how this problem bears on the norms they espouse. Perhaps surprisingly, there has so far been little explicit philosophical discussion of the emotional demands that cultural and political pluralism bring with them. However, a number of arguments have been put forward which implicitly sidestep this issue, either by contending that the problem I have identified is not a serious one, or by claiming that, demanding as it may be, we know how to deal with it. While these strategies may have succeeded in distracting attention from the difficult task of considering the emotional capacities on which pluralism depends, I shall argue that netither manages to establish that the task itself is unimportant or philosophically under control. After briefly touching on the first strategy, I shall go on to consider a prominent form of the second in greater detail.

One way to overlook the difficulty I have raised is to take a comparatively rosy view of existing liberal societies. Rorty, for example, sketches a picture of the United States as a community in which most people have internalised the emotional dispositions contained in practices that uphold norms of mutual respect and toleration, and are therefore not troubled by feelings that significantly interfere with their ability to function comfortably as decent capitalists, parents, students, voters, and so on. If we were to accept this image of a society emotionally attuned to the demands of respect and toleration, our problem would indeed recede into insignificance. It might even be replaced by the different concern that exercises Rorty: the worry that existing liberal communities may passively rest on their laurels. In some parts of the world, he suggests, conformity with liberal practices has become so habitual and entrenched that citizens are in danger of losing the ability to look beyond existing arrangements in order to identify hitherto unacknowledged forms of cruelty and oppression. The issue, then, is not to understand how people respond with compassion and decency to states of affairs that they recognise as intolerant. Rather, the main emotional challenge confronting liberals lies in cultivating the ability to respond to forms of oppression that remain largely unacknowledged.

The moral value of what Rorty describes as sentimental progress can hardly be denied. However, by giving it such a central position in his analysis, he occludes the equally important moral demand that we should manage to avoid practising forms of cruelty and oppression that are already familiar. His claim that the disposition to avoid these forms of behaviour has become habitual is surely empirically indefensible. And by introducing a fantasy about the character of existing liberal societies, it distracts attention from the ways in which they fail to live up to their own political norms.

The second and much more usual way in which theorists have sidestepped the problem I have identified takes the form of arguing that, imperfect as liberal societies are, we already understand how to set about reforming antisocial emotional dispositions and inculcating more constructive ones. While it may in practice be exceedingly difficult to get rid of the affects that fuel discriminatory behaviour, or to keep them within acceptable bounds, achieving this is a political and social task, and does not pose specifically philosophical problems. This stance assumes first that we possess a satisfactory philosophical account of emotional dispositions and the ways in which they alter, and secondly that this account vindicates the possibility of a way of life organised around such liberal values as freedom and equality. Among the philosophers who have recently argued that these conditions can be fulfilled are several influential advocates of a broadly cognitive conception of the emotions. Because cognitivism not only offers an interpretation of what the emotions are, but also indicates how they can be changed, it gives rise to a general account of the type of method that can best be used to sustain liberal values. As I shall argue, however, one of the weaknesses of this approach lies in its over-optimistic assumption that it is equal to this task.

A recent defence of cognitivism, richly articulated by Martha Nussbaum in her book *Upheavals of Thought*,[9] characterises emotions as judgments of value about items that we regard as important for our well-being, but do not fully control. Viewed in this light, emotions are intentional, and are organised around beliefs about their objects. To feel angry with a politician, for example, I must believe that she has done something that injures goals or ends that matter to me. It is simply my assent to this belief that makes it emotional, and explains the fact that it may shake me or gives me a feeling of tightness in the chest. On the face of things, this analysis can easily be extended to emotional dispositions. In order to be disposed to admire a political leader, I must assent to the belief that he or she somehow supports goals that matter to me, and to be disposed to criticise a government I must assent to the

[9] Martha Nussbaum, *Upheavals of Thought* (Cambridge, Cambridge University Press, 2003).

belief that it tends to undermine values to which I attach importance. Nussbaum also holds that the strength of our emotions reflects the degree to which we care about their objects, and if we add to this claim the assumption that strong emotions are usually harder to control than weak ones, it follows that emotions which are likely to disturb the political *status quo* will typically be about things that matter a lot to particular groups of people. For instance, the citizens of a town may feel intense hostility to migrant workers because of their shared assent to the belief that the migrants threaten employment opportunities on which the town's livelihood depends.

The view that an emotion consists in assenting to a belief implies that changes of belief will also be reflected in our emotions, and that our emotions are intimately linked to the way we describe and understand their objects. This claim serves to connect emotion with description, and thus with argument. Suppose the town mayor manages to persuade his constituents that the migrants do not pose a threat to their prosperity or way of life. Their beliefs about their situation will change, and if the cognitive theory is right, so will their emotions. Although their sense of outrage may not entirely vanish, their feeling of grievance will diminish, so that they are less likely to lash out at their new neighbours in ways that contravene existing norms of toleration and respect. An important feature of the cognitive view is therefore that it offers to explain how illiberal emotions can be altered. By subjecting the beliefs on which our feelings rest to criticism, and by seeing how they stand up to the cognitive forces of reflection and argument, we can both examine our emotions and test our commitment to them. These forms of interrogation are a familiar part of everyday life, and by making the formation of the emotions parasitic on them, the cognitive view suggests that the question of how we shape and change emotions is not much more mysterious than the question of how we shape and change our beliefs. We continually make judgments about how the world does or does not sustain the aims we care about, and modify our beliefs in the light of experience. Because this process is simultaneously cognitive and emotional, our emotions, as much as our beliefs, are change with our experience, including our experience of criticism and argument.

To accept this account is to accept that the key to altering violent or coercive emotional dispositions is to alter beliefs, whether one's own or those of other people. There are of course a number of indirect ways to achieve this; for example, if the trouble lies in a group's beliefs about its situation, one might try to change the situation. But a crucial role in creating the emotional dispositions on which democratic pluralism depends will presumably be played by various forms of persuasion, including persuasive argument. Insofar as we come to see ourselves as individuals whose way of life depends on certain kinds of emotional restraint, our beliefs about the significance of this aspect of our existence will bring with them a constellation of emotional dispositions, such as a tendency to feel shame when we fail to treat other people's practices respectfully. If we also come to believe that this self-image captures something that matters to us, the feelings it generates will be strong enough to help offset our disposition to express ourselves in ways that are cruel or oppressive, and will in turn modify the emotions on which these dispositions depend.

One of the attractions of this view is that, by presenting our emotions as susceptible to cognitive forms of reflection and criticism, it offers the prospect of a considerable level of control over them. It is true that we cannot simply choose what to feel, any more than we can simply choose what to believe; and it is true that mistaken beliefs may generate emotions that are inappropriate to our circumstances. But because the process of getting a rational grip on our individual and collective situation will also give us a grip on our emotions, the question from which we began—what does it take to be capable of the emotional restraint that pluralist democracy requires?—is by implication easily answerable. To give people this capacity, or to create it in oneself, it is enough to create and sustain a belief in the overriding value of practices in which norms of respect and toleration are embedded.

By bringing emotions closely in line with our evaluative beliefs, and claiming that the first generally track the second, cognitive theorists such as Nussbaum paint a picture of the self that is consonant with the image of the rational individual traditionally upheld by liberalism. Rather than conceiving of the emotions as obstacles to our processes of belief-formation, or presenting them as possessing an economy of their own, this view co-opts them as a motivating force that both links belief to action, and shapes our efforts at understanding. The question as to what entitles liberals to take for granted the forms of emotional restraint on which pluralism depends is thus reformulated in a way that writes out part of the worry on which it was based. The original worry was that we encounter, or belong to, groups of people who seem to be subject to emotions that play a part in creating and sustaining intolerant or inegalitarian practices. Reformulated, this becomes a claim to the effect that people have such emotions insofar as they assent to judgments that conflict with some of the key beliefs to which liberal pluralists attach exceptional value.

Two features of this reformulation are particularly worth noting. First, it carries with it a conception of the political tools and techniques on which it is most productive to rely. The emotions that move us to political action, it claims, are primarily shaped by our cognitive capacity to form and alter beliefs, and it is therefore primarily to beliefs, whether true or false, that we need to look if we want to bring about political change. Reform is therefore understood as a cognitive business. Secondly, the reformulation serves to uphold a familiar conception of autonomy. Just as we view ourselves as possessing the ability to revise our beliefs in the light of our experience, and thus to take a degree of individual and collective responsibility for them, so, it urges, we can take responsibility for our emotions. This is not to say that it is easy to get them right, any more than it is easy to get our beliefs right, or to deny that they may sometimes be misplaced or inappropriate. But because our access to a range of everyday techniques for testing and modifying our emotions constitutes part of our autonomy, the emotions do not threaten it, nor do they present a special problem as far as it is concerned. The outcome of the analysis is thus that, by assimilating emotions to states and capacities that philosophers have traditionally regarded as constituting the core of the self, and by interpreting them as within the reach of familiar forms of self-control, the theoretical dimensions of the problem with which we are concerned come to be domesticated. They are assimilated to the epistemological project of practising, and submitting to, forms of rational persuasion, which are seen as making us individually and collectively more autonomous.

There is much that is attractive in this approach. By analysing some of the processes through which we release ourselves from debilitating or destructive passions and put our emotions to constructive political use, cognitivism can be empowering. For instance, a group that once felt shame for what it believed to be its own inadequacies may, after examining and revising its beliefs, come to feel indignation at what it now interprets as its oppression, while a group that once took comfort from its understanding of its members as victims may use the same methods to generate confidence and determination. However, we can recognise the efficacy and political significance of redescriptive strategies such as these without conceding that emotions consist in assenting to beliefs, and it is easy to feel that cognitivism turns it back on aspects of our emotional life that are out of kilter with a liberal desire for individual autonomy. By allowing for non-cognitive aspects of emotion, we may be able to make space both for a fuller examination of the capacity for emotional restraint, and for a richer analysis of the conditions in which it arises.

A systematic analysis of the features of the emotions that cognitive theories fail to capture is beyond the scope of this paper. However, one can get a vivid sense of some of the things they leave out by considering a strongly contrasting position, recently defended by Teresa Brennan in her posthumous book, *The Transmission of Affect*.[10] Brennan argues that cognitive approaches are manifestations of a collective repression. In order to uphold a conception of the person as firmly bounded, and as more or less in control of his or her emotional states, they fail to mark the difference between affects that do indeed have their origins within the individual, and those that originate in others and are transmitted to individuals from outside. The latter, Brennan argues, do not possess the intentional form that cognitive theories dwell on, although they may acquire it by 'sticking' to an object that matters to an agent, as when I experience your transmitted hostility to the friends I have just been visiting as a feeling of guilt about turning up late to meet you.[11] Such emotions are not constituted by assent to the beliefs implicit in them; on the contrary, the beliefs in question are rather like garments that they can put on or take off. Defending a version of the position that Nussbaum labels 'The 'Adversary',[12] and Elizabeth Spelman calls 'The Dumb View',[13] Brennan claims that emotions are transmitted from outside, not only in comparatively rare cases of contagion within crowds, but also in the course of everyday social processes. It is therefore more than a metaphor to say that one can walk into a room and feel the emotions it contains.

Brennan's account is not without its difficulties; but it possesses a number of strengths. First, it draws attention to the mutually supportive relationship between the ideal of autonomy and cognitive theories of emotion. By ignoring or suppressing the phenomena on which her own account concentrates, cognitive

---

[10]   Teresa Brennan, *The Transmission of Affect* (Ithaca, Cornell University Press, 2004).
[11]   The image of an emotion 'sticking' to a belief is used by Sara Ahmed in *The Cultural Politics of Emotion* (Edinburgh, 2004).
[12]   Nussbaum, *Upheavals of Thought*, 33.
[13]   Elizabeth Spelman, *Fruits of Sorrow: Framing Our Attention to Suffering* (Beacon Press, 1998).

theorists uphold an image of autonomy in which affective transmission is not acknowledged. Secondly, Brennan's account focuses on emotional processes that are not easily captured by cognitivism, and yet cry out for attention, such as the ability of some emotions to 'stick' first to one belief and then to another. Confronted by this problem, cognitivists can always sustain their position by finding objects for the emotions in question, for example by representing them as reiterations of primitive beliefs formed in early childhood. It is not clear, however, that it is sufficient to describe such early feelings, or indeed many of our vaguer emotional states, in these terms. While it is true that we sometimes do our best to fill out our emotions by attaching them to objects, this does not commit us to concluding that the emotions we try more or less effectively to make sense of are always already states of assent. If we insist that this must be the case, we are liable to impose a limiting and distorting form of order on phenomena that are not straightforward to conceptualise. To take an example of Jonathan Lear's, when the Rat Man told Freud, 'I was afraid that you were going to hit me', he seems to have been trying to account for a feeling of fear which was too indeterminate to be traced back to a belief, and lacked the articulation that the cognitive approach presupposes. Something similar might be true of the townspeople of our earlier example, who attributed their hostility to a group of newcomers to the fear that they would be deprived of their jobs. If so, what cognitivism captures is not the full character of emotions, but the way that some of us, in our efforts to keep a grip on ourselves, imagine emotions to be.

Brennan's criticism of cognitivism rests on a distinction between emotions that originate in the self and emotions that impinge on it from outside. I think it is unhelpful to make too much of this opposition between inner and outer, and more fruitful to view emotions, in the manner of Spinoza, as manifestations of the way we experience our relations with both environment and self. While Nussbaum is right to hold that emotions chart the value and importance we attach to things, her view is mistaken in suggesting that our affects are principally cognitive. Rather, as both Brennan and Spinoza remind us, they are manifestations of our embodied existence, and encompass a far greater variety of sensitivities and responses than the cognitive view allows. An analysis that took account of these two claims would need to recognise that alterations in belief are often accompanied by emotional change, and that this process has an important part to play in politics. But it would also need to acknowledge that this is by no means the whole story. The task of finding ways to address and modify socially destructive passions therefore requires a richer interpretation of emotion than the one favoured by cognitivists.

This conclusion serves to revive the problem from which we began. It implies, first of all, that without a more powerful analysis of the emotions, we will lack the theoretical tools that are needed to understand the affective capacities and dispositions on which harmonious, yet pluralist, societies depend. Moreover, by questioning the cognitivist contention that we already have the makings of an adequate account, it challenges the view that, because we know in principle how to address it, the problem posed by the expression of illiberal emotions is not philosophically pressing. Rather than assuming that we do not need to worry much about the emotional capacities that people need to possess in order to live by liberal values, because these can be created by means that we understand pretty well, we need to address this issue in all its complexity. The current failure to do so is, I think, a kind of delusion, the fruit of an unwillingness to admit just how emotionally taxing these values turn out to be.

The current popularity of cognitive theories of the emotions provides an occasion to speculate about the political dimension of a philosophical trend. Cognitivism clearly illuminates some aspects of our affective experience. Moreover, by analysing emotions as a species of belief it makes them accessible to analytical philosophy, and prepares the way for them to be integrated into wide ranging accounts of rational thought and action. At one level, this is a free–standing philosophical project with its own rationale and aspirations. At another level, however, it is part of the political enterprise of defending a conception of the self that conforms to the preconceptions of contemporary liberalism. It is important to liberalism to be able to assume that citizens either possess, or are capable of acquiring, the emotional capacities on which pluralism depends. Cognitivism then offers the reassurance that creating and maintaining these capacities is a matter of creating and maintaining certain beliefs, and therefore presupposes just the cognitive capacities that are already central to a liberal conception of the self. Cognitive accounts of the emotions thus indirectly serve to strengthen the philosophical categories around which liberalism is organised. But in doing so, they perpetuate a an image of the citizen considerably removed from much of our everyday political experience.

Index

Index

For EU product safety concerns, contact us at Calle de José Abascal, 56–1°,
28003 Madrid, Spain or eugpsr@cambridge.org.

www.ingramcontent.com/pod-product-compliance
Ingram Content Group UK Ltd.
Pitfield, Milton Keynes, MK11 3LW, UK
UKHW010040140625
459647UK00012BA/1497